The Politics of Healthcare

THE POLITICS OF HEALTHCARE

Achieving Real Reform

Edited by
Eilish McAuliffe *and* Kenneth McKenzie

The Liffey Press

Published by
The Liffey Press
Ashbrook House, 10 Main Street,
Raheny, Dublin 5, Ireland
www.theliffeypress.com

© 2007 Eilish McAuliffe and Kenneth McKenzie
and individual contributors

A catalogue record of this book is
available from the British Library.

ISBN 978-1-905785-21-6

Printed in Ireland by Colour Books

CONTENTS

ABOUT THE CONTRIBUTORS

Frank Ahern entered the Civil Service after secondary school in 1961. He worked in the Department of Health and Children from 1987 until 2006. He worked as Principal Officer in the Hospital Policy Division until 1997 when he took over the personnel portfolio for the health services. He has a wide range of experience in the area of industrial relations and personnel development. In 2002 he became the Assistant Secretary with responsibility for strategic development and corporate services where he had a major role in the Health Service Reform Programme. He holds an MA in Change Management and is currently completing a PhD on the management of large-scale change.

Ruth Barrington is CEO of the Dublin Molecular Medicine Centre, and was the Chief Executive of the Health Research Board (HRB) from 1998–2007. Dr Barrington is a graduate of University College Dublin, the College of Europe in Belgium, and was awarded a PhD from the London School of Economics. She was awarded an honorary degree in laws by the National University of Ireland, Maynooth in May 2005 and is a Trustee of *The Irish Times*. She is the author of *Health, Medicine and Politics in Ireland, 1900–1970,* and other publications on health and research policy.

Fenton Howell is a Director of Public Health with the Health Service Executive – Population Health Directorate. He is a former Dean of the Faculty of Public Health Medicine in Ireland. He is a former President of the Irish Medical Organisation. He is a longstanding Board member of ASH Ireland and is a past Chairperson of ASH Ireland. He is also a Board member of the All-Ireland Institute of Public Health and the Research Institute for a Tobacco Free Society.

Michael Kelly is Chair of the Higher Education Authority. He was Sec-retary General of the Department of Health and Children from January 2000 to March 2005. During that period he played a leading role in the reform of the health service, including the preparation of the current health strategy "Quality and Fairness", the policy groundwork for much of the on-going reform programme and the re-structuring of the health system, leading to the establishment of the Health Service Executive. He has also played a prominent role in leading reform in the civil service, particularly in performance management.

Matt Merrigan is National Industrial Secretary for the Health and Local Authority Sector, for the Services, Industrial, Professional and Technical Union (SIPTU). He is also Joint Chair of the Health Service National Partnership Forum and a Board member of Beaumont Hospital.

Fergus O'Ferrall is Director of The Adelaide Hospital Society and au-thor of *Citizenship and Public Service: Voluntary and Statutory Rela-tionships in Irish Healthcare* (2000), and co-edited *Medical Ethics and the Future of Healthcare* (2000). He holds an MSc degree in Health Ser-vices Management from Trinity College Dublin and is part-time lecturer in Health Services Management in Department of Public Health and Primary Care, TCD. He is a Board member of The Adelaide & Meath Hospital at Tallaght, and has served as a member of the National Eco-nomic and Social Forum and the National Economic and Social Council. He is a past President of the National Youth Council and past Chairman of The Wheel.

Aileen O'Meara is a health journalist and broadcaster, with extensive experience of reporting on all aspects of the Irish health service. She was RTE's Health Correspondent for six years up to 2004, when she was awarded Medical Journalist of the Year for television and radio news coverage of the health services. She writes political and economic analy-ses of the issues facing the health services for *The Sunday Business Post*, and runs her own independent production company, Twintrack Media.

John Owens graduated from Queen's University Belfast in 1961. He has worked as a Consultant Psychiatrist since 1967, holding posts in Ireland and Canada. John was Chief Psychiatrist in St. Davnet's Hospital in Monaghan from 1972–2002. He was a member of both the Postgraduate

Medical and Dental Board and Comhairle na nOspideal. He served as Chairman of the Mental Health Commission from 2002–2007 and has co-authored two key policy documents in mental health, *Planning for the Future*, 1984 and *Vision for Change*, 2006.

Prof Anne Scott was appointed Deputy President of Dublin City University in February 2006; prior to this she was Head of the School of Nursing at DCU. Her research interests are in the philosophy and ethics of health care and in judgement and decision-making on issues of ethics and clinical practice. She currently supervises post-graduate research students in health care ethics, philosophy and ethics of health care and in clinical judgement and decision-making. Prof Scott is a member of the Board of the Health Service Executive.

Dedication

To Mac and our wonderful daughters Lara, Tess and Anna for making life fun! – *Eilish McAuliffe*

To Fiona Hayes – thanks so much for being with me every step of the way in my time in DCU and TCD – *Kenneth McKenzie*

Chapter 1

THINKING AND ACTING IN HEALTHCARE

Eilish McAuliffe and Kenneth McKenzie

Since the late 1980s, healthcare reform in OECD countries has been characterised by rationalisation, as governments try to control supply and ensure maximal efficiency of resources (Björkman and Altenstetter, 1997). More recently, governmental initiatives in this area have also been concerned with how to manage the ever-more complex healthcare system, as populations age, advances in technology gather pace, and previously foreign territory in the shape of the assorted biotechnologies intrude into the policy arena. Additionally, citizen demand for healthcare has ranked consistently towards the top of electoral concerns in all rich democracies (Wilensky, 2002: 628). Governments, then, are confronted by technical policy-making problems that often fall outside the expertise available to their advisors and civil servants, and are likely to be punished heavily at the polls if the healthcare package is seen to be diminished.

Ireland is an interesting case for healthcare policy comparativists. Unlike the rest of its OECD peers, in recent times rationalization has not dominated the policy agenda; instead, increasing uptake and the necessary rise in public spending have underpinned government policy since 1997 (DoHC, 2001: 10). Despite this largesse, there is as yet no objective needs-based element to the resource allocation system (O'Loughlin and Kelly, 2004: 272), while it remains difficult to assess the impact of increased funding against the backdrop of a radically altered system of health administration.

It is arguable that the perception of the quality of Irish health has been marred by a litany of scandals that have been uncovered, often accidentally or by the media, over the past decade and more. The list has an eerie familiarity – tainted blood transfusion; the handling of the Cole case (Hepatitis C contracted through blood transfusion) by Michael Noonan; the questionable legality of the elderly and their families paying for nursing home care; unacceptably poor standards of care and abuse of the elderly in the case of Leas Cross; the death in transit of two patients in Cavan and Monaghan; Michael Neary (flawed decision-making resulting in unnecessary hysterectomies being performed on young women) and the degree and quality of self-regulation of the medical profession. No wonder the one time Minister for Health, Brian Cowen, named the health portfolio as "Angola". Add to this roll call of embarrassment the level of public anger over the intractable A&E situation, and some observers would not seem out of place to regard strategic management of Irish health as maladroit, misaligned, and misdirected. It is thus feasible to affirm that as there have been so many problems, there must be flaws in systems or personnel, or both. Some argue that these flaws stem directly from a historically low funding base that was exacerbated by severe cutbacks in the 1980s, and that recent health spending, though hugely increased, is not sufficient to allow us to play catch up at a speed that matches ever increasing public expectations. Regardless of the funding debate, the reality is that in recent times remedying the flaws has occupied much of the energy of the serried ranks of healthcare administrators and practitioners.

Notwithstanding the well-known problems mentioned above, policy change has occurred and the practice and management of healthcare have also changed. Saltman and Figueras (1997: 259) do not look at the incentive of scandal as a driver of change in health; instead they have a deceptively simple checklist of important factors in successful healthcare reform.

1. Timing

2. Financial viability

3. Political will and leadership

4. Strategic alliances

5. Public support

6. Well-managed process

7. Technical infrastructure and capacity.

Academic checklists of reform processes can appear far too abstract when someone tries to apply them on the ground. For example, how much could one succeed if one took book-based models and applied them to try to resolve the problems of A&E, Hanly, or Leas Cross?

To remedy the shortcomings of a purely academic approach, we have invited a number of healthcare actors to contribute a chapter each based on their experience and unique perspective of the changing landscape of Irish healthcare. The recognition that academic models need to be complemented by context-specific pragmatic approaches (some of which can only emerge from experience) is a prime motivation for this book. Healthcare is often referred to as a complex environment and managing in this environment does not have direct parallels in any other industry or sector. The complexity of health systems arises not because of the structure of healthcare, but because of the myriad of complex relationships between the various stakeholders in health. The successful healthcare manager must be able to navigate through this maze, strategizing, negotiating, persuading, motivating, empowering, and making some tough decisions along the way. Take the first point from Saltman and Figueras (op. cit.) – timing. Wilsford (1994) writes that this can be quite difficult to operationalise, as it may incorporate the notion of a new "mood" for strategic thinking within a government or government department. Plainly, there has been a marked hunger for "blue sky" thinking in many areas of government over the last eight years, with major initiatives such as the *National Development Plan* (2000); the *National Spatial Strategy* (2002) and the *Decentralisation Plan* (2003). As these plans have substantial "lock-ins" (six years for the development plan and 20 for the spatial strategy), they seem to indicate a willingness to think in terms of the political long-term. Within the Department of Health and Children (DoHC), we note that a similarly strategic mindset has emerged just prior to 1997 and has persisted with the general tenor of government thinking described above. Michael Kelly in Chapter 2 links this shift in thinking to the Strategic Management Initiative and the role it has played in refocusing civil servants on their responsibilities and accountabilities.

This interpretation of a shift in thinking is supported by two aspects. First, there is the signalling of the DoHC's move away from operational management in setting up the Health Service Executive (2005). Second, the last twelve years has been a very busy period of policy formulation, with a raft of ambitious policies in a short space of time. Prominent and relevant documents here include the 1994 strategy, *Shaping a Healthier*

Future followed by the *National Cancer Strategy* (1996) and *Building Healthier Hearts* (1999), then the *National Health Promotion Strategy* (2000); the current blueprint, *Quality and Fairness* (2001), and the three reports that have informed the reform programme, the *Report on the National Task Force on Medical Staffing* (2003), *Audit of Structures and Functions in the Health Service* (2003) and *The Report of the Commission on Financial Management and Control Systems in the Health Service* (2003), as well as the *Health Service Reform Programme* (2003). Kelly traces the developing sophistication in the policy making process within the Department of Health over this time and interweaves his personal development and the many influences that assisted him in charting a particular policy course while maintaining a clear vision of what healthcare might become, a vision that garnered favour in some circles and disfavour in others. Kelly draws attention to the difficulties faced by senior civil servants in trying to frame strategic policy whilst keeping an eye on the bottom line of how the machinery of government responds to overtures of significant change. His contribution illustrates the tension between the role of civil servant and that of strategic planner and the difficulties of maintaining your course whilst being swept along by the political tide.

The reality of policy implementation, however, is that a much more short-term perspective seems to prevail and this is heavily influenced by where we are in the political cycle as well as (to some extent) the strength of the political opposition and the public voice. Frank Ahern's contribution (Chapter 6) on the influence of parliamentary questions underlines how the core activity of the Department of Health and Children has all too often been displaced by the pressure to give adequate responses to Opposition challenges to the incumbent minister. He describes how the introduction of "Leader's questions" in the Dáil has influenced the prioritisation of healthcare issues. Ahern notes that some questions focus on substantive policy details, but alludes to the fact that many also refer to instances of micro-management for which a minister cannot be realistically expected to have operational responsibility or adequate knowledge. The description of how civil servants would be diverted from concerted policy work by the latest bad news story on health brings to mind Nye Bevan's comment on the post-war British National Health Service – that his senior civil servants would hear every bed pan dropping in the country. Ahern's chapter illustrates the folly of such an aspiration.

Fiscality has been an enduring feature in the political debates on healthcare over the past several years with successive Ministers of Finance referring to the "black hole" in healthcare and the emergence of value for money reports and financial audits interspersed between the various strategy and policy documents. Although Kelly alludes to the increasing emphasis on costing in successive strategies, his account of the Ballymascanlon cabinet meeting serves as a reminder that when the real costs of healthcare are laid bare, the reaction is at best unpredictable. In contrast to this John Owens (Chapter 3) considers the thorny issue of how to push change through when the prevailing climate is for the maintenance of the status quo and no additional finances are forthcoming. Whether such reluctance to change is propelled by fear or doubts as to the worth of what is proposed as an alternative is a recurring question. Owens traces the history of mental healthcare from a point where the prevailing philosophy was one of caring for and protecting the person with a mental health problem, through the labelling, medicalisation and institutionalisation (largely shaped by the medical profession) to the current trend towards care in the community and enabling people to live fulfilling lives. His reference to successful efforts to alter mental health services in Cavan/Monaghan by shifting funds from one service to another serves as a capsule illustration of the difficulties encountered as well as the rewards reaped when people are willing to step outside of their professional boundaries and engage in purposeful, respectful and convincing interactions with other actors.

One of the great success stories of public health medicine has been the smoking ban in the workplace. Fenton Howell and Shane Allwright (Chapter 5) outline the thinking and tactics behind the campaign to remove smoking from the pub, which many had thought to be impossible. Their account of the lobbying that preceded the smoking ban draws our attention to the scale of change that is possible through the formation of the right strategic alliances. The successful implementation of the smoking ban also serves as an illustration of how strong and fair leadership that weighs up the evidence and takes decisive action is critical to any significant change.

A number of other chapters also address the importance of forming strategic alliances both within and beyond the health sector and how this coupled with effective leadership creates a powerful force for change. Anne Scott's chapter (Chapter 8) clearly illustrates the value of forming strong partnerships with all those concerned with the development of the nursing profession. She analyses the strategies and alliances as well as the "lucky breaks" that allowed the transition of nurse education into the university environment to happen rapidly and relatively smoothly and how this approach enabled the development of a vibrant School of Nursing in a very short timeframe. Kelly develops a robust approach to strategy and policy formulation that is built on the belief that building strategic alliances with stakeholders early in the process leads not only to greater ownership and involvement, but to a better product.

The place of trade unions as strategic allies in policy is of undoubted importance – social partnership is now an inveterate feature of public affairs. With ever-increasing amounts of money being spent on health since 1997, some pundits accuse staff of having profited at the expense of patient-centred reform. In his role as chief health negotiator for SIPTU, Ireland's largest general trade union, Matt Merrigan has argued the collective case for a broad swath of staff with very different skill bases and salaries. He (Chapter 7) looks at how his members have tried to provide feedback to middle and senior management on how to improve the delivery of services at the coalface, and he tries to explain why attempts at involving staff have sometimes proved very successful and at other times been dismissed by senior managers. Despite the variability in the attitudes of politicians and senior managers towards partnership, Merrigan argues that is has transformed the landscape of industrial relations and he remains optimistic about its potential to deliver real and lasting improvement in the health services.

Garnering public support for healthcare change is a thorny issue. It happened for the smoking ban. It didn't happen for the regional reorganisation of hospitals – as evidenced by the rapidity with which the Hanley report appeared and disappeared off the agenda. Traditionally, patients or the public have not been accorded the status of actors within Irish health. Fergus O'Ferrall (Chapter 10) follows the development of public participation in health governance. He outlines the difference between "republican citizens" (or active citizenship) and "liberal citizens". He argues that the only resources that people have for voicing their needs and for exercising influence over the health services is through their social relationships, social networks, community and voluntary organisations or through their political representatives. The latter, O'Ferrall argues, operate in a centralised clientelist political system, which does not co-exist happily with a participatory democracy such as "active citizenship" would create. "Re-imagining" or reconceptualising citizenship according to O'Ferrall, must address the deeper basis of economic and social dominance, in particular growing income inequality, and the State must be reconceived as an "enabling state", because "the state shapes its citizens".

Aileen O'Meara (Chapter 9) also writes about the issue of public support through her critical analysis of how the actors in healthcare engage with the media. She examines how the news agenda on health is invariably a negative one, and how poorly some major governmental initiatives have been communicated to media outlets, thus damaging the projects in the eyes of the public before they have even had a chance to take shape (the launch of the Hanley report being a good example of this). She discusses factors a health manager should consider in their relations with the media, and emphasises that a "one size fits all" communiqué is hamstrung from the start: managers should bear in mind that the agenda of local radio is very different from that of organs such as *The Irish Times.* They are often unprepared for the variety of media outlets and what each sees as important. Because of this and the general distrust of the media, healthcare managers have been poor at utilising the media as a vehicle to inform and engage with the public about healthcare issues. Interestingly, O'Meara comments on the lack of positive health stories in the media and concludes that unless the media are considered as healthcare actors, the likelihood is that managers will continue to fight media-fanned flames at the expense of planning for change.

Sometimes a number of these factors can come together in a form that provides a window of opportunity. For example, Anne Scott claims that a unique confluence of circumstances gave rise to a new status and vision for nursing. At other times it may be that the force of one can be used to influence another. For example, Howell and Allwright detail their media relations strategy and indicate how evidence was used to persuade the government of the case to introduce such strong legislation, despite much opposition from the industry sector. It is not hyperbolic to classify the policy change on workplace smoking as having achieved a significant cultural shift.

Taking a broader perspective on why health policy fails, why the system has a tendency to repeatedly go down blind alleys and demonstrate a reluctance to learn from past mistakes, Ruth Barrington (Chapter 4) continues this theme of evidence-based approaches and looks at the greater role research could play in guiding policy direction. She argues that more resources need to be targeted at health policy and systems research, and that we need to bring an evidence-based approach to policy formulation and policy implementation. We need to critically evaluate what lies behind successful initiatives as well as failed initiatives in healthcare. Research that provides answers to these problems is a necessary ingredient in achieving a high quality health system.

Howell and Allwright's account of the ripple effects of success and the interest shown by other countries juxtaposed with Barrington's criticism of this country's lack of awareness of the critical part research plays in healthcare highlights the importance of documenting and learning from our past failings but also from the many success stories in healthcare.

One cannot but be struck by the near obsessive focus on structures, infrastructures and capacity in attempts to reform our health service over the past decade, from the establishment and demolition of the Eastern Regional Health Authority in a timeframe of less than five years, the huge shift from health boards to a single authority in the form of the Health Service Executive and the speculation on a further move towards a regional authority structure, to the start-stop attempts to effect a dramatic increase in medical manpower in the system. Yet none of the contributors to this book gave a great deal of attention to any of this. The metaphor of the deck chairs on the Titanic springs to mind!

The rationale for this collection of writings is to address the gap between theory and practice in effecting change in healthcare. Previous works in the area have done a good job of laying out some of the key problems of Irish healthcare but are less inclined to consider how these problems might be overcome. Theory-led accounts of how to change things for the better can fall on barren soil when the reader finds that they are based on an idealised world that bears little resemblance to what they see piled up in their in-tray. This book aims to distil some of the collective wisdom of significant actors within and around the Irish healthcare system on how to push for change and how to deal with some of the obstacles one inevitably meets.

We believe that an understanding of the content and context of shifts in Irish healthcare politics requires both an expert input and a theoretical perspective. Without a theory or framework, the reader is confronted by a series of insights or anecdotes that do not lend themselves to a cogent analysis of the structural aspects of health which are critical to plotting and carrying out change. A myriad of theories for explaining strategic change may be chosen, but we have opted for a loose institutionalist approach (Steinmo, Thelen and Longstreth, 1992) which we feel helps to structure the varied inputs of the contributors. By "institutional", we mean any event or process which is structured by the political setting in which it occurs; for example, a government's response to lobbying would be institutional, as is the ability of government to act relatively freely in legislation because it has a workable majority. An institution can be defined as "a relatively enduring set of rules and organised practices embedded in structures of meaning and resources that are relatively invariant in the face of turnover of individuals and relatively resilient to the idiosyncratic preferences and expectations of individuals and changing external circumstances". (March and Olsen, 1989, 1995, 2005: 4) In this book we explore change in the health system as an institution. Some institutional factors are explicit, such as political leadership, whereas others are more implicit and difficult to pin down, but can include factors such as a new mood for strategic thinking that is found in both minister and civil servant at the same time, or the degree of respect traditionally accorded to the medical profession by other healthcare stakeholders. Accepted rules and practices within this institution prescribe appropriate behaviour for the various actors, based on their position in the hierarchy, the power base of their profession etc. There are embedded structures of meaning that give legitimacy to these behaviours. March and Olsen (2005) argue that in any institution there are structures on resources that create capabilities for acting. Institutions empower and constrain actors differently and make them more or less capable of acting within the prescriptive rules for appropriate behaviour. The stories of the actors in the ensuing chapters help us develop an understanding of the interplay that occurs between actors and their institutions in effecting meaningful changes in healthcare.

Although this book contains chapters by important healthcare actors, we are keen to point out that the chapters amount to more than mere autobiographies of how these actors have tried and in many cases succeeded in making their mark on the healthcare landscape. In particular, we would like to signal our intent to move away from the great man or great woman theory of change. The idea that one person can be driven to change what they see is found most strikingly in John Horgan's (2000) life of Noël Browne. It is true that the eradication of TB owes much to Browne's personal history, but the part played by the confluence of other factors – a theme that reverberates through all of the chapters in this book– makes it anomalous to have an overriding focus on the personal abilities and motivations of key actors. Instead, we prefer to see change as the outcome of competent, committed people working with clear processes – it is the interplay between the environment, the actors and the actions that is critical. To this end, we have structured the book so that each author addresses this interplay and in doing so conveys to the reader how they may transfer this understanding to their own particular role in improving healthcare.

In the final chapter, we extract the threads of wisdom from the various contributors to weave together a pattern of the enabling and inhibiting factors that are an integral part of the healthcare environment. We analyse the interplay between the actors and the environment and identify the personal, interpersonal and situational factors that are critical to succeeding in the quest to improve healthcare. In this way the book serves as a guide to managers and healthcare professionals on how to play a more proactive, strategic role in shaping healthcare, the argument being that regardless of one's level or scope of operation, there is always an opportunity waiting, an action to be taken. The varied and interesting stories in this book on the one hand illustrate the on-the-job learning that shape the actors and thinkers in healthcare whilst at the same time providing critical insights into the task of grasping opportunities to effect change in a complex, dynamic environment or *institution*. Of course, the real skill in the successful delivery of healthcare is in recognising these opportunities, assessing the climate for change and, whilst being mindful of the needs of other actors, pursuing one's goal with single-minded determination.

References

Bjorkman, J. and Altenstetter, C. (1997). "Globalized concepts and local practice: divergence in national health policy reforms". In C. Altenstetter and J. Bjorkman (eds), *Health Policy Reform, National Variations and Globalization.* Basingstoke: Macmillan, pp. 1-16.

Horgan, J. (2000). *Noël Browne: Passionate Outsider.* Dublin: Gill and Macmillan.

March, J.G. and Olsen, J.P. (1989) *Rediscovering Institutions*, New York: Free Press.

March, J.G. and Olsen, J.P. (1995) *Democratic Governance,* New York: Free Press.

March, J.G. and Olsen J.P. (2005) *Evaluating the "New Institutionalism",*

Working Paper No. 11, Arena, Centre for European Studies, University of Oslo. www.arena.uio.no.

O'Loughlin, R. and Kelly, A. (2004). "Equity in resource allocation in the Irish health service: A policy Delphi study". *Health Policy*, 67, 3, 271-280.

Saltman, R.B. and Figueras, J. (1997). *European Healthcare Reform: Analysis of Current Strategies.* Copenhagen: World Health Organization.

Steinmo, S., Thelen, K. and Longstreth, F. (eds) (1992). *Structuring Politics: Historical Institutionalism in Comparative Analysis.* New York: Cambridge University Press.

Wilensky, H. L. (2002). *Rich Democracies – Political Economy, Public Policy, and Performance.* Berkeley, CA: University of California Press.

Wilsford, D. (1994). "Path dependency, or why history makes it difficult but not impossible to reform healthcare systems in a big way". *Journal of Public Policy*, 14, 3, 251-283.

Chapter 2

STEERING A POLICY COURSE

Michael Kelly

Public Management in Ireland has been under-going wide ranging reform and modernisation over recent decades and over the past ten years
in particular. An agile and responsive public service is now seen as an
essential pillar to continuing economic and wider societal progress and
development. Much effort has been invested in the incorporation of the
essentials of strategic management into the operations of Government
Departments and public bodies more generally. Initiatives like the Strategic Management Initiative in the Civil Service and sectoral initiatives
in the wider public sector are a reflection of the determination of Government and senior levels in the civil and public service to bring about
the necessary reforms and improvements. (Department of the Taoiseach,
1996: www.bettergov.ie)

Improving the way we do things and, in particular, the way in which
we deliver a service to the citizen as client and paymaster, lies at the heart
of the public service ethos. Successive waves of public service reform
have aimed at accentuating this as a key motivation for those working in
the public service and the most recent iteration of strategic management
does reflect some measure of success in moving public service thinking in
this direction. Particular manifestations include the development of quality
customer service plans and standards and the very concrete improvements
in service delivery through, for example, on-line administration of many
services, better access to information electronically and in hard copy,
greater attention to customer complaints, and the more transparent setting
of service standards and monitoring of performance.

As somebody who studied the business of management at under-graduate level in the 1970s and subsequently wondered, on the basis of personal experience, what possible relevance much of it could have to the business of government at that time, the new emphasis on manage-ment as a distinct but intrinsic part of the public management role was something I could immediately and naturally identify with. It reflected a concern with the achievement of key results in output and outcome terms as well as the traditional requirements for good administration, sound policy analysis and advice and the safeguarding of public assets and re-sources.

Understanding and Charting the Terrain

As part of my own development, I was given the opportunity to build on my earlier studies and to undertake postgraduate training as a policy ana-lyst. This brought me into closer contact with the application of strategic thinking to particular issues and dilemmas in public policy making. Par-ticipation in this programme was also to be a key milestone in shaping the direction I would take in terms of career development and the ap-proach I was equipped to bring to any policy issue or agenda I came into contact with subsequently.

My first test came with my assignment as a Policy Analyst to the Planning Unit in the Department of Health in 1984. The project I was assigned was lead responsibility for the preparation of a green paper on the health service. Although the Paper was methodically and enthusiasti-cally drafted by a small team, it was never pursued or published. One of the explanations for this, I believe is that its strategic intent was never fully thought through or communicated to stakeholders. The manner of its preparation was also a distinct civil service production of its time– a tight drafting team with little involvement even by others within the De-partment and no engagement with any stakeholder outside the Depart-ment. However I gained enormously from its preparation in my under-standing of the functioning of the health system and the varied and com-plex policy issues it raised.

This was to be a considerable advantage in responding to the next similar request I received about two years later which was for a short consultation paper on the key issues in health policy. This emerged in 1986 as Ireland's response to the WHO Health for All by the Year 2000 Programme, under the title *Health – The Wider Dimensions* (DoH,

1986). It was complemented by a report published by the Health Education Bureau on Health Promotion and was one of the first examples of a strategic approach to the health system overall, which sought to simultaneously analyse key aspects of the system in some integrated fashion. Given the strategic nature of this response and the degree of public debate it engendered, the logical extension should have been a white paper setting out the Government's agreed policy decisions, following on a period of consultation. This was not to happen however, partly because of a change of Government and also I suspect because there was not sufficient commitment to push through some of the key developments and reforms being put forward.

The manner of its publication is significant in understanding some of the tensions around health policy at that time. Rather than a more orthodox approach involving a Green or White Paper, either of which would have required prior Government approval, it was decided to publish the document as "a consultative statement on health policy". My recollection is that this was done in the belief that a more dilute version of the document and its proposals would have emanated from any process of detailed examination by the Department of Finance in particular. While there were formal requirements for a Green Paper, for example, a mere consultative statement could enter onto the stage of public debate with much greater ease, thus preparing the ground for significant change in health policy.

Among the issues raised were the need for:

- A more explicit concern with the relationship between policy measures and desired outcomes through a stronger role for epidemiology in policy planning and performance monitoring;

- Addressing inequalities in health;

- An emphasis on health promotion and prevention of disease;

- Active community participation in developing and implementing strategies for health;

- The need for multi-sectoral collaboration in ensuring the prerequisites for health;

- An emphasis on primary healthcare;

- The need for international co-operation in tackling health problems across national boundaries (DoH, 1986).

The approach taken to preparing this paper did not provide for any broadly based consultation or involvement. Its publication and wide dissemination was followed some months later by the organisation of a national conference involving stakeholders, though with an emphasis on providers and funders rather than service users and the broader consumer viewpoint.

Although some of the policy changes which ensued over the following years, e.g. the development of health promotion, a stronger epidemiological basis for planning and decision making, continuing rationalisation of the acute hospital system and development of some primary care services were guided by the policy position set out in HWD, the implementation process fell short in a number of ways. In particular because it was a discussion paper rather than an action plan, there was no place for a well-planned and integrated action programme outlining key roles and responsibilities. It was also weak on analysis of resource requirements, reflecting a cautious approach to any positive commitment of resources at a time of significant financial pressure for the exchequer and in particular for the health system. Also, any proposals requiring new resources would have required prior submission for Government approval. It is significant that HWD was published at a time when annual Government spending on healthcare as a proportion of GNP was in decline, a trend which continued until 1989. As a consultation paper, it had limited value in leveraging positive action but it did provide a focal point for debate and strong guidance as to the type of policy interventions which were likely to contribute to improved health in the population. Overall therefore this exercise, while very useful in charting an approach to integrated policy analysis across the health system, fell short as an approach to strategic action.

All Hands on Deck

Having spent much of the 1980s working on various policy projects in the Planning and Health Promotion Units of the Department I found myself assigned as head of one side of the Personnel Unit in 1989. This led to a baptism of fire, where I had to learn very quickly about the processes of industrial relations, in order to survive. Not unusually, the Department very often found itself as the unfortunate meat in a sandwich, between unions and health service employers on one side and a rigid Department of Finance on the other. As employment or pay issues arose in local situations, health boards and other health employers would do their best to find solutions which would not breach public pay policy and could be afforded within budget. Too often, these requirements could not be met and disputes escalated to the national level.

Prior to the advent of the partnership framework and benchmarking pay agreements, the engagement by the Department in industrial relations was more frequent and intensive. I had particularly strong contacts with the nursing profession, both in negotiating issues with the four unions representing them and in regard to professional development through my membership of An Bord Altranais. Through this period, I learned a lot more about how to get things done by working with people, where possible, on shared agendas. An example will help to illustrate the point.

From the time I had first contact with the nursing unions in 1989 I began to hear about their demand for a major pay review, outside of the normal relativity based cycle which applied at that time. Under this system, a special pay claim would be processed for each group of public servants on a three- to four-year cycle. This cycle would be typically led by the Public Service Executive Union and through a series of arbitration findings or Labour Court Recommendations would eventually embrace all public service workers, with the aim of restoring pay relativity with selected groups of workers in the private sector. The nursing unions, while participating fully in this process and availing of all pay awards as a result, were also pressing the case for a more general review of nursing pay and conditions through all career grades. A major part of the job I was expected to do was to head off the demand for such a review – both for cost reasons in relation to the nursing pay bill and because of its precedent value for other groups in the public service.

The early stages of this battle of wits were based on tactical moves within the industrial relations processes which ensured that the special pay review was procedurally blocked. As time went on, it became clear that with frustration levels building up, something more constructive would need to be done. This led to a series of discussions with the leadership of the respective unions about progressing a number of non-pay developments instead. While difficult for some of the unions involved, I would have to acknowledge the responsible leadership they displayed during this period (although viewed from the perspective of the people they represented, the value of doing so may have been less apparent at least in the short term).

It was out of this set of discussions that the initial momentum for a radical change in nurse education and training as well as the drafting of a new Nurses Act first emerged. Both have taken some time to develop fully but this experience taught me about the value of thinking laterally and of constructing shared agendas for joint action as a substitute for old fashioned confrontation or extended periods of stalemate in negotiations with staff groups. The model of "pay for change" has, of course, since been mainstreamed into the design of pay arrangement for all public service employees.

A further stage in my own formation was my assignment to the post of Deputy Secretary in the Department of Justice from November 1996 to February 1999. The objective was to lead an organisation change programme in that Department, including the agencies it then managed e.g. Courts, Prisons, Probation and Welfare Service. This assignment put a premium on strategic planning and its close relationship to people management skills and, in particular, the building of a partnership approach to planning and managing the Department's business. Over this period I was also asked to take on a prominent role in developing a new Human Resource Management Framework for the Civil Service and, in particular, to lead the development of the Performance Management and Development System now in place in all departments.

Each of these experiences reinforced in my mind the absolute importance of being able to find ways to work with people, ideally in a win-win framework, in securing key business objectives. Much of my academic training and early experience had honed skills around planning and evaluating, these were concerned with trying to decide the right things to do in any given situation. My later experiences taught me a lot more about the politics of getting things done. This deepened my understanding of participative decision making and of the absolute folly of knowing what to do, if you had no way of translating that into action through the commitment and effort of other people.

Learning to Navigate

While numerous policy reviews and planning documents were developed on particular aspects of the health system over the following years, each of which was effective in providing a planning framework for a particular service or patient group, it was to be nearly a decade later that the next integrated strategy document was produced, in the form of the

Health Strategy – Shaping a Healthier Future in 1994. This document was concerned with many of the same policy questions as *Health – The Wider Dimensions* (e.g. the need for a stronger role for primary care and promotion of positive health), but also added new momentum for the strengthening of services for people with a disability, older people, and children in care. It was also more resolute in arguing the case for more resources and in pointing up the need for analysis and review of the delivery and organisation structure and strengthening of information systems and human resources management. Its preparation was supported by some degree of consultation with stakeholders. As its title implied, it was intended to lead into a re-shaping of the health system along a number of dimensions and it can certainly be seen as having provided clear guidance and a logical policy framework for policy makers and service deliverers over the following five to seven-year period (DoH, 1994). The fact that, unlike its predecessor, it had Government approval as a strategy statement on health added significantly to its influence in guiding decisions and actions in the health system.

There was also, for the first time, a clear attempt to translate strategic thinking into concrete action in the form of a four-year action plan. This set out for each of the main health services a statement of intent for the following four year period, supported in many cases by a statement of targets, though with varying levels of specificity. Although this framework can be criticised for not being sufficiently specific in regard to planned outcomes, time lines and key responsibilities, it did reflect a clear desire for co-ordinated action across the health system in pursuing a set of stated goals and targets.

The strategy was widely welcomed by those within the health system and more generally, both for the change of direction and re-shaping it promised as well as its value as a road map for decision makers at all levels in the health system. It was also an early expression of a new approach to strategic planning then being promoted as part of public management reform more generally.

As part of the preparation of the current strategy, Quality and Fairness, an independent review of the 1994 strategy was undertaken by the ESRI (Wiley, 2001). The motivation in doing this was to objectively establish some baseline as the starting point for a new strategy, to harvest the lessons and experience from the implementation process over the preceding six years and to incorporate these into the preparation of the new strategy in some methodical fashion.

Some of the key conclusions from this independent review can be summarised as follows:

- The incorporation of a performance monitoring process into a plan for the health system was innovative and in setting out a shared set of targets represented an enormous advance for planning and policy development.

- Substantial progress was achieved on a majority of the targets set out.

- There was not, however, a standardised framework for design of targets, leading to some inconsistency as to specificity and degree of challenge involved across the policy agenda.

- Among the many competing policy goals, clear priorities in terms of urgency and resourcing were not articulated.

- The performance indicators, means of achievement and key responsibilities should have been made explicit.

- The timeframes projected for target achievement should reflect both the necessary discipline of setting deadlines but also the need to retain some degree of flexibility in responding to unexpected events (Wiley, 2001).

Overall, the review pointed up the value of a strategy and action plan in providing a focus for integrated effort in a complex system, such as the health services. The review also conveyed important messages with regard to the preparation process. In particular it identified the importance of effective consultation and communication with stakeholders. More specifically, the following factors were identified as being of key importance in the development process:

- The scope of the process must be clearly specified at the outset.

- A project management plan needs to be developed and agreed.

- The consultation process needs to be open, transparent, balanced, manageable and effective.

- A small team of individuals committed to the development of the strategy and involved throughout the process is critical.

- Clarity of vision is essential; it is important that all parties to the health system can identify with the strategic vision being proposed for health system development.

- Ensuring appropriate responsiveness to unplanned events demands an acceptable degree of flexibility for strategy development and outcome.

- Targets and objectives must be appropriate and specified in an achievable manner.

- Adequate procedures for monitoring and evaluation are essential.

- An expansive and inclusive communications programme utilising the power of state-of-the-art technology is a prerequisite for ensuring that health system participants, consumers and the public at large take "ownership" of the health strategy for 2001 and beyond.

I have quite deliberately dwelt on the process involved in each of these strategic planning exercises as an important backdrop to the preparation of quality and fairness. The progression outlined above does reflect a developing momentum in the direction of more explicit and longer term planning with consistent growth in the depth and breadth of prior consultation employed. This form of strategic and joined up thinking was also very much in evidence in the preparation of a number of sectoral strategies developed in the late 1990s. In particular, the National Cancer Strategy (1996) and Action Plan (1997) and the Cardiovascular Health Strategy (1999) both employed a systematic planning approach, setting out clear goals and targets across the range of health service and other public policy areas concerned, were clear about the assignment of responsibilities for particular action points, and incorporated in a methodical way the expertise and views of the relevant stakeholders. Both strategies were strongly endorsed by Government with clear commitments to make the necessary level of investment in the development of key services over defined time frames. The commitment to implementation was also reflected in the creation of custom-designed implementation and governance structures, again involving the range of relevant stakeholder interests.

Working with the Elements

By the time I took on my next strategic planning exercise – to lead the preparation of a national strategy for children in 1999 – I was in a posi-

tion to incorporate into the design of its preparation, all of the key principles and the lessons derived from earlier experiences.

These included the need:

- To communicate a clear vision, sense of mission and understanding
  of what is required and for strong, political and senior management
  endorsement and collaboration;

- To trust and actively bring into the frame all relevant stakeholders
  and to err on the side of generosity in determining who was to be involved and what roles they would perform;

- To provide user-friendly points of access for any person or organisation prepared to contribute;

- To provide continuity from conception, through analysis and action
  planning, through to implementation and management of outcomes;

- For technical competence, both in regard to subject matter and in
  relation to process, both for planning and implementation stages;

- To establish a framework for implementation, making clear what was
  expected of whom on each action point and by when; what the monitoring and reporting relationship in relation to progress were to be
  and how public accountability for results and outcomes would be
  discharged.

Health and services for children across the range of public services involved, must count as two of the most challenging areas of public policy-
making. Both are intrinsically concerned with the well-being of the person, both are explosive in terms of emotional impact and acute public
interest, both are multi-faceted, involving a complex cocktail of interacting policy measures and professional contacts and both involve virtu-
ally the entire community as stakeholders in one capacity or another. To
state that these shared characteristics make for complexity in planning,
managing and developing the relevant services would not do justice to
the scale of the challenge involved in either. The maxim I adopted in
setting out on the road to strategy building in both cases was that as a
Department we needed all the help we could get from all available
sources and that our task would be to put in place an accessible and or-
derly process through which these multiple contributions could be woven
into a road map for the future, which would be meaningful to all stake-

holders and would secure the ownership, commitment and active participation of all relevant actors in delivering on the actions later required for
successful implementation.

In the case of the National Children's Strategy this involved a
structure that was designed to actively involve all relevant Government
departments and public bodies, NGOs, relevant groups of professional
practitioners and the relevant academic and research community, including both national and international expertise. An inter-departmental
group provided overall direction to the Strategy with expert advice and
guidance from an International and a National Research and Information Advisory Panel, a Non-Governmental Advisory Panel as well as a
Health Board Liaison Group. The Strategy was prepared by a cross-
departmental team. The process put in place provided for a well organised and accessible public consultation process, and a custom designed
means for consulting with the central stakeholder– the raison d'être for
this strategy – children and young people themselves. The resulting
blueprint found widespread support when published and this has continued through the implementation stage. Dedicated structures (e.g. Office of the Minister for Children, Ombudsman for Children) were put in
place to ensure continuing focus on the action points and to maintain
momentum over a medium- and longer-term implementation timeframe.

Taking the Helm

Against the background of these previous experiences I was appointed
Secretary General of the Department of Health and Children in January
2000. There are few events in life which can match the tsunami of feeling and emotion that goes with such an appointment. There is a sense of
pride and achievement, a feeling of honour, an anxiety to succeed, an
awesome sense of responsibility, a sense of confidence and optimism
about the future and a real sense of urgency about getting on with it and
making a start. I interpreted it as a role which required strong leadership,
an ability to think through to the future while remaining agile in responding to day to day pressures, an ability to work intensively with and
through other people and overall, an ability to project a strong sense of
direction and communication in an environment beset by crisis management and negative public commentary.

At the time of my appointment the department was feeling the impact of a number of pressures, the collective aftermath of a series of major shocks during the late 1990s. These included:

- Tribunal of Inquiry into the blood bank scandal

- The nurses' strike of 1997

- The on-going crisis in the acute hospitals, reflected in the accident and emergency pressures and acute public criticism of the length of waiting lists for elective procedures

- Long waiting lists for other services, e.g. orthodontics

- Ongoing friction about the pace at which the backlog in services for people with a disability was being addressed

- Constant pressure from the courts regarding the shortage of places for young people in care, and

- A fractious environment within the Department, with significant mistrust and divided loyalty at top management level.

I had the advantage of having spent a period over two years (November 1997-February 1999) on assignment with the Department of Justice, Equality and Law Reform, working full-time on the management of strategic change. During this period I had also been very centrally involved in thinking through some of the key elements of the Strategic Management Initiative as a member of a number of working groups on different aspects of the SMI. I had therefore been out of the "heat of the kitchen" for a period and had the opportunity for some reflection and creative thinking about how apparently intractable problems in public management could be tackled in a more business-like way. It was in these circumstances a natural instinct on my part to now think in more strategic terms about health policy and to think about a widely shared strategic view as a way of moving key actors onto a common pathway in terms of future progress.

It had also become clear to me that the annual estimates cycle was a very poor mechanism for achieving strategic change, although it had considerable strengths in copperfastening the role of the Department of Finance in controlling the volume of public spending. I had come to realise that if anything worthwhile was to be achieved, it would have to be on the basis of presenting a full analysis of the entire system and all of its strengths and weaknesses to Government, along with a set of suggested solutions and an implementation plan which of necessity would have to adopt a medium to long term timeframe for implementation.

It was also clear that any process like this could only succeed if it had full political commitment and involvement. The relationship between a Minister and Secretary General can be a delicate organism. It thrives on mutual respect, mutual trust and open communication. The absence of any of these attributes on the part of either party to the relationship makes for difficulty. Where none of the prerequisites are present, in either direction, the relationship fails. I was fortunate to work in my first years as Secretary General in a context where all of the prerequisites for a constructive working relationship were in place. The then Minister and I had both arrived into our posts at about the same time, neither of us with too many preconceptions, other than that we would have to work extremely hard and in a mutually supportive way. From our first contacts it became clear that we were both utterly determined to make a lasting impact on the capacity of the health system to deliver the results expected by the tax-paying public.

One of my early experiences as Secretary General was to lead and co-ordinate the response to a no-confidence (in the Minister for Health and Children) motion by the opposition parties during the early months of 2000. The experience reinforced in my mind the need for a serious engagement in the form of a genuine and more broadly based public debate about the real issues and challenges in health policy and that this required an approach substantially different to the usual mechanisms adopted by the Department for effecting change. I shared my views with the Minister and we were agreed on the need to seek some new means of focusing longer-term attention on health policy, rather than simply responding to the latest symptom of dysfunctionality in whatever part of the system was in crisis at that particular time.

During the late 1990s, and quite independently, the whole question of management–staff–union partnership working had become a live issue across the public service. Many examples of successful partnership working could be observed elsewhere and this new model of working together on problems was being seen as a central feature of future working relationships in public management. The management of industrial relations in the health service had also come in for some criticism, based on the perception that too many issues were being brought to the stage of confrontation before being resolved. While there seemed to be good rea-

sons for this, based on the need for health management to defend centrally determined pay policy, nonetheless there was a view abroad that a
more participative approach to management, employing greater flexibility on both sides, could lead to a more constructive environment in
which fewer issues of contention would reach dispute stage. During
1999-2000 the precise model of partnership best suited to the health environment was being considered and one of the major players in the latter stages of that process was the then Policy Adviser to the Minister.

The broad design of the process of developing the health strategy
emerged from a quite spontaneous brain storm discussion I had with the
Minister's Adviser as an addendum to an informal discussion about
some other matter. The context was an end of week chat, reviewing the
week's happenings and anticipating likely issues for the following week.
As we touched on the subject of the health strategy I was coming to it
with the experience of the various strategy exercises outlined earlier and,
in particular, a desire to involve a broad range of stakeholders so intensively and openly that they would feel fully committed to the outcome
and would be equally willing and enthusiastic in their active implementation of their part(s) of the plan. The adviser was thinking more narrowly
of workforce participation and in particular about how the newly developing partnership structures might be employed with benefit both to the
strategy and for an early win for a partnership approach to a genuine
business challenge. Our joint conclusion was that a process should be
designed which embraced both aspects. We ran through the implications,
pros and cons of such an open and participative approach to strategy
building and overall felt the idea should run. Following on from this discussion, the idea was fleshed out, was discussed with and cleared by the
Minister and ultimately put into practice.

This was a good example of the successful (and spontaneous) bond-
ing of policy and political thinking. I could see the need for broad participation for a number of good policy and operational reasons:

- We needed to incorporate the thinking of a wider group of stakeholders, for completeness. This was a frank acknowledgement that
  the Department could not pretend to have all the answers internally.

- Given the scale of the task we were now taking on, we needed to be
  able to share the administrative load with others e.g. health boards,
  other health agencies.

- The opportunity to participate and help to shape the strategy should engender broader awareness of it and support for its implementation.

From the political viewpoint, while all of these were valid considerations, there was also an opportunity to demonstrate serious commitment through broad and overt participation and to create an appeal for the health unions, by addressing their concerns also within this overall framework, to begin to put flesh on the bones of a partnership model. We were conscious too that such an open approach would be more challenging in a number of ways. In particular, the task of building consensus would be more demanding and the preservation of some degree of confidentiality in regard to proposals to be submitted to Government for approval would present obvious difficulties.

Formal proposals to prepare a health strategy were then put to Government and approved early in 2001. Now in the driving seat, I had decisions to make about how to successfully mount a task of this magnitude within the limited timescale indicated – about twelve months. The reaction of many people to whom I spoke at the time was that it was an overly ambitious undertaking and high risk. At the time I had taken on the leadership of the National Children's Strategy in 1999, it had seemed similarly over-ambitious within a similar timeframe and my plans had been greeted with a similar sense of pessimism and caution. With the experience of successful completion of that project behind me, I was confident that we could and would succeed. Spurred on by these sentiments, I made a number of decisions which I believe were key to the success of this project.

Unlike all earlier exercises, I took the view that the Department and Health Boards should work in partnership on its preparation. The mechanism for joint working was already in place in the form of the MAC (Management Advisory Committee)–CEO Forum which was co-chaired by the Secretary General of the Department and the incumbent Chair of the CEO's group. Adopting this framework meant that we could reach across the full spectrum of policy issues, including an understanding of the impact on the ground of particular measures being considered. Working within this framework also required a discipline on the part of senior health board management, both in contributing a significant amount of time to the project and in observing confidentiality in relation to the matters being discussed. Their contribution was exemplary on both counts.

Internally in the Department I also took the view that the strategy was everyone's business and would be the priority project for the Department during its preparation. Each member of the MAC was assigned responsibility for leading work on a particular aspect. As chair of the MAC I took a close interest in the progress made in each area and input to the strategy became the dominant issue in all of my dealings with my colleagues. A dedicated Project Team was put in place, again formed from across the Department and by staff assigned by the Health Boards. While there was some internal debate and doubt expressed about the release of key staff for this purpose, the attitude I took was that this was our most important task at that time and on that basis, merited the assignment of some of the best people in the Department and health boards. This model of Department staff working in close partnership with staff assigned by the health boards on a common team headed by the Department was also an innovation in the health services. It worked very well, aided by a high level of shared commitment by those selected to the task in hand and very able leadership by the Project Director.

The process put in place also involved the participation of many other people at all levels in the Department and in the Health Boards. This was a deliberate stratagem, both to ensure that we exploited all available knowledge and insight but also as a way of sharing the effort and building ownership of the outcome.

It also involved an acknowledgement that if we were to do justice to the strategy project, other activities which by definition were of lesser priority would have to wait. This approach in the context of a busy Government Department like Health is a lot more difficult to do than to plan. Inevitably, workloads built up and the pressure was relieved through the willingness of many people to carry additional tasks on top of their "day jobs". This indicated to me the extent of the commitment that existed for a project that many believed would yield long-term solutions to the main challenges facing the health system. The extent of this commitment was also reinforced by the belief that at the political level there was a genuine will to grapple with the difficult issues and that the many supporting political pronouncements would ultimately be under-pinned by concrete action and adequate resource allocations. The extent to which such expectations were subsequently fulfilled is a matter for debate.

The Government had adopted a practice of allocating some of their time to theme discussions, concentrating on particular policy areas for more in-depth analysis and discussion of possible policy solutions. This led to the agreement by Government to focus on health for one of its regional meetings. That meeting took place in Ballymascanlon in May 2001 and was formed around a series of presentations made to the cabinet by the Department. This was a unique opportunity in beginning a more serious and reflective consideration of the full set of measures required to put the health system right. It took the debate out of the restrictive framework of the estimates cycle and very properly brought it into a "whole of Government" domain. This was appropriate both because the scale of what needed to be done would require full Government support and because so many other ministers could influence health outcomes through the policies and actions of their own departments.

The preparation by the Department for this meeting was intensive. Each aspect of policy was covered in a series of audio-visual presentations each delivered by the relevant member of the top management team. Against the background of fraught relationships internally I could also see the real value of an agenda which would sufficiently motivate and excite the staff of the department generally to the point that it, rather than inter-personal frictions, became the dominant pre-occupation. In my experience, deep down, every official of the Department of Health stands first and foremost for a better deal for people who depend on the public health system and for securing good value for the tax-payers investment. The Department corporately tended to be much less concerned about the interests of the private deliverers of services or the users of such services. This was based on the belief that parties to private arrangements had the motivation either of private profit or preferential access to services and were generally well equipped to look after their own interests.

However, the agenda we were setting out to address – e.g. waiting times for various services for public patients, service for people with a disability, greater equity in access to care and in payment for services – were all of direct concern to thinking people in the Department. The opportunity to open up these issues and put forward solutions to be discussed directly with Government, provoked an enthusiastic and spirited response by a top management team, united in the task of persuading Government that more needed to be and could be done.

The rules of Cabinet Confidentiality do not permit me to comment on the meeting itself. However, our internal conclusion was that the meeting had gone well, we had been given the opportunity to present on all relevant issues and we were satisfied that the Government collectively had been fully briefed on the extent of the problems in the health system and on the underlying policy and resourcing questions. The constructive mood of the meeting itself was somewhat marred by the very different perspectives on its outcome expressed respectively by the Minister for Health and Children and the Minister for Finance subsequently. The tension between these perspectives was to be a constant feature of the policy debate about health over the ensuing years and, I believe, a key influence in limiting the progress that could be made in pushing forward with the development and reform agenda which was adopted by Government in late 2001 but much of which still remains to be implemented.

Highlights of the Voyage

Preparing the Strategy

In describing the approach to preparing the strategy I am choosing to be selective and to concentrate on aspects which I believe will be of greatest interest to students of policy making. Neither do I intend to cover the content of the strategy document itself in any detail. Rather, the approach taken is to outline the stages of development, the process involved, the structures through which we worked and a brief commentary on the handling of some key policy questions.

The Start Up

A good policy initiative usually starts with the definition of some problem in public policy and a desire to identify the best solution. In health, there has traditionally been no shortage of problems being identified often around the eruption of some crisis and it is also true that a good deal of quality policy development has taken place, as reflected in the plentiful supply of reports, reviews, working groups and related avalanche of policy recommendations about most aspects of the health system. Very often though, these exercises take place in isolation from each other and the proposed solution can be difficult to assemble into a coherent whole. The earlier review of "strategy making" in health reflects the periodic quests to arrive at some overall picture of what required to be done. For a variety of reasons, already referred to, the same strong feeling that some better approach was needed had taken hold during the year 2000. That culminated in a decision late that year to develop a new strategy document.

The first stage involved thinking through the broad approach, putting a dedicated team in place to drive the project and constructing the right

alliance around it to ensure broad involvement in preparation and commitment to the outcome. It became clear fairly quickly that the order of
effort involved, the breadth and openness of consultation required and
the need to secure strong political commitment to the outcome would
require whole Government support from the word go. The intention to
prepare a new strategy was made known to the Department of Finance
and the Department of the Taoiseach late in 2000. However, the formal
proposal to do so was first put by the Minister to the Government via an
aide memoire on 6 February 2001. That informed the Government that
work had begun on the development of a new health strategy, outlined
the main areas to be covered and also referred to the breadth and depth of
the supporting public consultation process then being planned.

The planned strategy document had also been discussed in detail with
the Taoiseach at one of the policy discussions he was then having with the
Minister and Secretary General of each Department. The Taoiseach expressed enthusiastic support for the project from the start and consistently
during its preparation he encouraged the Minister and Department to be
ambitious and to consider radical change where it was felt necessary. He
was unambiguous about his strong personal support for the project and,
more significantly decided that one of his advisers would be closely involved in its development as a way of keeping the project "at the centre
of Government work in the coming months". This very clear support at
the highest political level, and the influential presence at all key meetings
of the advisor in question, was to be a powerful stimulus in keeping
commitment and energy levels high during the following months of intensive discussion, negotiation and drafting.

The Project Structure

A project of this complexity and obvious political importance required a
supporting structure which would be sufficiently broadly based to include all relevant viewpoints but would also need to be well led and co-
ordinated to ensure a closely woven set of proposals as the eventual outcome. The fact that the Government wished to have the strategy by late
summer also imposed tight deadlines on the consultation and drafting
work programmes. The structure we designed to deliver on these multiple requirements is summarised in Figure 2.1.

Figure 2.1: Structure for Developing Health Strategy 2001

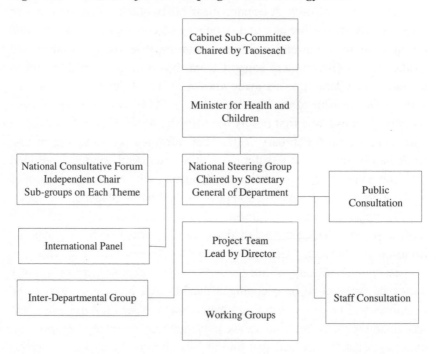

The role of each element of this structure was distinct and proved to have its own importance and value. A brief comment on how each element worked will assist in understanding the breadth of engagement involved and also the challenge of pulling the various strands together into a coherent whole.

Steering Group

This was the 17-member policy-making group made up of top management of the Department and the then health boards, representative of the Department of Finance and the Taoiseach's and Minister's advisers. It was chaired by the Secretary General of the Department and also included the Chair of the Project Team. Its role was to consider and approve all key proposals and to sign off on the content of the strategy overall, although final drafting was left to the Project Team. This was a novel structure in drawing together the top policy makers, the top managers of service and key political representatives into a single tight decision-making unit. Discussions tended to concentrate on the more sensitive and controversial proposals rather than to dwell on detailed preparation of more mainstream content. This group operated efficiently, meetings took place within a planned cycle, were well supported through preparation of position papers from the Project Team and Working Groups and, with few exceptions, the Steering Group quickly developed a common position on most topics considered.

Project Team

The 15-member Project Team was the motor for this entire project. It was made up of a group of senior managers from the Department and the then health boards from both administrative and professional backgrounds and led by a Director from the Department. A small number of people were released full-time for this project. However, many were asked to double-job for the duration but because the project generated a high level of enthusiasm throughout the health system, it was relatively easy to attract top quality people to become involved, even at considerable cost in terms of personal time and effort. Project elements were pursued with a relentless efficiency and the collective enthusiasm of the Team was both easily detectable and highly infectious. In summary its role was to manage, co-ordinate and develop to completion all aspects of the Project including the preparations of all drafts and the final document. It was supported in doing so by a number of other elements of the structure, outlined in the following paragraphs.

National Consultative Forum

This was a group of about 100 people, drawn from a broad range of backgrounds each with some particular relevance to the health system, which was convened specifically to provide input to shaping the strategy. Interests represented included patient and consumer representative groups, community and voluntary bodies, professional bodies, regulatory bodies, social partners, academics and others. The Forum was convened in plenary session on three occasions over the period of preparation. It had an independent Chair. Much of its detailed input came from the formation of sub-groups. Each of the sub-groups was formed so as to reflect a range of experience and knowledge and the mission assigned to each sub-group was to formulate ideas and proposals for change and to offer views on the key themes outlined in Figure 2.2.

Figure 2.2: Health Strategy 2001: Key Themes – Working Groups

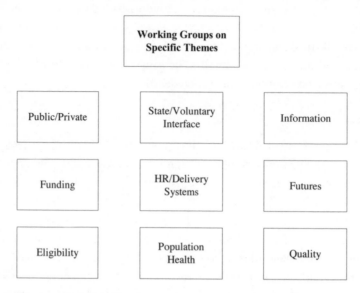

Each sub-group was chaired by a nominated person with a known inter-est or strength in that policy topic and the work of each sub-group was supported by a nominated member of the Project Team. It was also made clear to each sub-group that an important aspect of their role would be to test the validity and feasibility of proposals being put forward.

There was quite intensive interaction between Forum sub-groups and "official" working groups made up of Department and heath board staff with the objective of achieving convergence between both insider and outsider perspectives in regard to key questions around each of these themes. The conclusions from this joint working then fed directly into the work of the Project Team in preparing early drafts of the strategy document and the formal reports of the sub-groups were submitted to and considered by the Steering Group in its consideration of the overall content of the strategy.

The contribution made by the Forum was invaluable in bringing a re-ality check to the main thinking behind the strategy. This was as impor-tant around thinking through the early broad brush strokes, e.g. in adopt-ing a new vision and a set of four principles as it was in validating the overall thrust of particular policy initiatives in the latter stages.

The fact that this innovation in health policy development, which was conceived during an unplanned "Friday evening brain-storm", has now been adopted as a permanent feature of the policy-making process underlines the real value it delivered in the formation of strategy during 2001.

In addition, there was a very broad ranging consultation process with the general public. Advertisements were placed in national newspapers inviting the public to submit their views on healthcare. Consultation packs were provided to all who requested them. An overwhelming response was received from civil society organisations and individual members of the public. This proved beyond doubt that the public have a commitment to improving healthcare in this country. The Department collated all of this valuable information and as well as ensuring that it was reflected in the Strategy, it formed the content of a separate more detailed report entitled *Your Views about Health* whose publication accompanied that of the Strategy Document.

International Panel

The consultation that took place with a selected panel of three international experts was designed to ensure that the new policy direction would be consistent with most recent thinking internationally and that the lessons of reform in other health systems were taken onboard. The expected contribution from an international critique was the likely effectiveness or otherwise of particular initiatives based on experience elsewhere and any obvious misfits between the problems to be addressed and the solutions being proposed, again drawing on their knowledge of experience elsewhere.

Maintaining consistency with best international practice would have been an on-going concern in policy development at many levels in the health system. Through involvement with the work of the WHO, EU, OECD, Council of Europe and other international organisations with an interest in healthcare, the Department, senior health managers and professionals were already aware of the international developments of most relevance. It was not surprising therefore that the main task actually undertaken by the members of the International Panel was largely to validate and reinforce many of the policy positions being put forward in the context of the strategy.

Particular points of emphasis in the views they offered included:

- A stronger statement about health as a right, to be expressed in the context of a right by everyone to achieve full health potential.

- The absolute need to develop a full functioning primary healthcare system to which all members of the community would have access without impediment. The apparent policy paradox in the Irish health system between the system of eligibility and entitlements which seemed to favour secondary care, and the stated policy priority for primary care was a constant theme in these discussions.

- In discussing future scenarios, the panel emphasised the need to moderate public expectations from the new generations of apparent "wonder-drugs" with some discussion of demographic projections and the most rational use of limited resources.

- There was a positive endorsement of the participative approach being taken to strategy development and an equally strong rationale for continuing in this vein with a strong element of community involvement in the design of services on the ground.

These comments serve to illustrate the breadth of the perspective taken by the members of the panel and also the value of their overall endorsement of the process and emerging content of the strategy. They were required to operate under significant time pressures and their involvement was another significant re-enforcement in validating the overall shape and content by reference to best practice internationally.

Additional Valuable Inputs

The value of a strong input by the health workforce, both because of the technical knowledge it could offer as well as its importance as a "binding agent" in the future, was appreciated from the start. The medium employed was the national partnership structure for the health services, then in formation, and a similar process for the staff of the Department itself. The work undertaken by the Partnership Forum was important both in bringing new knowledge and a very practical perspective to bear on some of the policy issues being addressed but also in engaging the health workforce in a very meaningful way with the policy and business challenges faced by the health system.

The Quality Forum was established during 2000 as an informal grouping of professionals, service managers and policy-makers with a commitment to a much stronger focus on the positive management of quality at all levels in the health system.

The Forum was convened on a number of occasions over the period 2000-2001 and many of the ideas which it espoused can be readily identified in the approach to quality reflected throughout the strategy document. In particular the adoption of "guaranteeing quality of care" as a core principle, the emphasis placed on "national standards supporting best patient care and safety" as a core element of the national goal concerned with high performance and the putting in place of a permanent evidence-based focus for standard-setting and evaluation in the form of the Health Information and Quality Authority to drive the quality agenda forward underline the signal importance attached to quality management as a core theme running through the strategy.

The work done within the Quality Forum added real value in this respect and presented a ready made agenda for action in incorporating a strong quality focus into the overall policy agenda.

Any study of population health will quickly yield a conclusion that it is heavily dependent on many other factors and inputs, apart from healthcare per se. The establishment of a strong inter-Departmental dimension, as a pre-cursor to joined up thinking in developing and implementing solutions, was therefore a natural part of the overall architecture of strategy building. The pervasive nature of the health policy challenge is reflected in the involvement of nine other Departments in the Inter-Departmental Group (IDG). The process involved an identification of policy overlaps between the respective concerns of the particular Department and the health system in regard to specific care groups, e.g. older people, children, prisoners, homeless people, people with a disability or policy areas, such as, traffic accidents, drug dependency, and service delivery issues e.g. unique identifier, one-stop-shops, among others.

In each case the IDG was asked to identify issues and policy challenges and to put forward shared solutions involving some degree of joint action between different Government agencies. This process could be seen as responding to the government's wish to see more joined-up Government as well as positioning health concerns much more prominently on the agendas of relevant Departments and public agencies.

A Cabinet Committee was also formed to consider selected proposals in depth as a pre-cursor to formal submission of the completed strategy document to Government for eventual approval and publication. This proved to be an extremely valuable forum for examination of the net political issues. Again the rules of Cabinet confidentiality preclude any comment on the content of these discussions. However, media coverage of the health debate over this period and public comments made by individual Ministers graphically illustrated the breadth of views supportive and otherwise in relation to the proposals being discussed. It was also clear that a lot of behind the scenes work needed to be done to develop consensus around the final content of the proposals adopted. This would not be considered unusual for such an extensive, and in places controversial, policy agenda and one that signalled a commitment of serious levels of public investment into the future. It reflected a level of collective engagement by the Government and would also have suggested strong commitment to subsequent implementation.

Overall, this elaborate and time-consuming process of strategy development engendered widespread support for the Strategy. Staff working at all levels of the health system were provided with the opportunity to be involved and contributed willingly of their time and expertise. The response from the public was overwhelming. Senior officials across the health system and across government departments contributed significant time and effort to ensure that this strategy both accurately reflected the current state of the health system and set out a realistic achievable and integrated set of strategic priorities to improve services for the public.

I sometimes asked myself why this unusual level of obvious support and active engagement materialised. I concluded that it was born of a belief that there was a real determination to, not just analyse problems, but to develop imaginative solutions and make them happen. The extent to which this confidence was borne out by subsequent developments, I will leave to the reader's judgement.

Conclusion

There are a number of valuable lessons I take with me from my long involvement in developing and implementing health policy in this country. First and foremost is that substantial shifts in policy require careful planning and calculated preparation of the environment over time. Success will not come to those who are in it for the short-haul. It is critical in a sea of changing political interests and competing political personalities that at least some of the actors in healthcare stick fast to a course that they believe will lead to improvement – even if this seems a long way down the line. From Health – the Wider Dimensions in 1986, through Shaping a Healthier Future in 1994 to Quality and Fairness in 2001, a period of 15 years, a slow but steady shift occurred in our approach to healthcare in this country

Another critical component in my learning process was acknowledging that any one person rarely has the full answer to any problem and that best solutions in terms of lasting impact rely on active participation at both the design and the execution stages. Participation is important on several levels: different perspectives – user/provider, insider/outsider, front-line/senior management, health/other departments – bring added value that helps us to question our actions – what we are doing, how we do it and why; active participation brings a greater sense of ownership and involvement – working together *harnesses* energy whereas opposing each other *dissipates* it. Nowhere is this more evident than in the partnership approach that has been adopted throughout the health service over the past several years and the positive contribution to policy development and implementation this engendered. Continuing progress seems more likely to flow from collaboration rather than confrontation.

Finally, this story of an inclusive, comprehensive approach to the development of what I believe to be a visionary, integrated and holistic blueprint for how we achieve a health system that meets the needs of all of our population, serves to highlight that the tried and tested approaches are not always the best ones. When we hear a good idea and believe it can work, even if it is somewhat alien to our usual modus operandi, and it hasn't been arrived at by the usual mechanisms, it might just be worth a risk. Every now and then it helps to push the boat out!

Whether these lessons have been fully absorbed into the current processes of decision-making in the health system is to the outsider, at best, an open question.

References

Department of Health. (1986). *Health – The Wider Dimensions*. Dublin: The Stationery Office.

Department of Health. (1994). *Shaping a Healthier Future: A Strategy for effective healthcare in the 1990s*. Dublin: The Stationery Office.

Department of Health and Children. (1996). *Cancer Services in Ireland: A National Strategy*. Dublin: The Stationery Office.

Department of Health and Children (1999) *Building Healthier Hearts: The Report of the Cardiovascular Health Strategy Group*, Dublin: Stationery Office.

Department of Health and Children. (2000). *The National Children's Strategy: Our Children – Their Lives*. Dublin: The Stationery Office.

Department of Health and Children. (2001). *Quality and Fairness: A Health System for You*. Dublin: The Stationery Office.

Department of Health and Children. (2002). *Your Views about Health: Report on Consultation*. Dublin: The Stationery Office.

Department of the Taoiseach. (1996). *Delivering Better Government: Second Report to Government of the Co-ordinating Group of Secretaries – A Programme of Change for the Irish Civil Service*. Dublin: The Stationery Office.

Government of Ireland. *Strategic Management Initiative*. http://www.bettergov.ie (accessed 8th May 2007).

Wiley, M. (2001). *Critique of Shaping a Healthier Future: A Strategy for Effective Healthcare in the 1990s*. Dublin: Economic and Social Research Institute.

Chapter 3

MENTAL HEALTH POLICY IN IRELAND

John Owens

Mental health has never been a topic of abiding interest within the Irish health services. The pattern is very much one of long periods of disinterest and neglect, followed by short intervals in which major attention is focused on the service, often in response to negative incidents of one sort or another. These long periods of neglect are difficult to understand, particularly from a public health point of view. Mental ill health is a ubiquitous phenomenon. Point prevalence in Ireland and other advanced countries suggests that, at any one time, around 17 per cent of the population will have a diagnosable mental health problem. Put another way, 25 per cent of people will develop a substantial mental health problem at some stage in their life and depressive illness will shortly overtake coronary artery disease as the main cause of health related disability (World Health Organisation, 2001). A number of reasons contribute to this disinterest in mental health services. Stigma is a major factor. Mental health problems can be seen by some as not having the legitimacy of physical health problems and there is still confusion in the mind of the public as to whether mental illness is a character problem or an illness phenomenon. In addition there is often a misplaced association between violence and mental illness. Facilities available traditionally for the treatment of mental illness have only heightened feelings of fear and rejection. People are often reluctant to acknowledge having a mental health problem and patients may be too ill to advocate effectively for improved services.

There have only been three national policy documents in relation to mental health services since the establishment of the State. *The Commis-*

sion of Inquiry on Mental Illness was published in 1966 (Department of Health). In 1984, the seminal policy document *Planning for the Future* was published (Department of Health). In January 2006, a third policy document *Vision for Change* was published (Department of Health and Children). The relative infrequency of national policy developments relating to mental health services has been matched by slowness in modernising mental health law. It is quite extraordinary that the Mental Treatment Act 1945, with relatively minor amendments in 1961, regulated mental health services and patient rights until the Mental Health Act 2001. This is in spite of increasing levels of awareness of human rights issues characteristic of the 1970s and 1980s. Patients can still be detained indefinitely, with no automatic independent right of the decision to detain. Similarly, modern safeguards of the rights of patients in regard to a range of treatments are not ensured. The long survival of an anachronistic law governing the rights and management of the mentally ill speaks volumes for the low priority given to these particularly vulnerable groups. This situation will only change when the remaining sections of the new 2001 Mental Health Act are commenced. In contrast to the past, Ireland is currently experiencing a surge of activity in relation to mental health services, as evidenced by the enactment of the Mental Health Act of 2001, the establishment of the Mental Health Commission in 2002 and the publication of *Vision for Change* in 2006. It remains to be seen whether the current level of interest is maintained.

The origin of mental health services in Ireland, as in the rest of the western world, was the setting up of asylums in the late eighteenth and nineteenth centuries. A range of county asylums came into being, the majority founded in the early and mid-ineteenth century. Initially these institutions were established to provide asylum, in its true sense of being a safe place and refuge for individuals who were socially derelict or behaviourally disordered. The role of the asylum gradually changed, however, and came to be seen as providing care for people with a mental illness of some sort. The emphasis in care gradually switched from a social to a medical model, at a time when mental illnesses were not understood and were essentially untreatable by medical means. This institutional medical model had the effect of separating people with mental illness from the community from which they came. It also led to an acceptance of long term disability and therapeutic despair. As a result of the lack of discharges and continued admissions to the asylums, they progressively increased in size. What were initially reasonably acceptable conditions, rapidly deteriorated in the context of over crowding and chronic under-funding. These asylums were seen as housing potentially dangerous individuals and rapidly became prison-like in their construction and general layout. They became total institutions, self-reliant and sealed off from the community at large. They had their own life routines, with uniform patient clothing, hospital farms, and their own churches and graveyards within the walls of the institution. These institutions became large employers in the areas where they existed, employing doctors, attendants, nurses and a wide range of trade staff such as farm manager, carpenters, tailors and butchers. Doubtless, they contributed in a major way to the economic life of their local communities.

The numbers resident in Irish asylums/mental hospitals peaked in 1958 at over 25,000. From the late 1940s, a range of new treatments were becoming available such as ECT, neuroleptic medications and anti-depressant medications. The effective nature of these treatments allowed the discharge of significant numbers of patients. The asylums/mental hospitals began to decline rapidly in size to the extent that in 1984 the number of inpatients in mental hospital units was 12,484 (Mental Health Commission, 2005). The asylum origin of mental health services, however, has had ongoing effects on the modernisation of services. At the structural level, services inherited an out-of-date institutional, stigmatised and often dilapidated physical structure on which to base services. This institutional background has had a lingering effect on the attitudes of both the general public and mental healthcare staff. Many mental healthcare professionals have had difficulty in adapting to non-bed based community programmes. There has been considerable reluctance to shed the secure employment associated with the institutions and the prison-like appearance of these institutions still lingers in the mind of the community, likely perpetuating attitudes of stigma.

The modern era of mental health service development started in the 1960s. This was a simultaneous development throughout the developed world and took the form of the espousal of community-based treatment programmes and a move away from institutional care. While there have been legitimate criticisms of community care in mental health services this model has been broadly accepted and remains the cornerstone of modern service developments. In Ireland this new approach was given expression by the policy documents *Commission of Inquiry to Mental Illness* in 1966 and *Planning for the Future* in 1984. This latter document, in particular, has been central in the development of mental health services in Ireland over the last 20 years. Its main recommendations were that services should be comprehensive, integrated, catchment-based and structured to allow continuity of care. It recommended the setting up of multidisciplinary community mental health teams, with services being provided in community mental health centres and outpatient clinics. It emphasised the importance of close links with primary care. The major thrust of the document amounted to a plan to provide alternative community-based care to individuals with chronic illness. Under this heading, it suggested the setting up of day centres, sheltered workshops and a range of group homes and hostels to provide community-based accommodation as an alternative to long term institutionalisation. *Planning for the Future* also recommended that all acute inpatient care be provided in psychiatric units in general hospitals. These have been slow to develop but the stage has now been reached where over 60 per cent of all acute admissions occur to these units and it is planned that, by 2009, all acute admissions will be to such units. At that time the large mental hospitals should have no further role in service provision.

Planning for the Future received widespread acceptance but its implementation by the different health boards varied to a significant degree. While under-funding was citied as a main reason for this limited implementation, it is evident that the main difficulty was the inability of service managers to release and shift existing resources from the institutional care programme to the recommended new service model. *Planning for the Future* did not give major consideration to management systems within the mental health service and this omission, to a certain extent, limited the full implementation of its recommendations. Despite this, the policy was associated with a dramatic reduction in the numbers of people in mental hospitals, with a decline in inpatients from 12,484 in 1984 to 3,475 in 2005 (Mental Health Commission, 2005). Four mental hospitals had closed, with the remainder having reduced greatly in size. While at first sight this might seem to be quite a dramatic success, the reduction in inpatient numbers was accompanied by the setting up of a range of hostels and group homes which, by 2005, was providing accommodation for over 3,000 people, the majority of whom were former long-stay residents of mental hospitals (Mental Health Commission, 2005). While the physical conditions in these community residences are generally superior to what existed in the mental hospitals, there has been valid criticism that the quality of care provided has not improved.

Despite the progressive, albeit slow and incomplete implementation of the recommendations of *Planning for the Future* the mental health services continue to be seen as inadequate, of poor quality and stigmatising. This view has been expressed not just by users of the services but by the service providers themselves. The nature of the criticisms and the reasons for them vary significantly between these groups (Keogh, Roche and Walsh, 1999; Dunne, 2006; Mental Health Commission, 2006; O'Keane, Walsh and Barry, 2005; Crowley, 2003).

It is only in very recent times in Ireland that the rise of consumerism has resulted in service providers talking to and taking on board the views of users. Users see services as being difficult to access, provided in poor quality, stigmatising premises, inordinately medication-dominated, and allowing them little opportunity to have inputs in deciding their care plans. Community-based services for people with acute illness are frequently restricted to the limited contact available in often overcrowded outpatient clinics. For those with enduring illness, rehabilitation services are often rudimentary and limited to repeated and frequently fruitless admissions to acute units or to accommodation in what may amount to little more than a community-based long stay ward sited in a hostel (Mental Health Commission, 2005). For both groups, a narrow medical model very much under-emphasises the importance of psychological and social factors with resulting under-investment in potentially effective, individualised care programmes directed at reducing areas of disability and disadvantage. This situation has been significantly contributed to by the failure to develop truly multidisciplinary community mental health teams, encouraging a narrow medical focus in assessment and treatment.

Clinical professionals regard lack of resources as being the major limiting factor in service development. Psychiatrists stress, in particular, lack of staffing and beds. Non-clinical professional managers also stress lack of resources as being a major problem, despite the very substantial resources potentially at their disposal in a rapidly declining institutional base. They cite industrial relations issues, arising from clinical professionals' reluctance to adapt to new ways of working, as hindering the redeployment of staff resources. In turn, clinical professionals describe difficulties in achieving meaningful roles in management. However, within the management structure that does exist, clinical professionals do not seem to have shown sufficient interest or confidence in their roles. This is manifest in the very limited interest in service research in Irish mental health services and a reluctance by many clinicians to be innovative in using the resources at their disposal. Conflicting viewpoints and a dysfunctional management system within the mental health service underlie the failure to provide high quality, accountable, efficient and easily accessible services. In this conflictual situation morale has been adversely affected and responsibility for service deficiencies has been shifted from one group to another.

Management of mental health services in Ireland has been disappointing, particularly in its failure to transpose the substantial staff and capital resources available in the declining institutional model to support new community developments. Clinical management has not yet begun to introduce widespread clinical governance systems to ensure the delivery of safe, effective and efficient services. The result of these failures is that mental health services nationally vary to a remarkable degree across a range of service measures. These include admission rates, new long stay rates, certification rates, rate of ECT use, hospitalised morbidity, range of specialty service availability and availability of alternatives to bed use (Mental Health Commission, 2005). Staffing and funding levels show high variability across catchments, reflecting the location of mental hospitals established over a century and a half ago. For example, funding in 2005 varied from €79 to €493 per head of the population, bearing no relationship to rates of deprivation. So it is that users of mental health services in Ireland find themselves in a lottery situation in regard to the services available to them. It is evident however, that funding is not the defining factor in service quality variation. Some poorly funded catchments have been innovative in service development and have relatively high quality services. Similarly, some well funded catchments have shown little sign of local initiative and have services that are still predominantly institutional in character. Many clinical professionals nominally aspire to the provision of community services but continue to practice a bed-based service, complaining bitterly when beds are no longer available in the planned reduction in institutional care.

Impediments to Change

Irish Mental Health Services have changed substantially in the last two decades, with *Planning for the Future* being the major force driving this change. Its implementation, however, has been incomplete and patchy. It is useful to reflect on factors which have retarded the obvious need for service reform and modernisation. These factors include:

- Limited public interest and engagement

- Limited political interest

- Stigma

- Professional self-interest and inter-professional rivalry

- Under-availability of a range of clinical staff

- Centrality of beds as a locus of care in service delivery

- Separation of the mental health services from community services

- Paternalistic professional attitudes

- Fragmented and inefficient management structure

- Financial constraints

- Lack of mental health service research.

The long-awaited and recently published national mental health policy document *Vision for Change* attempts to address these issues.

Limited Public Interest and Engagement

Public interest and engagement in mental health service issues follow on public knowledge. Both the educational system and the media have major roles to play here. The public will not be interested in mental health issues if they see mental health problems as having little relevance for them. In the light of 17 per cent prevalence of substantial mental illness at any one time and the fact that mental illness directly impinges on the lives of families and associates, its relevance for all is evident. The financial implications of mental health problems demand that the burden of mental ill health be taken very seriously. The cost of mental ill health has been studied in a number of countries including Northern Ireland (Sainsbury Centre for Mental Health, 2004). Extrapolating these studies to the Republic of Ireland it is likely that the annual cost of mental ill health is in the region of €10 billion. Most of this cost relates to social and personal costs, with less than €1 billion being incurred by the cost of treatment.

In many ways, the media reflect the general public's apparent lack of interest in mental health issues. What limited reporting occurs is more often negative, focusing on untoward events within the service or highlighting, in a non-substantiated way, associations between violence, crime and mental illness. A reasonable and more valid approach might be more frequent publication of measured articles on the nature of mental ill health, its prevalence, the services available for its treatment and the negative consequences of stigma.

Limited Political Interest

Political interest, in general, responds to community concerns highlighted by the media, as evidenced by the political response to rising suicide rates. The limited public interest in broader mental health issues however, as expressed in the media, underlies the lack of political interest and engagement in these matters. In these circumstances it behoves government to ensure that this poorly represented aspect of health services is adequately prioritised and funded.

Stigma

The policy document *Vision for Change* defines three approaches in dealing with stigma. These are described as contact, education and challenge. Stigma is understandable in the context of a predominantly institutionally based care system and there is no doubt that the past asylum model contributed greatly to fear of mental illness and reluctance to acknowledging having problems of this nature. The development of more advanced models of community care, where mental illness of both acute and chronic nature can be contained and managed within visible community settings, should go a long way to dissipate these irrational fears. Normalising and mainstreaming mental healthcare systems, apart from having the potential to substantially increase the resources available for the mentally ill, should have the effect of informing the public that mental illness and mental health disability are in the same category as all other illnesses and disabilities. Health professionals are not immune from stigmatised attitudes and, in the move towards community care, people with mental health problems have had to suffer a degree of discrimination in their entitlement to other specialist services and programmes.

Educational programmes, in which mental health and emotional problems are seen as an essential part of health education, are now beginning to develop in schools. While these programmes remain to be evaluated information of this sort should be helpful in making young people more aware of emotional and mental health issues and give them greater understanding and ability to deal with these aspects of their lives.

The state has a role in challenging discriminatory practices, particularly in the areas of employment and housing for those with chronic illness. The state itself should not indulge in discriminatory practices. Given the ongoing lack of a natural constituency for the mentally ill, the state should ensure that mental health services are allocated a reasonable percentage of total health spending. There has been a progressive decline in the percentage of total health expenditure devoted to mental health service, from 13 per cent in 1984 to 6.7 per cent in 2005 (Department of Health and Children, 2006). A significant portion of this decline is related to the rapid deinstitutionalisation of mental health services and redesignation of former mental health units. However, the stage has now been reached where mental health services are not being allocated a fair proportion of health funding.

Professional Self-interest and Inter-professional Rivalry

The multidisciplinary approach to the delivery of modern mental health-care arose from the acceptance of the importance of biological, psychological and social factors in the origin and treatment of mental illness. Despite the recommendations for multidisciplinary community mental health teams in *Planning for the Future* in 1984, these teams have been slow to develop so that, currently, there are very few fully staffed, appropriately-functioning teams of this nature. In addition, differing perceptions of the relative importance of the biological, psychological and social factors across clinical disciplines have, in some cases, not been successfully bridged, so that when teams do exist, the disciplines tend to work in isolation. Medical dominance remains the norm and there has been a reluctance to allow non-medical team members to contribute to the elaboration of comprehensive care programmes. For some of the minority clinical professions, such as psychology, social work and occupational therapy, this has resulted in what might be regarded as a "cold house" and is likely to be a factor in the limited availability of these clinical professional groups. There has also been a limited acceptance of alternative community approaches in mental health treatment within the nursing profession. Nursing career structures and salary premia are still linked excessively to bed-based models of care, leading to a considerable reluctance to accept any radical move in the direction of community services. Nursing forms, by far, the majority of clinical professionals in mental health services and their willingness to adapt to new models of care will be essential in their modernisation.

Under-availability of a Range of Clinical Staff

Irish mental health services are notable for their lack of a range of mental health professionals. These professionals are essential for the establishment of the multidisciplinary mental health teams necessary for the development of community mental health services. This has come about because of the dominant bed-based model of care. Professional groups such as social workers and occupational therapists were traditionally given limited roles, often concerned with serving the interests of institutions. There is an urgent need to extensively increase professional resources in these areas. This will require major reform in professional training, with significant increases in training places and extra finance. Given the duration of training, resolution of these shortages will necessarily take considerable time.

The training of all health professionals, in general, tends to be narrowly clinical, with limited emphasis on concepts of community health and models of service provision. Similarly, clinical professionals are poorly trained in principles of management and, at a very practical level, in team-working with other professionals. These are issues which will need to be addressed by the relevant training bodies at both undergraduate and postgraduate level.

Centrality of Beds

Though mental health services in Ireland are now developing a community orientation, most services still operate from an institutional base in close association with beds, either in a psychiatric hospital or a psychiatric unit in a general hospital. Inpatient care still remains the hub of interest and is clearly overused as a way of dealing with both acute illness in crisis and illness which does not fully recover. This situation continues, despite clear evidence that much illness, both acute and chronic, does not respond satisfactorily to bed-based care. Seventy-five per cent of all admissions are readmissions (Daly, Walsh, Doherty et al., 2004). Many inpatient units are "silted up" with patients who remain ill and disabled despite prolonged inpatient care (Keogh, Roche and Walsh, 1999). Most acute inpatient units exhibit a pattern whereby a small number of patients make up a substantial proportion of all admissions and occupied bed days, through a pattern of very frequent readmissions. This pattern is allowed to continue despite its manifest failure to benefit patients. The need to move away from this futile activity, demoralising for both patients and clinical professionals, has been slow to be fully realised. More advanced models of community care, allowing for home-based and assertive outreach treatment, provided by specialist teams, have only recently begun to make their appearance.

Separation from Community Services

Mental health services still remain separate from community care services. While links with general practitioner/primary care services have improved, these links are still limited and successful models of coordinated care are still the exception. A great deal of mental ill health is related to social disadvantage in a range of areas including housing, education, employment and family dysfunction. Community care programmes working in these areas have significant potential to become allies in delivering comprehensive mental healthcare programmes. Unfortunately, mental health services, coming from their historical institutional base, have remained aloof from these potential partners in treatment. In turn, community care services, in the light of their own limited resource, have often not been welcoming in sharing resources with mental health services. The synergy involved in an appropriate alliance between these services would have major potential, not only to radically increase the efficacy of services, but also to go a long way towards reducing the stigma associated with mental illness. This type of coordination might seem to be self-evident, but for a variety of reasons, it has not happened. An example of this separation between mental health and community care services was the concern expressed by the majority of consultant psychiatrists when, in the recent health reforms, mental health services were included in the Primary, Continuing and Community Care Programme, rather than in the Hospital Programme.

Paternalistic Professional Attitudes

All health professionals face a significant problem in their relationship with their patients. On the one hand they are responsible for elaborating treatment programmes, with reasonable expectation that patients will be compliant in carrying these out. On the other hand they must respect patients' views and attitudes in relation to treatments suggested. This can be a particular problem for mental health professionals when patients' understanding of treatment issues may be limited by the nature of their illness. Indeed, in certain cases, mental health professionals may recommend that patients' liberties be restricted under relevant legislation. In this setting, mental health professionals may find themselves in danger of not always recognising patients' autonomy and rights, so that treatment decisions may not be adequately discussed, side-effects of medications not fully recognised and the basic rights of full citizenship not taken seriously. Healthcare professionals, in some situations, have not been welcoming of the recent development of patient advocacy in representing patients' interests.

Fragmented and Inefficient Management Structure

Mental health services, like health services in general, have suffered from difficulties in achieving competent structures of management. The management system within mental health services remains based on the management structure of the traditional asylum/mental hospital. Mental health catchments are managed by a Resident Medical Superintendent, now known as Clinical Director, a Hospital Manager, now known as Service Administrator and a Chief Nursing Officer, now known as Director of Nursing. These management teams look after catchments of varying populations, again largely reflective of the population base of the original asylum/mental hospital. While in some catchments management has been impressive, in others management deficiencies have been very evident. Some professional and clinical managers involved in these management teams have not had any formal management training. In addition, there has been little scope for management input by the broader range of clinical professionals involved in the service. Limited catchment size has hampered planning for appropriate specialities and there has been no scope for input in broader strategic or national service development matters. The origin of this type of management, coming as it does from the management of large institutions, has been inclined to bias the service perceptions of managers in the direction of bed-based models of care. The dominance in this management structure has been exercised by the Service Administrator, who in essence, controls the service budget. In some areas, management has largely taken the form of administration, with the emphasis being on budget control rather than on service planning and development.

Financial Constraints

A common perception in many local mental health services has been that desired new developments are being held back by financial constraints. Yet, within the current mental health system, there are extensive resources whose value has in no way been optimised. With regard to capital resource, the value of land and buildings in the current mental health service is potentially enormous. A significant portion of the institutional base is now redundant and this redundancy will become more widespread as services become more community-based. The value of this capital resource has never been estimated but is likely well in excess of the capital funding required for a quality community-based mental health service. The failure to estimate and realise the value of this resource and to apply it to fund the new structures required in a community service is reflective of the rigidities in central health service management with the regard to the more appropriate use of redundant assets. Eighty-five per cent of mental health budgets are spent on salaries, thus increased financial efficiency and service development necessarily imply radical reorganisation of staff deployment. New revenue resources will be required for staffing the necessary range of specialist community mental health teams but, with appropriate retraining and redeployment of existing staff resource, the new revenue funding required should be relatively modest.

Lack of Mental Health Service Research

Research in the area of health service delivery has been historically neglected. Doctors, understandably, have been more interested in clinical matters and the effectiveness of medical procedures. It is not possible to define the financial input to health service delivery research, but anecdotally it is minimal. In a health service which is budgeted to spend over €13 billion in 2006, it is extraordinary that there has been so little interest in the assessment of current models of care. Within the mental health service, research into models of care is even more important, in the context of the development of new community-based care programmes. There has been some published research but this has been the exception. The Mental Health Commission has taken the initiative in beginning to resolve this issue and, following the publication of its research strategy, is currently considering the establishment of a Mental Health Service Research Centre to help stimulate, support and coordinate mental health service research (Mental Health Commission, 2005a).

Given these impediments to change, the modernisation of the Irish mental health service has been slow and the full recommendations of the 1984 planning document *Planning for the Future* have still not been implemented. This has affected morale of service providers and has led to significant disillusionment. The situation, however, has not been universally bleak. Against the odds, a small number of catchments have been successful in modernising their service provision. In these areas, models of advanced community care have been established, introducing, what has been for Ireland, a new concept of home-based treatment for acute illness in crisis, with an equivalent service of assertive outreach treatment for those with severe and enduring illness. These treatment models permit the management of most acute illness in crisis in home and community settings and allow a real alternative to use of inpatient beds. The Tallaght and Cavan/Monaghan catchment areas have developed these models to the most significant extent. The effects of these developments have been evident in a dramatic reduction in the use of inpatient beds and have been associated with high levels of patient, relative and general practitioners satisfaction. In both these services, rehabilitation psychiatry (services for those with severe and enduring illness) has been developed as a specialist service. In Cavan/Monaghan it has been possible to begin the establishment of a specialist community mental health team in rehabilitation with, in addition to an assertive outreach team, the appointment of a range of relevant specialist staff. This rehabilitation service has successfully tapped in to community care and local authority services for those with chronic mental disability. The success of the Cavan/ Monaghan programme can be measured in the disappearance of the new long stay category of patients and the decline of alternative community residential units. Indeed, this service has been open in its acknowledgement of the need for ongoing treatment and rehabilitation of those with chronic illness, in a way that traditional mental health services have not been. This service has also demonstrated the potential for recovery for this group of individuals, given appropriate, albeit expensive, treatment resource. There have been other innovative service developments across a range of specialty areas. A recent example is the DETECT programme in Dublin, a new service for the early detection of psychotic illnesses. There have been other innovations within specialty areas. These innovative services are examples of bottom-up developments, reflecting leadership and initiative at local level. While being localised in their effect, they do demonstrate the potential to release and more effectively apply local resource. Significantly, successful pilots of this nature have not been taken on board nationally and have been slow to extend to other areas. It is unrealistic, however, to expect major service change to occur without a new national mental health policy and a strategy for its implementation.

With the new interest in mental health issues following the introduction of the Mental Health Act 2001, the need to modernise mental health services was recognised. An expert group was set up in 2004 to draw up a new national mental health policy. This policy document *Vision for Change* was published in January 2006. The expert group, following consultation with users, providers and other interested parties, recommended radical reform. It suggested that services in the future be based on a range of well-staffed, fully trained, specialised, multidisciplinary, community-based mental health teams. It recommended that these teams provide the full range of integrated services for catchments in the region of 400,000. Larger catchments were seen as necessary to provide for the full range of current and developing specialities. Home-based and assertive outreach care was recommended as standard practice. Maximum links between specialist mental health services, primary care services, voluntary services and community services were suggested. Maximum involvement of service users at all levels of service activity was prioritised. A new management structure was described at team, catchment and national level. The importance of service evaluation and meaningful performance indicators were stressed. A firm recommendation was made to close all existing psychiatric hospitals in the seven-year roll-out of the policy. New mental health information systems were recommended. It was recommended that planning, funding and training for mental health professionals be centralised in new HSE structures, as part of a multi-professional mental health service manpower plan. Substantial extra funding was recommended for the full implementation of the seven-year plan.

Core recommendations of *Vision for Change* are the development of the necessary range of new specialised community mental health teams, financial investment, real user involvement and the provision of new management structures. If deinstitutionalisation was a central feature of the previous policy *Planning for the Future*, the development of true multidisciplinary community mental health teams is the central feature of *Vision for Change*. The difficulties in developing such teams relate not only to the provision of adequate numbers of the required range of pro-

fessionals but also to the establishment of true multidisciplinary working. This process might be facilitated by opportunities for limited joint
training at undergraduate and postgraduate level. Psychiatrists, as the
lead profession, will have particular influence and responsibility in facilitating the move to multidisciplinary team working.

The non-capital cost of the new service envisaged under *Vision for
Change* will involve an additional €151 million. In the seven-year roll
out of the plan, this additional funding is relatively modest and attainable
at €21.6 million each year. However, if this funding is to be realistic,
available current staff will have to cooperate in a radical redeployment to
the new community services. To ensure the success of this redeployment,
the new management structures will need to be sensitive to the interests
of current staff and ensure that they have appropriately rewarded and
more satisfying roles within the new service. The capital funding required is much more substantial, involving the procurement of a large
number of purpose-designed community mental health centres. Altogether, a capital funding requirement of €796 million is suggested. This
extra funding is very realistic, given the substantial resource already existing within the current antiquated system. The capital requirement can
largely be met by realising the financial worth of the extensive and redundant institutional base and prioritising the resulting monies for the
new mental health service.

Vision for Change spells out in some detail how users can be more
actively involved in the new mental health service. Apart from being
given opportunities for realistic involvement in their own care plans, it is
recommended that users have a place on catchment management teams
and the new national mental health service directorate. If this increased
user involvement is to be successful, it will necessarily involve specific
training programmes for selected individuals with interest and commitment in mental health service development. Individuals with these qualifications are, in recent years, coming to the fore. However, it may well
be that such high level user involvement in mental health services may
take a number of years to evolve.

Vision for Change recommends radical reform of the management of
mental health services. It is seen as essential that management functions
are exercised jointly by clinical and management professionals. Community mental health teams will be required to be self-managing. They will
prepare service plans, agree service budgets and be responsible for delivering stated service goals. The new catchment management system will

be multidisciplinary and have representatives from core mental health professional and users. It will have, as a central function, the integration of a wide range of specialist community mental health services. The proposed national mental health service directorate, again multidisciplinary in make-up and with user participation, will be a new departure enabling mental health services nationally to be planned and coordinated on a rational basis. It will be linked to senior management within the Health Service Executive and will have significant inputs into national mental health service budgeting and manpower training issues. One of its more difficult tasks will be maintaining the integrity of the new specialist mental health service, while facilitating close working relationships and, to a degree, integration with community care and primary care services.

If the new management structure is to be successful it will require a radical improvement in the availability of accurate information on a whole range of service activity. What information is available at the moment is largely limited to inpatient activity – admissions, discharges, diagnostic category and legal status. Limited information is available for outpatient activity and attendances at day centres and day hospitals. Data are also available on numbers of places in group homes and hostels. No information is available on the extent and value of clinical inputs across the whole range of clinical professional activity, making it impossible to implement even the basic principles of clinical governance or to plan for the more effective use of clinical resource. The availability of this service information, so essential in effective planning, will need to be a high priority for the new national mental health service directorate.

So, what does the future hold? What can be anticipated in mental health service development at this point? Despite past experience, there is reason to hope that the Irish mental health services will achieve the radical modernisation that is so badly needed. Mental health law has been modernised and all parts of the Mental Health Act 2001 will shortly be commenced. The new national policy document, *Vision for Change,* spells out in detail the requirements for the evolution of a high quality mental health service and its implementation does not present a major financial challenge. There must, however, remain some concerns that the necessary service reforms will not be fully and promptly implemented. Previous mental health policy documents have been characterised by slow and incomplete implementation. All systems, by their very nature, resist change. The majority of resource within the mental health system is currently spent on institutions and the salaries of the individuals working to serve them, thereby supporting a model of care that is antipathetic to the real needs of service users. The greatest challenge will be to persuade current care providers to accept what will be, for some, radically new ways of working in the new advanced community services. The new management systems will have responsibility for bringing about this change and their establishment must be the first step in the roll-out of the new policy document. The Health Service Executive (HSE) has the responsibility for the implementation of *Vision for Change* and must show urgency and vigour in so doing. The concern must be that, if progress is not made in the short term in delivering on the recommendations for mental health service reform, the momentum for necessary service change will be greatly reduced.

A very significant step forward has been the establishment of the Mental Health Commission. The Commission is an independent, statutory body, set up under the Mental Health Act 2001. It has the dual responsibility of protecting the rights of detained patients and of fostering high quality in the delivery of mental health services. It has, fundamentally, a user-oriented approach in fulfilling these responsibilities. As a result, there is now a body with ongoing responsibility for ensuring user rights and quality in mental healthcare. The Mental Health Commission has endorsed the main recommendations of *Vision for Change* and will have a crucial role in advocating for their implementation. Through the Inspector of Mental Health Services, the Commission is uniquely qualified to exercise this role in having up-to-date knowledge of the quality of care delivered throughout the mental health services. In the pursuit of its quality agenda, the Commission has produced a series of reports and discussion documents relating to core areas of service provision which will be helpful in guiding services in the implementation of the recommendations of *Vision for Change*.

At long last, the wind seems set fair for the modernisation of Irish mental health services. It will be the responsibility of all involved stakeholders to ensure that this really comes about.

References

Crowley, F. (2003). *Mental Illness- The Neglected Quarter*. Dublin: Amnesty Ireland.

Daly, A., Walsh, D., O'Doherty, Y., et al. *Activities of Irish Psychiatric Units and Hospitals 2004*. Dublin: Health Research Board.

Department of Health. (1966). *Report of the Commission of Inquiry on Mental Illness.* Dublin: The Stationery Office.

Department of Health. (1984). *The Psychiatric Services – Planning for the Future. Report of a Study Group on the Development of the Psychiatric Services.* Dublin: The Stationery Office.

Department of Health and Children (2006) *Vision for Change: Report of the Expert Group on Mental Health Policy.* Dublin: The Stationery Office

Dunne, E.A. (2006) *The Views of Adult Users of the Public Sector Mental Health Services.* Dublin: Mental Health Commission.

Keogh, F., Roche, A., and Walsh, D. (1999) *"We Have No Beds…" An Enquiry into the availability and use of Acute Psychiatric Beds in the Eastern Health Board Region.* Dublin: Health Research Board.

O'Keane, V., Walsh, D., Barry, S. (2005) *"The Black Hole". The Funding Allocated to Adult Mental Health Services: Where Is It Actually Going?* Dublin: Irish Psychiatric Association.

Mental Health Commission. (2005). *Fourth Annual Report.* Dublin: Mental Health Commission.

Mental Health Commission. (2005a). *Research Strategy.* Dublin: Mental Health Commission.

Mental Health Commission. (2006). *Quality in Mental Health – Your Views.* Dublin: Mental Health Commission.

Sainsbury Centre for Mental Health. (2004). *Counting the Cost: The Economic and Social Cost of Mental Illness in Northern Ireland.* London: Sainsbury Centre for Mental Health.

World Health Organisation (2001). *The World Health Report 2001: Mental Health: New Understanding, New Hope.* Geneva: WHO

Chapter 4

KNOWLEDGE FOR HEALTH

Ruth Barrington

Introduction: Setting the Scene

What has knowledge ever done for health? For some, this question does not need to be asked, let alone answered; the contribution of knowledge, from the basic to the social sciences, to modern medical care and health systems is so obvious that the connection barely needs explanation. For them the question is how best to organise research and innovation systems to ensure that new knowledge is created and applied to the benefit of human health. There are others who do not see the connection so clearly or who are not persuaded of the need to organise ourselves in Ireland to create and use knowledge to improve health.

New knowledge, gleaned through research, has three major impacts on our health (Frenk, 2006). First, people use knowledge about health to change their own and societal behaviour. The research findings of Richard Doll and subsequently Richard Peto on the effects of smoking on health are an excellent example of knowledge that has helped change people's behaviour in the 50 years since the research was published (Peto, 1994). Second, knowledge generated through research helps to develop a consensus on the need to address health problems and how they should be addressed. The ban on smoking in the work place in Ireland is an example of the result of a consensus between different interests that formed following the publication of a report by the Office for Tobacco Control of research findings on the negative effects of inhaled smoke on the health of bar workers (Office for Tobacco Control, and the Health and Safety Authority, 2001). The reluctance of the South African government to accept the overwhelming evidence from research of the link between HIV infection and AIDS has, as an example of where knowledge has not been acted upon, resulted in years of delay in effective interventions to control the spread of the disease.[1] Third, the fruits of new knowledge that are translated into new therapies and interventions have greatly increased the effectiveness of medical interventions. Imaging that allows more accurate diagnosis; increasingly effective drugs to treat cancer; sophisticated implants for joint replacements; transplant surgery; stents that restore blood flow to the heart; vaccines to prevent meningitis; and anti-retroviral therapies that control the development of AIDS, are just some examples of where new knowledge has contributed and is continuing to contribute to better health outcomes. Advances in knowledge about information and communications technology, as applied to health systems, are transforming the efficiency and effectiveness of the way healthcare is delivered (Harno, 2007).

What evidence is there that this knowledge and its application make any difference to health as distinct from healthcare? The Society of Actuaries has estimated that those born in Ireland in 1940 are twice as healthy as those who were born in 1910 and this better health is now being reflected in dramatic falls in death rates across all age groups.[2] Mortality rates for men aged 55-64, for example, have halved since 1970. While one cannot claim that the dramatic fall in mortality rates that has occurred in this country over the past forty years is solely a result of more effective health interventions (improved nutrition, improved sanitation, and better lifestyles have all played a part), the application of new knowledge through health policies and interventions has been a major factor. Take the reduction by one half of the deaths from coronary heart disease between 1985 and 2000, for example. An important paper published in 2006 explores the relative contribution of different factors to this decrease in deaths from coronary heart disease (Bennett et al., 2006). The authors distinguish the relative contribution of medical and surgical treatments to reducing the mortality rate, on the one hand, and deaths prevented or postponed as a result of changes in population risk factors, such as smoking, lower cholesterol and lower blood pressure. They found that new treatments accounted for 43.6 per cent of the reduced mortality and control of risk factors for 48.1 per cent. For both categories, it was the generation of new knowledge through research that provided the evidence to change behaviour, for more effective health policies and more effective treatments. Interestingly, the paper shows that advances made in the last generation in controlling cardiovascular disease are being reversed by increased inactivity, obesity and diabetes. So a new set of challenges is being posed for research and health policy even as one problem is being solved.

There is a clear connection between the application of new knowledge and reductions in mortality and improved quality of life. In the past decade, research published by the World Health Organisation has drawn attention to the important link between the standard of health of the population to the overall development of a country (World Health Organisation, 2001). In much of the developing world, poor health is one of the major factors holding back economic progress. In the developed world, those countries that have high levels of health also tend to have high levels of economic growth and high standards of living. Those countries, that invested early in research for new knowledge to improve health have benefited economically from the development of new therapies, diagnostics, medical devices and health informatics. The pharmaceutical and medical devices industries are built on the outcomes of research and rely on a process of innovation that fosters the transfer of knowledge from the authors of peer-reviewed publications, through patient trials to the production of drugs and devices. Countries such as the US, Britain, Denmark and Finland that have recognised the importance of this process of innovation and fostered it have reaped the dividends in new products, companies and jobs. A report commissioned by the US Congress has found that the return on health research spending is of the order of 15 per cent.[3] The generation of new knowledge for health through research creates the classic "win-win" situation – the application of new knowledge increases health, provides a foundation for economic and social development and adds value through the production and sale of new health products. It is not surprising, as will be described later in this paper, that the contribution of health research to securing this country's place in the global knowledge economy is increasingly being recognised.

This paper describes efforts to define the role of research in the Irish health system and to position health research within the government's overall science and research policy. The story begins in the late 1990s and is far from concluded. At one level, it is a story about engaging the health system on the issue of research and the generation of new knowledge. At another, it is about mobilising the health system to work in cooperation with the third level sector and with economic and social development agencies so that the potential of health research to generate new knowledge is captured for the social and economic development of the country.

The background to this story is the low priority afforded to science and research nationally from the independence of the state to the late 1990s. A society that for the first 40 years of its existence tried to insulate itself from the intellectual tumult of the wider world was not one in which new ideas or innovation were likely to thrive. The policy shifts in economic policy and educational access in the late 1950s and 1960s and the decision to join the European Union, in addition to favourable demographic and global economic trends, brought Ireland unprecedented prosperity in the 1990s. However, this prosperity was largely thanks to the skill of Irish people manufacturing products which had been developed by scientists in other countries. The pharmaceutical and medical devices industries that have thrived in Ireland are good examples of high quality manufacturing operations based on the output of research and development that took place in other countries (Forfás, 2004).

As the prospect of losing much of the manufacturing base of Irish industry to lower cost economies became more likely, Government was persuaded of the need to invest in research and development, both to move up the value chain with existing manufacturing and to generate the new ideas for products or services that would underpin the next phase of economic and social development. A Technology Foresight exercise, begun in 1998, was quickly followed by decisions to prioritise investment in research and development in information and communications technology and bio-technology, the commitment of over €1 billion for research and development under the National Development Plan 2000-6, the Programme for Research in Third Level Institutions managed by the Higher Education Authority and the establishment in 2000 of Science Foundation Ireland. The impact of this policy change, led by the Department of Enterprise, Trade and Employment and the Department of Education and Science, has been profound, transforming the capacity of third level institutions to do research and to engage with those with an interest in how new knowledge can be transferred to the world in which we live. Where stands health research and the health system in this seismic shift in government policy?

The attitude to research within the health system in the mid-1990s was equivocal, to say the least. While there were excellent health researchers, there was no official recognition or commitment to research as a core activity, along with service and education, of the health service. No one was responsible for research in the Department of Health and Children, in the health boards or in hospitals, some of which were changing their names to include the word "university" in their titles. Research was undertaken by committed individuals in the health service with minimal support from their host institutions. The Health Research Board (HRB), through its long standing commitment to supporting high quality research, had kept "the flame" of health research alive but in 1996 its budget was Ir£3.5 million. In 1998 total expenditure on health research in Ireland was equivalent to $16 million or 0.3 per cent of health expenditure (0.02 of GDP). In the same year, Finland spent $200 million on health research or 2.3 per cent of health expenditure (0.16 of GDP) (Global Forum for Health Research, 2001).

However, in 1997, there was an important breakthrough. A matching funding arrangement was agreed between the HRB and the Wellcome Trust, then the largest medical research charity in the world. Under the agreement, the Trust and the HRB each made a commitment to invest the equivalent of IR£3 million each in building health research capacity in Ireland over three years. Pre-dating the Government's wider commitment to research referred to above, the Matching Funding Agreement was the first glimmer of light that health research had a brighter future in Ireland.

It was my good fortune to join the HRB as CEO in 1998 just as the funding from the Matching Funding Agreement was coming on stream. The Trust and the Board invested the funding wisely, mostly in supporting people to do high quality research. The funding was used to support eight career "New Blood" fellowships (the first full-time, permanent research posts ever filled in Irish universities); to provide research funding for new lecturers in health-related disciplines; in grants for health research equipment; in north/south research awards; and for new fellowships in health services research. At the end of the three years, the additional funding the HRB received under the Agreement from government became part of its core budget.

While the matching funding agreement was an important initiative, its initial benefits were mainly felt in the third level sector. The agreement did not address the problem created by the absence of a policy or ownership of research in the health services. In fact, there was, and perhaps still is, a school of thought in the health services that does not accept the need for active support of research. The arguments for non-engagement include "we're too small a country to do research"; "it's cheaper to send our people away to get their research, which they can then bring home"; "how can we support research when there are people in A&E on trolleys?"; "the health services should not get into bed with the drugs industry". Given the level of scepticism about research in the health services, it seemed to me that without a formal commitment to research as a core part of the health service, it would be difficult to secure the resources to support research to the level taken for granted in other developed countries or to remove the institutional obstacles that prevented the health system contributing its potential to research. The issue then became one of how to secure the commitment of government to health research.

The Story:

1. Promoting Research within the Health System

Before I became chief executive of the HRB, I was a senior official in the Department of Health and Children. Coming from this position, I was acutely aware of the importance of policy statements on health and social service issues that committed government and the health services to a certain course of action. They are not a guarantee that action will happen but, without them, action is most unlikely.

To address the absence of a formal statement on the role of research within the health system, the Board, under the chairmanship of Professor Michael Murphy, proposed to the Department in 1999 that the HRB would prepare a draft policy statement on health research for consideration and, hopefully adoption by the Minister and Government. The Department agreed with this approach and the HRB took up the challenge. In 2000, having looked at how health research was supported in a number of other countries, the HRB issued a consultation paper on health research, and in April 2000, held what turned out to be a most important conference in Dublin Castle to garner feedback on the contents of the paper. The conference was a unique occasion in that researchers from all disciplines engaged in health research came together to make common cause as to why health research should be better supported and funded. Mr Micheál Martin, TD and Minister for Health and Children, addressed the conference and provided the first ministerial endorsement of the importance of health research and of the Government's commitment to greater support for health research in the future.

Following the conference and further feedback from many people, including the Irish health research diaspora around the globe, the HRB finished its draft policy on health research and forwarded it to the Minister. In October 2001, following government agreement, the Minister launched *Making Knowledge Work for Health – A Strategy for Health Research* and announced his intention to implement the commitments in the strategy. It was a major step forward, but for reasons discussed below, did not lead to the degree of change for which the HRB had hoped.

Making Knowledge Work for Health endorsed the value of health research

- As a key factor in promoting health, combating disease, reducing disability and improving the quality of care

- To underpin more efficient and effective health services

- To the training of health professionals

- To achieve other government objectives, such as implanting the healthcare industry in Ireland.

The strategy recognised there were two major deficits in support for health research in Ireland. On the one hand, there was no formal commitment by the health system to research and development and on the other, financial support for "bottom-up", science driven-health research was inadequate by international standards. The strategy envisaged support for the two complementary aspects of health research – the establishment of a research and development function within the health system and enhanced support for science for health. The establishment of a research and development function within the health system, which was the most radical and innovative commitment in the strategy, involved a commitment by the Minister to:

- Appoint a Research and Development Officer in the Department of Health and Children to lead on the health research strategy

- The appointment of research and development officers in health boards and specialist health agencies to implement the strategy at regional level

- The preparation by health boards and specialist agencies of institutional research strategies reflecting health service priorities and appropriate linkages with third level colleges and with the healthcare industry

- The establishment of a Forum for Health and Social Care Research to advise on agreed research agendas addressing the main objectives of the health service

- The submission of proposals for funding for research initiatives consistent with these research strategies for peer review through the HRB, with awards made for five year periods to successful applicants.

In relation to support for "science for health" the strategy promised increased resources for the HRB to support open-call research programmes, fellowship and career awards, equipment, ICT and biological banks. In launching the document, the Minister committed to increasing funding for health research to the level necessary to achieve the objectives of the research strategy.

The publication of *Making Knowledge Work for Health,* carrying as it did the endorsement of the Minister and government, was a major advance. It enabled the HRB to be more explicit in its role, both in funding "science for health" and supporting the emergence of an R&D strand in the health system. The HRB addressed these challenges in the corporate strategy 2002-2007 and over the next five years made significant progress in building support for "science for health" and in supporting research and capacity building linked to the priorities of the health system.

In 2004, the Tánaiste and Minister for Enterprise Trade and Employment, Mary Harney TD, became the Minister for Health and Children. Recognising her interest in research and its contribution to economic development, the HRB, under the chairmanship of Professor Desmond Fitzgerald, proposed to her a programme of investment in research that would benefit health and contribute to wealth creation. The programme was also rooted in the commitments of *Making Knowledge Work for Health.* The programme was agreed and an additional €50 million over five years was made available to support investment in people, programmes and infrastructure for health research.

By the end of 2006 the HRB had greatly increased its support for research programmes, funded the first structured PhD programmes in Irish universities, appointed the first clinician scientists, supported a national health research imaging centre and successfully engaged with the Wellcome Trust and the Health Service Executive to fund three clinical research centres in Dublin, Cork and Galway. The HRB also supported research programmes that explicitly addressed problems facing the health system, to fund the first all-island network for cancer clinical trials under the Ireland/Northern Ireland US Cancer Consortium, to support nurses, midwives, clinical therapists and other health professionals to undertake research fellowships, to work with the Cochrane Collaboration to develop capacity in evidence-based practice and to partner with Irish Aid to fund research projects linked to the country's overseas aid programme and to co-fund research projects with the Medical Research Charities Group.

The budget of the HRB gives an idea of the scale of change that followed the adoption of the health research strategy, increasing from €14.8 million in 2001 to €55 million in 2007. Of the HRB's research investment portfolio of €100 million approx in 2006, €43 million was awarded to support people, research programmes and infrastructure linked in a direct way to the health service, with the remainder allocated for more fundamental health research programmes in third level institutions. The increased role for the HRB has also enabled it to play a much greater role in the developing national research system, described in more detail below.

While the increase in HRB's funding for research was significant, it was not on the scale of the investment under the Programme for Research in Third Level Institutions (PRTLI) which has transformed the commitment to and capacity of our universities to undertake research of the highest quality.[4] In the absence of financial incentives on the scale of the PRTLI, it has been difficult to persuade the health service and the institutions that make up the health service, to embrace research as a core activity of their business. Building the research capacity of the health system is just one of the capacity problems it faces and is not seen as a priority by many. The need to secure the scale of investment required was a major stimulus for the HRB to engage with the development of the national science and research agenda.

The HRB was also disappointed with delays in implementation of other commitments to support research in *Making Knowledge Work for Health*. Shortly after the launch of the national health research strategy, the Minister published *Quality and Fairness – A Health Strategy for You* that provided direction for the health system as a whole. The Health

Strategy recognised the importance of research and development to the health service. Despite this recognition, no progress was made with appointing a senior figure to the Department to be the person responsible for research. By 2003, the health system was embroiled in major structural changes, which were not signalled in *Quality and Fairness*, and that led to the replacement of the health boards with the Health Service Executive. This meant that the organisational structure on which the commitments in *Making Knowledge Work for Health* were made was fundamentally altered. Organisational change on the scale embarked on in 2003 is not conducive to the stable environment in which research and innovation thrive. An acute disappointment was the failure over many years to agree a new contract for medical specialists that would have enabled the HRB to attract to Ireland leading medical researchers who wish to focus the majority of their time on research, with smaller commitments to service and education.

With the announcement by government of its decision in June 2004 to establish the Health Service Executive, the HRB directed its efforts towards shaping the legislation establishing the new organisation. Thanks to the efforts of the HRB and others, the Act establishing the HSE includes support for research as one of the functions of the new organisation.[5] Just how that support will be expressed is one of the questions still to be resolved by the HSE more than two years after the legislation was passed. A committee of senior officials of the HSE, chaired by an external expert, Professor Muiris Fitzgerald, is currently preparing a research strategy for the HSE, in conjunction with its obligations to support medical education and training.

The HRB's view is that the HSE should take on the responsibility for developing a strong research culture in the health services to underpin its service and educational commitments; that this commitment should be expressed by assigning responsibility for research at a senior level in the organisation; that it should prioritise its research needs and facilitate staff to conduct research; that it should streamline procedures for ethical review of health research and that it should strengthen links with both the third level colleges and with the healthcare industry. In relation to funding programmes of research to address health service priorities, the HRB's view is that the HSE should contract the HRB to fund such programmes on the basis of competition and peer review to guarantee the excellence and relevance of the research. Positive signs at the beginning of 2007 include the agreement in principle by the HSE to fund the building costs of clinical research centres in Cork and Galway with the HRB agreeing to fund the research programme costs for five years; the joint funding by HSE and HRB of the establishment costs of the Irish Clinical Research Infrastructure Network (ICRIN) and the joint funding of studies to investigate the impact of demographic change on the planning and delivery of health services, and on a resource allocation model for the health service. The HRB hopes to develop a more formal agreement with the HSE in relation to each organisation's respective role in supporting research and development for health.

2. Promoting Health Research within the National System for Science, Technology and Innovation

In addition to promoting research within the health service, the HRB has been acutely aware, since about 2000, of the need to promote the profile of health research within the emerging national system of science, technology and innovation. This awareness stemmed from our understanding of the importance of health research to achieving the government's objective of building a knowledge society and economy in Ireland and because of the possibility that engagement with the national agenda would be the key to securing much greater levels of investment in health research. The immediate spur for engagement was the rapidly changing environment in which the HRB found itself. From being one of two research "councils"[6] providing funding for research on a competitive, peer-review basis, HRB found itself in new territory with the Higher Education Authority funding strategic research priorities of the universities through the Programme for Research in Third Level Institutions and two new research councils – the Research Council for Humanities and Social Sciences and the Research Council for Science, Engineering and Technology – funding principal investigator research and career development. Even more significant was the establishment of Science Foundation Ireland in 2001, with a well resourced mandate to fund research in ICT and biotechnology linked to economic development. In recognition of the need for coordination between the research funding bodies, the HRB was one of the parties that established in 2001 the Standing Committee of Research Funding Bodies that played a role in aligning the funding policies of the main research agencies.

The need for greater coherence was also recognised at government level, especially between the Department of Enterprise, Trade and Employment, Education and Science and Health and Children which, with their agencies, are major players in achieving the science and research objectives of government. In 2002, the Irish Council on Science Technology and Innovation established a commission, under the chair of Professor Edward Walsh, to advise government on how policy on science, technology and innovation should be coordinated. I was appointed to the Commission as the representative of the Minister for Health and Children. It was a difficult assignment as there was a strong view that science policy should be driven primarily by the enterprise agenda and that responsibility for coordination should be exclusively the responsibility of the Department of Enterprise, Trade and Employment and its associated agencies. The rationale for funding research for purposes broader than economic benefit, as is the case in the HRB, HEA and the research councils, was called into question.

The HRB, under the chairmanship of Professor Hugh Brady, made a strong submission to the Commission which provided me with a mandate to argue the case for a broader and more inclusive view of national research objectives (Health Research Board, 2002). The submission made the case for the separate organisation of health research within an overall national system of research and innovation based on the unique characteristics of health research. Its uniqueness stemmed from the importance of health research to the health system, the involvement of people as research subjects, the ethical dimension of such research, its close association with both the health and education systems, the involvement of research charities as well as its contribution to economic development.

For this reason, the HRB argued that the coordination of research policy should not be the responsibility of any department involved in funding research but should be the responsibility of the Department of the Taoiseach which could act as a *primus inter pares* between the Departments more directly involved. This was and is the arrangement in Finland, for example, which has one of the most effective systems for coordinating research policy of any EU member state (and which the Commission visited in the course of its work). Since the majority on the Commission favoured a system of coordination led by the Department of Enterprise, Trade and Employment (the representative of the Minister for Education and Science, Dr Don Thornhill, and I dissented on this point),[7] I was pleased that the arrangements that were subsequently put in place to coordinate science and research policy, while implementing the core recommendations of the Commission, also acknowledged the need for balance between the different Departments and their differing, but complementary reasons, for funding research.

While it was difficult to see how the cause of health research was advanced as a result of the time spent as a member of the Commission, the articulation of the arguments as to why health research should not be driven solely by economic motives may have helped to gain acceptance of the wider role that health research and the HRB serve. In any event, the logic of a body funding health research for a variety of reasons was accepted by an OECD expert team that visited the country in 2004 (OECD, 2004).

The preparation of the National Development Plan, which began in 2005, provided an opportunity to promote health research as part of the national system for support for science and research. As part of that Plan, a strategy for science, technology and innovation was developed. Meetings chaired by the Chief Science Adviser proved useful in developing a common approach to objectives and priorities across the research funding bodies. The HRB also worked closely with the Department of Health and Children to ensure that they articulated the priority needs of health research in the Inter-Departmental Committee on Science Technology and Innovation that advised the Department of Enterprise, Trade and Employment on the shape of the strategy. The Strategy, published in June 2006, is a sophisticated document that recognises that research serves a variety of complementary objectives of vital importance to the future economic and social development of Ireland.

The *Strategy for Science, Technology and Innovation (SSTI) (June 2006),* recognises the important role of the HRB in strengthening research capacity to improve health and the health services and increase the contribution of health research to achieving the Government's objective of a knowledge-based economy and society. The HRB is working to achieve its objectives in partnership with other agencies in an increasingly sophisticated, national research environment. Key actions for health research in the *Strategy for Science, Technology and Innovation* are to:

- Develop health research as a frontline health service to guarantee world class healthcare for patients, to resolve health problems facing the population, to attract and retain health professionals of the highest quality and to improve the efficiency and effectiveness of the health sector.

- Build a strong research culture in the health services through targeted investments, on the basis of competition and peer review, and by a strong corporate commitment to research by the Health Service Executive and other health agencies.

- Support the R&D pillar of *Making Knowledge Work for Health* to ensure that the crucial "population health" element of the Health Strategy has a sound research base to underpin appropriate disease prevention measures, redress social inequalities in health status and to ensure best practice in health service delivery and policy developments.

- Develop a number of centres of world significance in translational health research, each of which has strong foundations in both academia and the health services and which will act as a magnet to the pharmaceutical and medical devices industries, nationally and internationally. To build these centres through strategic investment in research infrastructure, people and programmes by competitive, peer-reviewed awards through the HRB and other funding agencies.

- Maintain the confidence of the public in health research by observing the highest ethical standards in research and provide for greater public engagement in relation to the benefits of health research and the complexities of undertaking such research.

The inclusion of health research explicitly in the Strategy for Science, Technology and Innovation opens the way for health research to be funded under the National Development Plan to an extent not previously envisaged. The HRB has been awarded €10 million in 2007/8 for priority research initiatives under the Strategy, with the prospect of significant additional funding in subsequent years.

The contribution of health research to achieving the economic objectives of government was endorsed in an important report produced by the Science Advisory Council, the successor of ICSTI (2006). The Report recommends a step change in the level and quality of health-related research and innovation, both to enhance the health of the Irish population and to capture in Ireland the benefit of the effective commercialisation of the intellectual property created. Their vision is to make Ireland the destination of choice when advanced technology for health is being conceived, tested or implemented. The Council recommends that the Department of Health and Children takes responsibility for health research policy and strategy, that the HRB, SFI, HSE and the higher education sector share responsibility for implementation and that the activities of the relevant bodies be coordinated through an extension of the inter-agency arrangements established to implement the Strategy for Science, Technology and Innovation. The Science Advisory Council's Report was being finalised at the same time as the HRB was agreeing its corporate strategy for the period 2007–2011. The corporate strategy, agreed at the end of 2006, plots a course for the HRB to support research within the parameters set out both in the SSTI and in the Science Advisory Council's report.

It is encouraging that the Science Advisory Council's Report endorses much of the analysis of *Making Knowledge Work for Health* and of the HRB over the years. As in the SSTI, the health and economic reasons for funding health research are seen as complementary and mutually reinforcing. The logic of its recommendations has been recognised with the decision in April 2007 of the Minister for Health and Children and the Minister for Enterprise, Trade and Employment to establish a Health Research Group, chaired by an Assistant Secretary in the Department of Health and Children, with representatives of the HRB, HSE, Higher Education Authority, IDA and Enterprise Ireland and other agencies with an interest in health research. The terms of reference of the Group require it to identify strategic research priorities; the resources required to address them; an investment strategy; the steps required to make Ireland a location of choice for translational research; and the priorities to be addressed in health services and population health research. The Group is to work closely with the enterprise agencies and key stakeholders in the health service in formulating its proposals.

So, by early 2007, an important point has been reached in the story of health research in Ireland. The value of health research to both the health service and to the economic future of the country has been recognised by government. The establishment of the Health Research Group provides a means by which the different perspectives on health research can be reconciled, priorities agreed and deficits addressed. The work of the Group is likely to stimulate a higher profile for research within the health service. It marks the beginning of a new chapter in the story of how knowledge will be harnessed in this country to improve health and generate wealth.

Reflections

At a macro level, the Irish health service appears to be reluctant to recognise the importance of new knowledge, its generation and application, as a core activity in the way that is the norm in Scandinavian countries, in the best US health institutions and in the British NHS. The process of innovation – whereby new knowledge is transferred to new ways of doing things or new products and services – is not well understood. If knowledge for health was static, this might not be so serious but, given the revolution that is underway in relation to knowledge of relevance to health and health systems, this is a serious systems failure. There are still too many people who believe that it is enough to copy or imitate knowledge applications in other countries. However, the pace of knowledge creation is now so great that unless health systems support significant numbers of people who are staying abreast of and interpreting new knowledge and who in turn are contributing to it, they will quickly become second rate.

Nor do many people working in the health service yet recognise its value as a resource for the economic development of the country. The lessons from the education sector have not been learned. Expenditure on education was seen as a "drain" on public resources until the 1960s when the economic value of an educated population was belatedly recognised. The economic value of a healthy population and an innovative health service are important assets that will give Ireland a competitive economic advantage in the future if harnessed correctly. While the objectives of the health system in knowledge generation and those of the commercial sector are complementary, it will be important to ensure that the highest ethical principles are observed in the relationship between the health system and the entrepreneurial world of drug, diagnostic and ICT development.

Future Challenges

The health system is at a crossroads in relation to knowledge for health. The people of Ireland aspire to a world class health service to which all have access regardless of means and that is organised in the most cost efficient way. Such a service cannot be achieved without a commitment to supporting and generating knowledge for health and an ability to absorb that knowledge. A key challenge facing the health service is whether it can change quickly enough to stay abreast of, absorb, and in turn contribute to the unprecedented advances in knowledge that are changing the nature of healthcare. The key to addressing this challenge is to recognise the three mutually reinforcing functions of every health system – delivering services to customers; educating the next generation of health professionals; and contributing to new knowledge about health and disease – and to organise around them. There is already much evidence from other countries (Finland, for example) of the transforming effect on the quality and cost effectiveness of the delivery of health services by the application of new information and communication technologies in a systematic way. A health system-wide approach to ICT in turn has the capacity to transform the way in which health professionals are educated and provides the information on the clinical manifestation of disease that is needed to complement advances in molecular and cell biology to find new and more effective ways of protecting health and combating disease. A truly win-win situation.

What is needed to transform the health service into a system that supports the acquisition, application and absorption of knowledge?

The experience of the past decade with building the research capacity of our universities suggests that a combination of clear strategy, strong commitment and the right financial incentives are the key drivers of change. In relation to knowledge for health, there is still work to be done to refine research strategy at national level through the newly formed Health Research Group, to gain the commitment of health service institutions to embrace research as a core part of their business and to provide the right level of financial incentive to ensure implementation. Bringing the universities and third level colleges into more formal relationships with the health system will be one of the ways that the capacity to develop and absorb new knowledge will be enhanced and the benefits of public investment in science and research maximised.

There is some urgency about making the health system more knowledge-friendly. On the one hand, the public's confidence in the quality of the health system has been seriously eroded over the past few years and needs to be regained. On the other, the challenge of keeping abreast of the unprecedented levels of knowledge that underpin healthcare is becoming more and more difficult. Delay risks creating a vicious cycle of continued loss of public confidence and a growing gap between what it is possible for healthcare to do for people and what is available in the Irish health system. If we do not act soon, we face the prospect of a health service that is compromised in its ability to deliver a standard of diagnosis, treatment and care equivalent to that available in other countries, a health service in which the public has little confidence. This erosion of confidence is already evident in that those who can afford to do so make private arrangements in Ireland or go to other countries for their medical care. The less well off are left at the mercy of a second-rate service. That is the burning issue facing healthcare in Ireland.

Lessons Learned

What lessons can one draw from the experience of promoting knowledge and research for health? It helps to have system-wide vision of what is needed while, at the same time, trying to relate what one is trying to do to the institution or the people who are involved. Having a national strategy such as *Making Knowledge Work for Health* that sets out a vision, a mission and strategic objectives, that supports other objectives of the health system and that has the buy-in from the key stakeholders is a necessary condition for action but it is not sufficient to ensure implementation. Implementation, as ever, is the difficult bit, requiring sustained commitment, adequate resources, organisational stability and good luck. In Ireland one can never overestimate the impact a relatively small number of people can have, either to move an agenda forward or to hold it back. Putting in place the right incentives to change the way the system supports knowledge for health is also crucial. These incentives are primarily financial, but building reputations and increasing the status of those involved in knowledge generation are also important. Strategy and implementation need to be continually reviewed in the light of changes in the environment and adjustments made accordingly.

One of the most significant lessons learned was the importance of aligning the strategy for building health research with that of the national strategy for science, technology and innovation. This would have been important on its own merits, but it became crucial to persuading health policy makers of the need to engage on the issues of building knowledge for health in the wider national interest. This required much thought and analysis in the HRB and learning from other countries that had embarked earlier or with more enthusiasm on this journey: the willingness of people across the globe to share their experience and learning about generating and applying knowledge for health is a unique resource that is freely available to this country. While the process of integrating the knowledge for health agenda with the national science and research agenda is far from complete, it is under way. Again, the implementation of the next phase will be crucial.

Working as the HRB does in close contact with the health system, the higher education sector and the enterprise agencies, I have been struck by the very different pace at which decisions are taken in the three sectors. In the enterprise sector, (Department of Enterprise, Trade and Employment, Forfás, Science Foundation Ireland, IDA and Enterprise Ireland) reviews are conducted, recommendations made and decisions taken quickly to implement them. The pace of decision making in the higher education sector (Department of Education and Science, HEA, the Research Councils) is slower but still impressive. However, in the health system, the pace of decision making can be so slow as to be imperceptible. The establishment of the Health Service Executive seems to have slowed it further, if that is possible. Given what I describe above as the burning question of the health system, the need to speed up decision making and implementation in and about the health system is urgent.

Endnotes

[1] For a summary of the problems caused by the reluctance of the South African Government to accept the international consensus on the link between HIV and Aids see *The Irish Times*, Health Supplement, 1 November 2006.

[2] See the Society of Actuaries in Ireland (2003), *Report of the Population Studies Working Party*, and "Population Ageing in Ireland and its Impact on Pension and Healthcare Costs", presentation at "Ageing Ireland", Progressive Democrats conference, January 2004.

[3] Joint Economic Committee, The Benefits of Medical Research and the Role of NIH, US Congress, May 2000.

[4] In 2007, the HRB's budget represents no more than .39 per cent of estimated total exchequer spending on health services.

[5] Health Act 2004.

[6] The other being Enterprise Ireland. Enterprise Ireland's functions in funding basic research transferred to Science Foundation Ireland in 2004.

[7] Although the report was never published, the main recommendations of the report were reported in *The Irish Times* on 17 February 2003.

References

Advisory Council for Science, Technology and Innovation. (2006). *Towards Better Health: Achieving a Step Change in Health Research in Ireland.* Dublin: Forfás.

Bennett, K., Kabir, Z., Unal, B., Shelley, E., Critchley, J., Perry, I., Feely, J., and Capewell, S. (2006). "Explaining the recent decrease in coronary health disease mortality rates in Ireland, 1985-2000". *Journal of Epidemiology and Community Health*, 60, 322-327.

Frenk, J. (2006). "Bridging the divide: global lessons from evidence-based health policy in Mexico". *The Lancet*, 368, 945-61.

Enterprise Strategy Group (2004). *Ahead of the Curve.* Dublin: Forfás.

Global Forum for Health Research (2001*). Monitoring Financial Flows for Health Research.* Geneva: WHO.

Harno, K. (2007). Paper presented at seminar on Innovation in Healthcare: Present Opportunities and Strategic Partnering between Ireland and Finland. Dublin City University, 25 April 2007.

Health Research Board. (2002). Irish Council for Science, Technology and Innovation Commission – HRB Submission. Dublin

Office for Tobacco Control and the Health and Safety Authority (2002). *The Health Effects of Environmental Tobacco Smoke (ETS) in the Workplace.* Dublin.

Organisation for Economic Co-operation and Development (2004). *Review of National Policies for Education: Review of Higher Education in Ireland – Examiners' Report 2004.* Paris: OECD.

Peto, R. (1994). "Smoking and death: the past 40 years and the next 40". *British Medical Journal*, 309, 937-939.

World Health Organisation: Commission on Macroeconomics and Health. (2001). *Investing in health for economic development.* Geneva. World Health Organisation.

Chapter 5

SMOKE-FREE WORKPLACES IN IRELAND: CULTURE SHIFT THROUGH POLICY CHANGE

Fenton Howell and Shane Allwright

Introduction

On March 29 2004 Ireland became the first country in the world to implement legislation[1] creating smoke-free enclosed workplaces that included bars and restaurants (Howell, 2004). Implementation has proved to be extremely popular and successful (Howell, 2005). In a one year review, 96 per cent of people polled felt the law was successful, including 89 per cent of smokers (Office of Tobacco Control, 2004).

It is important to recognise that the Irish legislation to create smoke-free workplaces did not emerge overnight, or in isolation. For over 20 years tobacco control advocates in Ireland had fought hard for a comprehensive tobacco control strategy dealing with key issues such as price and taxation, advertising and sponsorship, sales to minors, smuggling, cessation, and health promotion campaigns, as well as protection from the harmful effects of passive smoke. Concentrating on all aspects of tobacco control proved critical in engaging politicians, public servants, trade unions, and non-governmental organisations in the fight for a tobacco free society and helped to underpin the evolution of the legislation that is in place today to protect workers from passive smoke.

There has been considerable interest in how Ireland achieved this major public health legislative breakthrough. In telling the story, three distinct time periods are evident:

1. The period before the announcement of the legislation, pre-30 January 2003

2. The period between the announcement of the legislation and its implementation, February 2003 to 29 March 2004, and

3. The period after the legislation came into effect, March 2004 to date.

The Period before the Announcement of the Legislation, pre-30 January 2003

Towards the end of the 1980s, as evidence of the harmful effects of passive smoke began to emerge (US Department of Health and Human Services, 1986), Irish politicians were persuaded that passive smoke was harmful and that there was a need to bring in legislation to protect people from it in certain public places such as government public offices, cinemas, theatres and schools.[2, 3] This first attempt at legislating to protect people from passive smoke had no direct application to the workplace.

Research began to emerge that workers were concerned about passive smoke (Howell and Doorley, 1991), yet despite the growing evidence of the harmful effects of passive smoke, in the early 1990s only a voluntary code of practice on smoking in the workplace was agreed between the government, employers, and trade unions (Health Promotion Unit, 1992, 1994). This voluntary code offered little in the way of protection for those exposed to passive smoke at work, and nothing for those working in the hospitality sector.

Tobacco control advocates continued to lobby for further legislative measures to protect people from passive smoke and were rewarded with legislation that further extended the public places where smoking was no longer allowed. Although the legislation still did not offer any protection for those in the workplace, it did introduce the concept that 50 per cent of seating in restaurants was to be smoke-free.[4]

Tobacco control advocates pressed for further action. Politicians, public servants, and trade unions were extensively lobbied on a range of tobacco control actions including the need to protect workers from passive smoke. International research on the health effects of passive smoke and tobacco control developments in the United States (California Environmental Protection Agency, 1997) were kept to the fore in the media. The overriding strategy was to get tobacco control issues firmly on the agenda of policymakers in all sectors. With regard to passive smoke, the strategy was simple: this was a health and safety issue, involving all workers, including those in the hospitality sector, and needed to be tackled accordingly. The overall strategy had a fair degree of success. At a political level, the influential all-party Oireachtas Joint Committee on Health and Children examined the issue of smoking and health. It sought input from a wide range of groups, including the tobacco industry. The tobacco industry insisted that there was insufficient evidence to link passive smoke to any illness in non-smokers. The Committee, made up of politicians from across the political spectrum, rejected this argument however, and in 1999 unanimously recommended a new national anti-smoking strategy, to include restrictions on smoking in workplaces, including bars (Joint Committee on Health and Children, 1999). In a follow-up report, published in 2001, the Committee reiterated its commitment that all workplaces, including bars should be smoke free (Joint Committee on Health and Children, 2001). Perhaps more importantly, in the consultation phase for this second report, tobacco industry representatives refused to come before the Committee. This was viewed as an insult to the national parliament. This adversarial position and dispute with the political system effectively negated their behind-the-scenes influence and undermined their ability to successfully lobby politicians once the legislation on tobacco control was published.

Senior health officials from within the Department of Health and Children (DOHC) and the regional health authorities were also engaged in trying to address the tobacco issue. In 2000, they published a blueprint document for creating a tobacco-free society, "Towards a tobacco free society", which was adopted by government (Department of Health and Children, 2000). And in 2001 a key governmental health strategy document highlighted the importance of tobacco control (Department of Health and Children, 2001).

Subsequently an Office of Tobacco Control (OTC) (www.otc.ie) was established in 2001 by the government to build capacity for tobacco control measures. The OTC drew on international expertise on how to deal with the issue of passive smoke and brought experts to Ireland so that politicians, policymakers, the media, and trade unions representing hospitality workers might understand how best to proceed. Of particular importance was the input of James Repace, a renowned US health physicist, who estimated that up to 150 Irish bar workers could be dying annually as a result of their exposure to secondhand smoke.[5]

Given the evidence base that was emerging on the health consequences of passive smoking, the Health and Safety Authority might have
been expected to take a lead role in driving worker health and safety
forward. Whilst their 2001 work plan committed them to establishing a
working group to look at the issue of passive smoking in the workplace,
no such group was established and curiously, passive smoking in the
workplace did not appear as an item for action in the 2002 work plan. A
subsequent 2002 Freedom of Information request from ASH Ireland to
the Health and Safety Authority showed that the Attorney General's office had advised the Health and Safety Authority in 1999 that it could
deal with the issue by way of a Statutory Code of Practice under the
Safety, Health and Welfare at Work Act 1989. Regrettably, the Board of
the Health and Safety Authority decided not to proceed down the legislative route, but rather to continue with the Voluntary Code of Practice
dealing with smoking in the workplace. Armed with this information,
ASH Ireland approached Mr Tom Kitt, TD, the Minister of State with
responsibility for the Health and Safety Authority, to try and get a more
positive approach from the Health and Safety Authority in dealing with
passive smoking in the work place. The Minister responded positively
which greatly facilitated the newly appointed Director of the Health and
Safety Authority in becoming much more proactive in the whole debate.

In 2001 a new tobacco bill was published which was intended to
bring together and further enhance existing tobacco control legislation
and in particular it gave the Minister for Health and Children the power
to create smoke-free workplaces. It was supported by the opposition parties and was signed into law in 2002. Further discussions continued on
how widely restrictions on smoking in the workplace should extend. To
help that debate, the OTC and the newly involved Health and Safety Authority commissioned local independent scientists to review the evidence
on workplace passive smoke. Their report concluded that passive smoke
was harmful, that employees needed to be protected from it in the workplace, and that as ventilation was ineffective legislative measures were
needed (Allwright, McLoughlin, Murphy, et al., 2002). So definitive
were their findings that, at the launch of this report on 30 January 2003,
the Minister for Health and Children, Mr Micheál Martin, TD, announced that he would make the necessary orders to ensure that all enclosed workplaces, including bars, would be smoke-free from 1 January
2004. In the event, various technical issues delayed the implementation

of the legislation until March 2004. However, in the interim, there was much heated debate on just how the new legislation would be received.

The Period between the Announcement of the Legislation and Its Implementation, February 2003 to 29 March 2004

Once the Minister for Health and Children announced the legislation, it quickly became apparent as to where the battle lines would be drawn. Whilst the legislation was to apply to all indoor workplaces, it was the hospitality industry, most notably bar owners and their representatives, the Vintners Federation of Ireland (VFI) and the Licensed Vintners Association (LVA) who objected most vociferously to the legislation. A flavour of their objections can be gleaned from their many press releases and public statements throughout the following 14 months available on their respective websites.[6, 7] In addition to these well established representative bodies, a new organisation, the Irish Hospitality Industry Alliance, emerged out of nowhere to fight against the proposed legislation. This new organisation claimed to have widespread membership amongst the hospitality sector which has never been authenticated and they appeared to have significant financial and public relations support at their disposal, the source of which has never been adequately explained. Incidentally, since the successful introduction of the legislation the Irish Hospitality Industry Alliance appears to have disappeared completely without further comment. This type of development will not have surprised others who have had experience in introducing a similar type of smoke-free legislation (Dearlove, Bialous and Glantz, 2002).

Throughout this 14-month period, the hospitality industry argued that a complete ban on smoking in their venues was unnecessary, unworkable and unenforceable. Whilst they accepted that smoking was harmful, they continually disputed the findings of the commissioned report (Allwright, McLoughlin, Murphy et al., 2002). They argued that further research was needed and cited the findings of one new and controversial study of passive smoking which found little evidence of adverse effects (Enstrom and Kabat, 2003). They claimed that ventilation and separate no-smoking areas were a better way to address the health issue. This was not surprising as they had been engaged in a campaign over the previous three years, supported by the tobacco industry, in trying to persuade their members to install ventilation systems. In addition they predicted that a ban on smoking in bars would have serious negative economic consequences for themselves and for the country as a whole with massive job losses and a stem in the flow of tourists coming to Ireland. They suggested that there would be significant public order problems as a result of the ban and cited the experience in New York where a barman was tragically killed some time after a similar ban was enforced there. They used their long established connections with the political system to try and get the legislation diluted, overturned or postponed. They suggested alternatives to the ban by way of "customer choice and common sense". They threatened to withhold VAT payments to government if the legislation went ahead. They also threatened to run candidates against the government parties in the local elections and they proposed to challenge the legislation in Irish and European courts. Incidentally, they continued to pay VAT, did not put up any candidates for the local elections, and their legal challenges to the legislation never materialised.

There were others who questioned the need to bring in such legislation. The Irish Cigarette Machine Operators Association, which supplies cigarette vending machines to bars, campaigned vigorously against the legislation citing a possible decline in their business should the legislation come into being. The Irish Business and Employers Confederation (IBEC), one of the country's most powerful lobby groups representing 7,000 top businesses, said more research should be conducted before the ban was implemented and they supported the retention of designated smoking rooms in the workplace. The tobacco industry also contributed to the debate, but in a muted fashion, having run foul of the political system some years earlier as described above. The tobacco industry argued that the science underpinning the legislation was flawed and that ventilation and designated smoking areas were the way forward.[8]

Whilst there was extensive lobbying against the legislation by vested interests, they did not have it all their own way. In the lead up to the legislation, there was recognition by the pro-legislation side, both governmental and non-governmental organizations (NGOs), that this was going to be a tough battle for the hearts and minds of the community at large. Three distinct groups were evident in their support for the legislation: the Minister for Health and Children and other politicians; the public service sector including the OTC, the Department of Health and Children, the Health and Safety Authority and the regional health authorities; and the NGOs, most notably ASH Ireland, the Irish Cancer Society, the Irish Heart Foundation and MANDATE trade union which represents hospitality workers. Together with others, these groups played significant but

different roles in ensuring that any arguments put forward by those
against the legislation were immediately countered. Whilst they all had
different roles to play, all recognised early on that the message going out
to the public needed to be simple, straightforward and consistent.
Agreement was reached that the message would revolve around the following key tenets:

- Passive smoking is a significant health and safety issue

- Passive smoke is a serious cause of ill health

- All workers, including hospitality workers, deserve protection

- Ventilation will not remove the harmful constituents of passive
  smoke

- Separate areas do not work – passive smoke cannot read

- Smokers are reasonable people and most want to quit

- Provide assistance to help smokers quit if they wish to.

In addition, all parties were clear that the primary objective of the legislation was to protect workers from the harmful effects of second-hand
smoke. The legislation was not presented as a means of protecting the
public or encouraging smokers to quit smoking or reduce tobacco use.
Thus, it was held that if the public – patrons of a hospitality venue, for
instance – benefit from smoke-free workplaces, or if smokers cut down
or quit smoking as a result of the workplace smoking ban, these would
be welcome consequences but not central objectives of the legislation.

Not surprisingly the Minister for Health and Children who proposed
the legislation was to the fore in defending the legislation and explaining
how it would be implemented. Whilst he had the support of most of his
colleagues in government, he also had the backing of the opposition parties who had declared their support previously via the Joint Committees
on Health and Children. Unfortunately, during the course of the 14-
month debate in the lead up to the implementation of the law, some senior and junior ministers buckled under pressure from the hospitality
lobby and called for the Minister for Health and Children to modify his
proposals. With support from the NGO community, their arguments
against the legislation were promptly dealt with and the Taoiseach continued to support his Minister for Health and Children and the proposed
legislation.

The NGO community played an important role in this period. They recognised the need to quickly bring together as many organisations as possible with an interest in this area and to ensure that they all sub-scribed to the messages outlined above. ASH Ireland, The Irish Cancer Society and the Irish Heart Foundation combined their limited resources to mount a public health media advocacy campaign in favour of the smoke-free initiative and to provide leadership and support for other NGOs who wished to be involved. The NGO media campaign was un-derlined by the principle that someone must always be available to the media in order to outline the pro-health side. This involved key spokes-persons being available round the clock for all elements of the media, be they national or local. All opportunities to get the health and safety mes-sage across and to counter the arguments of those who were hostile to the smoke-free legislation were to be maximised. Tobacco control advo-cates were encouraged to pro-actively write letters to the editors of all newspapers and to pen opinion pieces for national and local print media in support of the legislation whenever possible. Linkages were also es-tablished with many international tobacco control organisations who readily gave of their support and advice. GLOBALink, the leading inter-national tobacco control internet network serving all those active in to-bacco control, was an important source of support throughout the cam-paign and its members ensured that the Irish tobacco control advocates had the most up-to-date- information at their fingertips.

Trade union support was critical during the debate: those represent-ing the hospitality sector played a crucial role, and those representing the medical and nursing professions provided support at key times. In addi-tion to the three NGOs outlined above, many healthcare professional or-ganisations such as the Irish College of General Practitioners, Environ-mental Health Officers' Association, and other NGOs such as the Asthma Society, supported and contributed to the campaign.

The OTC played a key role, not only in advocating for the smoke-free initiative but also in running a campaign to build public compliance with the smoke-free workplace legislation for which they subsequently won a public relations award. In doing so they utilised the power of local radio to its full extent in getting their key messages across. They ensured that the experiences of those charged with enforcing similar legislation elsewhere, especially New York and Boston, were brought to the atten-tion of all concerned in Ireland. They were also responsible, in associa-tion with the Health and Safety Authority and the Department of Health and Children for ensuring that all the necessary information and signage was available to those who were expected to enforce the legislation when the legislation came to be implemented.[9]

The Department of Health and Children also played a key role in ensuring the success of the initiative. The Chief Medical Officer in the Department issued a clear and unambiguous view on the potential health impact of the legislation which was widely reported in the media.[10] In addition, the Department ran a multi-media campaign on the harmful effects of smoking to the individual using the *Every Cigarette Is Doing You Damage* catchphrase. They also ensured that adequate supports were put in place for those who wished to quit smoking in advance of the legislation coming into effect. Additional smoking cessation staff were identified and an enhanced national telephone Quitline with back-up support was put in place in association with the Irish Cancer Society and local health authorities. A dedicated website dealing with all aspects of the legislation was also launched and this provided the public with clear answers to many questions posed concerning the implementation of the legislation.[11]

Throughout this period not everything went smoothly. Whilst the legislation was initially scheduled to come into force on January 1, 2004, and to include all indoor workplaces, problems arose as to how to deal with the constitutional ramifications of a workplace that was also a home. As a result of legal advice, some exemptions were eventually allowed for places that could legally be regarded as a person's temporary home, such as hotel bedrooms and prison cells, and the ban was postponed from its initial implementation date of January 1, 2004, partly because of the debate over exemptions, but also because of the legal requirement to provide a minimum period of notice to the European Union. Once all the legal niceties had been resolved, the Minister for Health and Children announced on the 18 February 2004 that the legislation would take effect from the 29 March 2004. This announcement was widely welcomed.[12]

March 29 was fast approaching and tension was rising as to how the public would react. Although opinion poll after opinion poll suggested that there was grassroots support for the initiative, would the reality be otherwise? Just before the implementation date, the hospitality industry finally called off their proposed legal challenges to the legislation and asked the public to help them in their efforts to be compliant with the law.

In the 14 months from the announcement that smoke-free workplaces were to be introduced, the media coverage was extensive. Barely a day went by in that period when there was no opinion piece or Letter to the Editor in the print media, and radio talk shows covered the issue extensively. Against this background it was interesting to see how the media would respond to the actual implementation of the legislation.

The Period after the Legislation Came into Effect, March 2004 to Date

On 29 March 2004, the day the smoke-free initiative was to come into place, all three national broadsheet newspapers (*The Irish Times, Irish Independent* and *Irish Examiner*) and the three main tabloid newspapers (*Sun, Mirror* and *Star*) carried positive stories on the ban on their front page, and all editorialised in favour of the initiative. This was an important start to the day. The NGO community also decided to seize the initiative by organising a series of events throughout the day to celebrate the event. ASH Ireland hosted Ireland's first smoke-free breakfast at 8am in a popular city centre restaurant. The Minister for Health and Children and the many supporters of the smoke-free initiative were invited to attend, as were the media. Local and international media interest was high and ASH Ireland provided the media with a steady stream of spokespersons to discuss the issue in a positive light. Later in the day the Irish Cancer Society and the Irish Heart Foundation organised similar types of events which facilitated the media in covering the story. The story from day one was that the smoke-free initiative was working – as was loudly proclaimed on the front page of the *Evening Herald* on the March 30, 2004.

Very high levels of compliance with the ban were immediately apparent to the environmental health officers and health and safety inspectors who were charged with enforcing the ban. This was confirmed by the media who dispatched reporters far and wide in an attempt to find bar owners and customers who were prepared to defy the ban. Instances of non-compliance with the ban even in bars in the toughest neighbourhoods and in rural locations were few. Within a month of the ban, it was officially reported that 97 per cent compliance has been achieved in all workplaces, including bars (Office for Tobacco Control, 2004)

There were some high profile attempts to defy the ban. In one case, a few days after the ban came into force, a prominent front-bench politician and member of the opposition shadow cabinet openly defined the ban by smoking three cigarettes in the Dáil bar. Although this defiance gained much publicity, the politician involved was promptly fired from his front bench position and the matter died down. In another case in July 2004, the owners of several bars in Galway claimed that they had suffered a 30 per cent fall in sales as a result of the ban and were now going to allow smoking in their bars. This story was also covered extensively in the media. However, the local health authority intervened quickly and the owners were subsequently fined some €10,000. This sent a very clear signal that any open defiance of the ban would be met with the full rigour of the law.

A one-year review of compliance with the legislation demonstrates that implementation has been successful (Office for Tobacco Control, 2004). In particular, the review found that:

- 94 per cent of all workplaces inspected under the National Tobacco Control Inspection Programme were smoke-free

- 92 per cent of all workplaces inspected by the Health and Safety Authority were smoke-free, and

- 93 per cent of all hospitality workplaces inspected were smoke-free.

The review also found that 96 per cent of all indoor workers reported working in smoke-free environments since the introduction of the smoke-free workplace law and that air quality in bars had improved dramatically (Office for Tobacco Control, 2004). This subjective view is supported by a study of 249 staff working in rural and urban pubs in the Republic of Ireland and Northern Ireland both before and after the Republic's ban was implemented. This study showed that the smoke-free workplace law has provided protection for this heavily exposed group by reducing their exposure to secondhand smoke (assessed by salivary cotinine and self report) both in and out of the workplace. Furthermore, after the ban there was a significant drop in the proportion of these bar staff experiencing respiratory symptoms (Allwright, Paul, Greiner et al., 2005)

A public opinion survey conducted for the OTC in advance of the one-year anniversary of the law (Office for Tobacco Control, 2004) showed that there is extensive support for the legislation among smokers and non-smokers alike:

- 93 per cent thought the law was a good idea, including 80 per cent of smokers

- 96 per cent of people felt the law was successful, including 89 per cent of smokers

- 98 per cent believed that workplaces are now healthier because of the smoke-free law, including 94 per cent of smokers.

Before the introduction of the smoke-free legislation, bar owners consistently stated that the smoke-free legislation would have a negative impact on their business.[13] Since its introduction, some bar owners claimed that sales are down between 15 per cent and 25 per cent with significant job losses evident, as a result of the legislation.[14] However, in advance of the legislation, market research from the drinks industry showed that the number of regular bar-goers had fallen by at least 20 per cent since 2000.[15] In addition, volume sales of alcohol in Irish bars reached their peak in 2001 and had fallen by 15 per cent before the smoke-free legislation came into force in March 2004.[15] Many reasons have been postulated for this shift: changing demographics, increasing price of drink in bars, health concerns about alcohol, commuting times, and drink-driving legislation, to cite but a few. Recent objective data on bar sales and volumes in Ireland from the Central Statistics Office show that seasonally adjusted turnover in bars had fallen by around 3.8 per cent in value and 5.8 per cent in volume during the first nine months after the smoke-free initiative was implemented. However, more recent data indicates that bar sales volume increased by 0.1 per cent in 2005, the first increase since 2001, with more recent data showing that bar sales have climbed by 2.3 per cent in both value and volume terms between September and November 2004, and have continued to improve into 2006.[16] The claim by the Vintners' Federation of Ireland that sales fell by 25 per cent since the smoking ban was instituted is, therefore, unsubstantiated.[17, 18]

Despite all the negative rhetoric from vested interests surrounding the introduction of the smoke-free initiative in Ireland, the impact that it has had on the Irish population was perhaps best captured on a programme broadcast on national television on New Year's Day 2005. Market research carried out for the programme "2004: How was it for you" found that from a list of 30 positive events that happened in Ireland in 2004, including many memorable international sporting achievements, the implementation of the smoke-free initiative in all workplaces topped the poll. Not only did it top the poll, but it was a clear 15 per cent above the second-placed event.

Reflections

The implementation of the smoke-free workplace legislation was a brave decision for the Minister for Health and Children. The success of the initiative has confounded many observers. In this section we outline factors that contributed to the success of the ban.

International Support

It is important to look back at how similar initiatives fared elsewhere. Of particular interest is what happened in New York and Boston. Both cities went smoke-free in advance of Ireland and advised us that whilst they had similar concerns, once the legislation became law, compliance was very high from the outset. This underscores the fact that most people are law abiding most of the time, irrespective of what the law is. In addition to personal contacts developed in the United States and elsewhere, GLOBALink (internet group of tobacco control advocates), provided a truly international support network. This international fraternity of shared experience provided instant information and advice as different situations arose.

Smoking and Smokers

Before the introduction of the legislation, experienced tobacco control advocates from the United States and Canada privately suggested that with a background smoking prevalence of 27 per cent, it might be too soon for Ireland to embark on such an initiative and that it might be best to wait until the prevalence rates fell by at least another 5 per cent. Fortunately, they have been proved wrong. Whilst about a quarter of the population are smokers, the corollary is that about three-quarters of the population are non-smokers, so from day one, over 70 per cent of the population were going to obey the smoking ban.

In addition, opinion poll after opinion poll tells us that 70 per cent of current smokers wish they could quit smoking.[19] Smokers are ambivalent about their smoking and many saw this as an opportunity to either reduce their consumption of cigarettes or quit altogether. The multi-media campaigns on the harmful effects of smoking and of passive smoking, coupled with the additional supports provided to smokers to quit during the debate on this issue, facilitated many smokers in their endeavour to cut down or quit. This was borne out by reports of decreased sales of cigarettes in Ireland in 2004, increased access to quitlines[20] and some indication of decreased smoking prevalence.[21] However, it will be at least another year before the true effect of the workplace smoke-free initiative on the prevalence and consumption of cigarettes can be properly estimated. The majority of smokers are reasonable people. This active engagement of smokers may have helped dampen down their opposition to the smoke-free initiative. After the media campaign, there was greatly heightened awareness among the Irish population that passive smoking is harmful, and smokers and non-smokers alike now share the view that workers should not be exposed to second-hand smoke.

Legislation

Past experience in Ireland and elsewhere has shown that voluntary agreements are observed more in the breach than in the observance. Legislative underpinning was therefore essential and it is likely that the comprehensive nature of the Irish legislation was a key factor since this made it clear to all, employers, employees and customers, where they could or could not smoke. This was especially important within the hospitality sector where exemptions to allow smoking in some bars depending on whether they served food, or if they could provide separate ventilated rooms, would have caused confusion and could have undermined the principle behind the legislation.

Scientific Basis

The sound scientific base for the legislation provided a secure platform for the political leadership and for advocacy groups alike. A number of extensive scientific reports detailing the evidence base had accumulated by the early 1990s but the commissioning of an Irish report by "homegrown" scientists (Allwright, McLoughlin, Murphy et al., 2002) seemed to have had a major impact. Minister Martin chose to use this report to launch the legislation and to convince his parliamentary colleagues of the need for the legislation.

Capacity

The Tobacco Free Society document (Joint Committee on Health and Children, 2001) proved to have made many wise recommendations, including the creation of the OTC. The OTC played a crucial role in build-ing the knowledge base of key players in the political, civil service, NGO and academic arenas, and in orchestrating the preparation for the legisla-tion together with the Department of Health and Children.

What was unexpected however was the overwhelming nature of the work input required by all the agencies involved in the months prior to the implementation, leading in some cases to neglect of other aspects of tobacco control and other health areas. Even more unanticipated was the continued drain on human resources after the ban due to monitoring the impacts of the ban, follow-up on legal challenges, and perhaps most of all, the (tobacco tourism) visits by and to the many interested govern-mental and NGO bodies from other countries.

Media Debate

Also important in the success of the smoke-free initiative was the 14 month media debate in advance of the legislation being implemented. Through this widespread and prolonged debate, everyone became aware of what was involved. It has been estimated that in that time period the smoking ban occupied in excess of 20 million words, equivalent to some 10,000 pages of newsprint and 2,000 hours of national and local broad-cast time (Gilmore, 2005). In this regard, the ban on tobacco advertise-ments in newspapers which came into effect in 2000 was critical. Prior to 2000, few anti-tobacco stories were carried by newspapers other than the Irish Times, which had voluntarily refused to carry tobacco advertise-ments for many years. This situation changed noticeably after the com-mercial incentive to stay on-side with the tobacco industry was removed. Indeed, print media analysis conducted by MediaMarket (an independent agency that carries out media monitoring) found that the pro-legislation lobby gained the lion's share of the coverage: 65 per cent of "share of voice" and 70 per cent of the positive-influence' element of the overall coverage (Gilmore, 2005).

The fact that the thrust of the legislation was to protect worker health was critical as it deflected the nanny state and individual freedom argu-ments. The tobacco control lobby kept their messages simple and clear cut, based on facts and on expert knowledge, and focused on health is-sues such as saving lives and protecting workers who were vulnerable. This was in contrast to those who opposed the measure whose main thrust was business rather than health. GLOBALink helped the pro-legislation lobby to stay up-to-date with developments elsewhere and was a rich source of media advice. The OTC ran a masterful campaign as previously mentioned. ASH's foresight in building a wide healthcare coalition was demonstrated by the consistency of the media inputs and breadth of support. And a statement of support signed by all the major health bodies came at a critical time in the campaign.[22]

People

Committed advocacy by ASH Ireland over many years, starting back in the 1980s when anti-tobacco crusades were far from fashionable, set the ball rolling. The energy and dynamism of the fledgling OTC also had a major impact.

Committed political leadership was also critical. The Oireachtas Joint Committee on Health and Children paved the way with their detailed analysis of the issues in their 1999 report (Joint Committee on Health and Children, 1999) which led them to the – at the time – startling conclusion that all workplaces, including pubs and restaurants, should be smoke-free. The Tobacco Free Policy Review Group recommended further far-sighted initiatives (although they did not recommend smoke-free pubs and restaurants).

After he was appointed Minister for Health and Children in January 2000, Micheál Martin came to have a strong personal belief in the need for this legislation and was very supportive of the Tobacco Free Society recommendations published in 2000. Because the cross-party Oireachtas Report had already recommended smoke-free workplace legislation in 1999, he was assured of all party support, which was vitally important for such ground-breaking social legislation.

If there was one person responsible for convincing the Minister that this legislation was necessary and that it would be popular, it was Tom Power. Tom Power was the senior civil servant in the public health division in the Department of Health and Children from 1992 to 2001. From day one, his analysis of the relative importance of the various issues that came within his brief led him to conclude that tobacco control was the single most important health issue. He acquired an encyclopaedic knowledge of the area and worked tirelessly to reduce its impact on the population. It was he who convinced Minister Martin to support the Tobacco Free Society blueprint, who showed him just how important the smoke-free legislation was, and who persuaded him that if he showed leadership on this, that the entire NGO community would come in behind him – as indeed happened. It was Tom Power, initially as a civil servant with a passionate belief in the enormous and unnecessary harm done to society by tobacco, and subsequently as the chief executive officer of the newly formed OTC, who persuaded the Department of Health and Children to adopt the Tobacco Free Society blueprint and who then drove it forward. He convinced the major stakeholders to support it and he made the legislation happen. An unassuming man who shunned publicity, he is the unsung hero of this ground-breaking social legislation. His untimely death on 25 November 2005 is a blow to tobacco control both nationally and internationally.

Over the last year, many policymakers have visited Ireland to learn how success was achieved; so many indeed that the term "tobacco tourism" has been coined. For most, actually going out to visit bars and talking to bar owners, staff and customers – both smokers and non-smokers – has provided the best insights into why the legislation has worked and the best demonstration that unambiguous smoke-free policies in public places are successful, popular, and highly effective.

Future Challenges

It is important to ensure that compliance remains high. Although the ban is largely self-policing, continued support for the enforcement officers and maintenance of the complaint line will be required. The somewhat vague legal definition of outdoor smoking shelters is leading to all sorts of ingenious constructions that are possibly legal but are certainly contrary to the spirit of the law. And concern has been raised about the extent to which outdoor smoke from such areas migrates indoors (Mulcahy, Evans, Hammond et al., 2005). However, the exposure levels from these situations are very low in comparison to the continuous high-level exposures experienced previously. Nevertheless it is important to ensure that these do not become the thin end of the wedge.

Another challenge will be to extend the legislation to protect staff in hitherto exempted areas such as prisons, psychiatric institutions, hotel bedrooms. There is also a duty of care to protect non-smoking prison and psychiatric inmates, particularly juvenile detainees.

And finally, perhaps the most important challenge of all will be to provide protection to children without intruding on the privacy of the home. Ongoing information drives are required to ensure that the public remains aware of the harmful effects of passive smoke and to ensure that people realise that smoking at home harms their nearest and dearest. There are fears that the smoke-free workplace legislation would lead to increased smoking in homes; in fact there is indirect evidence that the opposite has occurred (Allwright, Paul, Greiner et al., 2003; Fong, Hyland, Borland et al., 2006)

Lessons for Healthcare Managers

* Vested interests can be tackled and beaten.

* A firm evidence base provides a secure platform enabling parliamentarians, government officials etc. to withstand pressure from vested interests.

* Media debate is not necessarily a bad thing. There is a natural tendency for public servants to shun the media. Although the media debate was bruising, the debate played a major role in informing the public about the issues.

* Keep the media messages straightforward and consistent. The ability of the tobacco control/pro-legislation coalition to stay on message and to avoid getting deflected into the side debate on the economic impacts was very important.

* International networks are very useful. These enabled the pro-ban lobby to learn from others' experience and to avoid "reinventing the wheel".

* Advocacy has a powerful role in changing attitudes and policy. But advocacy takes time, decades and years rather than months, and requires champions.

* Major social change requires a champion(s). The emergence of a behind-the-scenes champion (Tom Power) and a public champion (Micheál Martin) was critical.

Endnotes

[1] Public Health (Tobacco) Acts 2002 and 2004. Dublin: Stationery Office, 2004.

[2] Tobacco (Health Promotion and Protection) Act, 1988. Dublin: Stationery Office, 1988.

[3] Tobacco (Health Promotion and Protection) Regulations, 1990. Dublin: Stationery Office, 1990.

[4] Tobacco (Health Promotion and Protection) Regulations, 1995. Dublin: Stationery Office, 1995.

[5] Repace, J. "Right to life overrides right to smoke". *The Irish Times*, February 11, 2002.

[6] http://www.lva.ie/page.php?intPageID=3 (accessed 3 May 2005).

[7] http://www.vfi.ie/aboutvfi/news_events.asp?article_type_id=1 (accessed 3 May 2005).

[8] O'Brien, C. "Tobacco firms say no justification for smoking ban". *The Irish Times*, 27 August 2003.

[9] http://www.otc.ie/communication_smokefree.asp. (accessed 3 May 2005).

[10] http://www.dohc.ie/press/releases/2003/20030821.html (accessed May 3, 2005).

[11] http://www.smokefreeatwork.ie/ (accessed 3 May 2005).

[12] "National and united force representing at least 1.1 million people living in Ireland fully endorse smoking ban and welcome date". www.smokefreeatwork.ie/news/detail.asp?id=10 (accessed 3 May 2005).

[13] Vintners' Federation of Ireland. "Research Shows 10 per cent job loss in New York pub sector since introduction of smoking ban." http://www.vfi.ie/ aboutvfi/article_detail.asp?article_type_id=1&article_id=38.(accessed 3 May 2005).

[14] Vintners' Federation of Ireland. "Smoking ban seriously hurting rural pub businesses - Drinks Suppliers confirm 15-25 per cent drop in sales." http://www.vfi.ie/aboutvfi/article_detail.asp?article_type_id=1&article_id=89. (accessed 3 May 2005).

[15] O'Kane, P. "Calling time on the pub?" *The Sunday Tribune*, 22 February 2004.

[16] http://www.cso.ie/releasespublications/documents/services/current/rsi_retrospective.ls (accessed 11 August 2006).

[17] McCaffrey, U. "Retail sales rise of 2.8 per cent marks turnaround – CSO." *The Irish Times*, 22 January 2005.

[18] Curran, R. "Pub sales dip raises doubt on impact of ban." *The Irish Independent*, 25 January 2005.

[19] http://www.irishcancer.ie/quitting/cycle.of.change.php (accessed 11 August 2006)

[20] Department of Health and Children. *7,000 fewer smokers in Ireland: Quitline and smoking ban attributed to 33 per cent decline in prevalence of smoking*, 26

September 2004. www.smokefreeatwork.ie/news/detail.asp?id=22 (accessed 11 August 2006).

[21] Cigarette smoking prevalence. http://www.otc.ie/research_reports.asp#cigarette (accessed 27 July 2006).

[22] http://www.otc.ie/article.asp?=42 (accessed 11 August 2006).

References

Allwright, S., McLoughlin, J.P., Murphy, D., Pratt, I., Ryan, M.P., and Smith, A. (2002). *Report on the Health Effects of Environmental Tobacco Smoke (ETS) in the Workplace*. Dublin: Office of Tobacco Control and the Health and Safety Authority.

Allwright, S., Paul, G., Greiner, B., Mullally, B.J., Pursell, L., Kelly, A., et al. "Legislation for Smoke-Free Workplaces and Health of Bar Workers in Ireland: Before and After Study". *British Medical Journal*, 331, 1117-1120.

California Environmental Protection Agency. (1997). *Health Effects of Exposure to Environmental Tobacco Smoke*. Sacramento, CA: California Environmental Protection Agency.

Dearlove, J.V., Bialous, S.A., and Glantz, S.A. (2002). "Tobacco Industry Manipulation of the Hospitality Industry to Maintain Smoking in Public Places". *Tobacco Control*, 11, 2, 94-104.

Department of Health and Children. (2000). *Towards a Tobacco-Free Society: Report of the Tobacco-Free Policy Review Group*. Dublin: Stationery Office.

Department of Health and Children. (2001). *Quality and Fairness – A Health System for You*. Dublin: Stationery Office.

Enstrom, J.E. and Kabat, G.C. (2003). "Environmental Tobacco Smoke and Tobacco Related Mortality in a Prospective Study of Californians, 1960-98". *British Medical Journal*, 326, 1057-66.

Fong, G.T., Hyland, A., Borland, R., Hammond, D., Hastings, G., McNeill, A., et al. (2006). "Reductions in Tobacco Smoke Pollution and Increases in Support for Smoke- Free Public Places Following the Implementation of Comprehensive Smoke-Free Workplace Legislation in the Republic of Ireland: Findings from the ITC Ireland/UK Survey". *Tobacco Control*, 2006, 15, 3, 51-58.

Gilmore, N. (2005). *Clearing the Air: The Battle over the Smoking Ban*. Dublin: Liberties Press.

Health Promotion Unit, Department of Health. (1992). *Clean Air at Work*. Dublin: Department of Health.

Health Promotion Unit, Department of Health. (1994). *Working Together for Cleaner Air*. Dublin: Department of Health.

Howell, F. (2004). "Ireland's Workplaces, Going Smoke Free". *British Medical Journal*, 2004, 328, 847-8.

Howell F. (2005). "Smoke-Free Bars in Ireland: a Runaway Success". *Tobacco Control*, 14, 2, 73-74.

Howell, F. and Doorley, P. (1991). "Employee Attitudes to Involuntary Smoking at the Workplace". *Irish Medical Journal* 1991, 84, 3, 94-96.

Joint Committee on Health and Children. (1999). *A National Anti-Smoking Strategy: A Report on Smoking and Health*. Dublin: Houses of the Oireachtas.

Joint Committee on Health and Children. (2001). *Second Interim Report of the Subcommittee on Health and Smoking*. Dublin: Houses of the Oireachtas.

Mulcahy, M., Evans, D.S., Hammond, S.K., Repace, J.L. and Byrne, M. (2005). "Second-Hand Smoke Exposure and Risk Following the Irish Smoking Ban: An Assessment of Salivary Cotinine Concentrations in Hotel Workers and Air Nicotine Levels in Bars". *Tobacco Control* 2005, 14, 384-388.

Office of Tobacco Control. *Smoke-Free Workplace Legislation Implementation: Progress Report, May 2004*. http://www.otc.ie/Uploads/Smoke-free per cent20workplace per cent20legislation per cent20progress per cent20report per cent20may per cent2004 per cent20FINAL.pdf (accessed 3 May 2005).

Office of Tobacco Control. *Smoke-Free Workplaces in Ireland: A One-Year Review*. http://www.otc.ie/article.asp?article=271 (accessed 3 May 2005)

US Department of Health and Human Services (1986). *The Health Consequences of Involuntary Smoking: A Report of the Surgeon General*. Washington, DC: US Government Printing Office.

Chapter 6

BALANCING ACCOUNTABILITY
AND RESPONSIBILITY

Frank Ahern

In this chapter I hope to give the reader an insight into how the Oireachtas holds the health service to account and the interaction that takes place between Ministers, Parliament and the Civil Service. It also shows how the accountability process works. I will describe what goes on every day to ensure that Parliament keeps a watchful eye on what is going on in the health services. All of what I describe can be seen very publicly each day in the Dáil chamber and is often carried as part of news stories by the media. On important occasions in the Dáil and Seanad you can see the relevant Ministers in the front bench on the Government side of the House with the opposing parties across the floor. Civil Servants may be seated to the right of the Minister (in the Dáil) or behind the minister (in the Seanad). Only members of the Houses can of course speak in the chambers so you don't hear from the Civil Servants, but their job is to provide the briefing or in the case of legislation to draft the proposed legislation. I have tried to show how the continuous interaction between Parliament and the executive wing of Government takes place and through my first-hand experience shed some light on how civil servants deal with this on a daily basis.

Accountability to the Dáil

Health staff at all levels and in all disciplines have their salaries paid from taxes and those that allocate the funds to pay those salaries and provide the buildings and equipment to allow the service to function (i.e.

the government) deserve to know how the service is being delivered, where the problems are and what solutions might be put in place to maintain and improve service to the public.

The last ten years of my life would see my day starting with the 6.30 am news. This meant that if a health story was hitting the headlines I had to know this and make plans to stay on top of the day's work. The first thing I would ask was, "is this on my side of the house?", i.e. within my domain of responsibility. If the answer was yes then I was already at work. While the Department was in theory a policymaking organisation it could never become too distant from the reality of day-to-day activities and needed to be up to date on the situations making the news where health was an issue. We would often have been criticised for "fire-fighting" but my answer was that fires had to be fought or you got burned.

Let me borrow a phrase from the musical *Oklahoma* by saying "I'd like to say a word for the politician". I was always impressed with the long hours worked by modern politicians and feel that they are not given due credit for the immense efforts that large numbers of politicians make by way of long hours worked. Quite a lot of these hours are devoted to health issues since politicians tend to be hugely interested in health. I found during my years in the Department of Health and Children that large numbers of health staff around the country had no appreciation of the intense interest the political world has in health and were also un-aware of the hours that politicians work on all sorts of issues. All the criticism of long holidays and short Dáil sittings takes little account that members are rarely off duty and when not in the Dáil are busy in their constituencies. They have the ultimate performance management system in that they must ask for their job back every few years based on the voter's evaluation of how well they have done their jobs. Very few people have so little fixity of tenure.

It has therefore always amazed me that amongst health service staff, Dáil Deputies and Senators are not perceived to be central to the health services. When addressing staff in the health services, I was regularly asked "What does the Department think?" or "What does the Minister think?" but was rarely asked what the Dáil thought about health issues. This surprised me since 85 per cent of all the money spent on healthcare in the public service is provided from voted monies by the Dáil. The money to run the health and personal social services is collected by the Office of the Revenue Commissioners as agreed by the Dáil and is then allocated to run the various elements of Government services through a process where the money is "voted " by the members for specific purposes. My first question to the reader is "Is there any group of people more entitled to know what is going on in healthcare than those who allocate the money to run the service on behalf of the citizens?" That power is exercised by the Dáil as part of the mandate that politicians get when we, the citizens, elect them to office. It is therefore logical and proper that the representatives of the citizens should be fully informed on what is happening with health monies. Some might have unrealistic notions of how much information they should have, especially in cases involving individuals, and the dividing line between accountability and seeking minute details of cases has often been a subject of lively debate.

So how do the parliamentarians keep track of what is happening and hold the system to account? First of all they will insist that one of their own members with responsibility for health services (the Minister) or indeed the Taoiseach tell them what is happening and tell them what is being done about the issue. The person providing this information could be the Taoiseach, the Minister for Health and Children or one of the Ministers of State at the Department of Health and Children, depending on the manner in which the issue is raised in the Houses of the Oireachtas and/or the availability of Ministers that day. Each House has an arrangement in place to allow Ministers to be questioned on issues and the job of the civil servant is to guess what line of questioning might ensue and prepare adequate briefing notes. Any issue that is deemed important enough to be raised in the house that day requires input from an Assistant Secretary to ensure that the Secretary General and the Minister are briefed on the matter and a draft of the Department's position is prepared.

This invariably involved a team effort. The mobile phone or e-mailing to blackberries has become very useful in recent years in allowing us to get started with the task of finding and preparing the information even before the working day begins. The tight deadlines imposed by the Dáil and the constant quest for information are generally not understood outside of the small group that deals with Dáil business. As a deadline approaches frantic activity becomes commonplace in the corridors and stairways in Hawkins House. The advent of electronic communication has eased the problems significantly. I still remember being offered a glass of water by an usher as I arrived breathless having run from Hawkins House (Department of Health) to the Dáil to get a speech to a minister in 15 minutes.

There are strict rules about how matters can be raised for discussion in the Dáil and the Ceann Comhairle will decide which of the matters can be raised. Three matters can be raised each day. While an issue might often get a quick airing when the Order of Business is announced at the start of the day, the proper arrangement is for motions to be put down for debate by written notice. Business is interrupted to take any matters to be debated at 8.30 pm on Tuesdays and Wednesdays and at 5.30 pm on Thursdays.

There is also an arrangement in place under Standing Order 30, which provides for a debate on matters of urgent public importance where a specific matter has arisen suddenly and requires immediate debate. The Ceann Comhairle will rule on this and if a situation is likely to develop significantly before the Dáil has a chance of discussing it then the Ceann Comhairle may allow a discussion.

The role of the opposition is, of course, to oppose and all sides are very good at this leading to lively parliamentary debates. The Civil Servant's job is to be prepared should an issue be raised such that he or she can brief the Minister on time and most of all accurately. Every senior Civil Servant lives in constant fear on these occasions of being the cause of "misleading the Dáil". This is viewed as the "mortal sin" by those who work on the preparation of briefing material for issues raised in the house. This preparation is done under extremely tight time limits, especially on Thursdays, but the tight time limits do not absolve you from blame if you are the cause of misleading the house. My advice to new staff was always to take these duties very seriously and constantly to check the facts before writing any statement. Where a lot of data must be processed a team of four to five people might be involved in preparing a brief. My second piece of advice to my staff therefore was to get started quickly on getting the accurate information from the system. Prior to the establishment of the Health Service Executive the Department had a series of networks, which allowed us to telephone the people responsible in the Health boards or in the Eastern Regional Health Authority (ERHA) directly. Prior to the establishment of the ERHA the Department had a network in the acute hospital sector in Dublin but the establishment of the ERHA meant that, by and large, only one phone call was required to get a picture of what was happening in Dublin. That was a great help to the Department especially in putting a national picture together. The establishment of the ERHA did mean that the collection of data on waiting lists, bed closures, etc. was done for the Department and this eased workloads.

Changes in the Civil Service

Since I entered the Civil Service back in 1961 the whole world of government services has changed. Certainly in the 1960s and the early 1970s the Civil Service was not a very responsive organisation and my mentors at that time saw careful wording of letters as being far more important than provision of quick customer service. A lot of effort was expended on drafting letters telling members of the public why we could not provide a service and the common belief in the Department was that provided the letter was accurate and grammatically correct then the job was done and we had earned our pay. In hindsight, it was a cosy enough place to work and the pressures were nothing compared to what they are today. While I was then a junior official the folklore was that not every Minister was at the top of the class in running a government department. I never met a Jim Hacker style Minister as portrayed in the "Yes Minister" series but I am assured by older colleagues that comparable versions might well have existed. It is equally true however that some senior civil servants could be said to portray at least some of the style of Sir Humphrey. Stories exist in the folklore of incidents that might not be totally out of place in that series. Such characters would not survive in today's Civil Service environment since the levels of accountability and responsibility being applied are much tougher than they were over 30 years ago.

The responsiveness of Government departments has improved over the past few years. Today's Civil Service is light years away from the one I entered. The focus now is on responsiveness and service to the members of the public. Some of this has been driven by the public themselves. Wood (1995) saw a situation where "citizens are demanding a higher level of service and greater responsiveness from public service organisations". In the mid 90s this movement was reflected in Irish public services with the publication of Delivering Better Government (1996) which is generally seen as the foundation of the Strategic Management Initiative. The Strategic Management Initiative (SMI) has moved the whole focus of government from making sure the wheels are going around to making sure we are going in the right direction. It has changed the focus from one of activity to one of outputs and begins with the question "Why are we here?" I believe that the answer is that Government Departments are there to serve the Government and ultimately the members of the public. Members of the public can seek the services being provided and if they encounter a difficulty in getting the service they are entitled to seek the help of their public representatives. This right must be respected but if they are seeking something they are not entitled to then it becomes a more difficult situation and merit rather than influence should be the deciding factor.

McKevitt and Keogan (1997) point out that the citizen lies at the heart of public management and constitutes the primary reason for the existence of the public service. The political process therefore focuses on the citizen's requirements and as such is a vital part of what is happening as long as the system is taxation based.

Responsibilities of the Civil Servant: Policy or Operations?

This brings me to one of the key debates over the last few years in the Department as to how much the Civil Servant should know about the operational level before they can brief a Minister on key issues. We do have general agreement that the Department should get out of the operational work and concentrate on the strategic elements of the service. The Department should, of course, be freed up from the operational issues but it cannot quite disconnect itself completely from what is going on in the service. The Minister of the day will be expected to have all the facts. The Dáil will require the facts and will expect the Minister to furnish these facts to the House. To accomplish this task the Department must be in constant contact with the delivery system. This contact however is not designed to interfere in the operational work but to get the relevant information to enable the Minister to reply to the questions raised on the issue. Where an executive agency (i.e., the Health Service Executive) has been set up to carry out the operational work they should be allowed to carry out their duties without undue interference but there is still a need to provide the Dáil with a reasonable amount of information when it is requested.

I do not believe that a clear line of territory can be drawn between the Department and the Health Service Executive. While clarity of roles is very important to ensure that no unnecessary duplication takes place it is my belief that working together on issues and sharing information on issues provides the best service from both organisations to the Minister. The Minister is ultimately responsible and as such must get 100 per cent support at all times in getting the relevant information. There were times during my working life when I found it difficult enough to get information urgently from the delivery system, being seen as "somebody from the Department annoying us for more information". My approach was to try and explain why it was vital, in a democracy, to bother busy people to get information.

There is often a view on policymaking that imagines a few people working in a quiet room far from the noise of day-to-day activity, "shooting the breeze" and hoping to come up with some inspirational thoughts. It is true that the writing up stage of policy formulation takes place in a quiet room but the actual policymaking goes on all the time and the reality of what is happening on the ground drives the policymaking. When the new Health Service Executive was being set up there was a very clear message from the Government that it would be given the operational role of running the service and taking the day to day decisions to provide and improve the service. There was also a realisation in the Department that the Executive would have to be a major player in informing the policymaking. I believe that the final decisions on policymaking take place at political level and assistance on policy making takes place in the space between the Minister, the Secretary General of the Department and the Chief Executive Officer of the Health Service Executive. Policymaking is one of the roles of the Minister and the department is there to assist the Minister in that task. The Executive has a role in assisting the Minister also and it will increasingly take on more of this role in the future.

However, policymaking in healthcare is not just in the remit of the Department of Health and Children. There will be occasions when the Department of the Taoiseach and the Department of Finance will be fully involved in policymaking. A coherent Government policy means that departments can't go on solo runs and thus central direction must always be provided. It is not possible to have decentralised decision making on policy in Ireland since everything else is nationally organised. For example, the existence of national trade unions cutting across sectors means that different departments of state cannot have different sets of policies for the one trade union.

Policy on funding however will continue to be made by Government. The share of funding which will be available for health services will continue to be decided by Government as long as we retain the current tax-based system. This, in turn, has led to the current situation where the Government will always insist that the allocated budget for the health service must be adhered to.

The Parliamentary Debate

Parliamentary debates are at the very heart of a democratic society and are a key element in holding the political heads of the department providing the services to account. It may be that the issue will be raised at leaders' questions, which can take place at an early stage of the Dáil proceedings. If so, a draft note will have to be prepared which must be short and bullet-pointed and deal only with the facts of the case and must arrive on the Secretary General's desk in time for the Dáil. Of course this does not finish the business of Parliament for the day. The Houses of the Oireachtas have many other ways to hold the system to account. It is not unusual at all to have a number of live "hot topics" on your table on any one day. A number of these may be matters to be raised on the adjournment of the house, which operates as follows.

Where matters are raised for debate on the Adjournment, the debate will take place later that evening so there is no time to waste. The issues raised by members will be sent electronically to the Secretary General's Office and transmitted to all relevant staff immediately by email. This was always my early warning that an issue on my side of the Department might be taken later on that day and some preliminary consideration is immediately given to these issues. Since many more issues are raised on the Adjournment than can be taken on any one day, the Ceann Comhairle must decide what the priority issues are. At the appointed time the decision is made on what issues will get raised. As soon as this decision is made the issues chosen are indicated to the relevant staff and the work on the draft speech and the brief begins in earnest. I always had the habit of getting the work started as soon as I heard that an issue had been raised with the Ceann Comhairle as it was likely to be chosen and if not would, in all probability be chosen the following day. I found that if the issue were important enough it would find its way on to the Dáil or Seanad agenda sooner or later. Again we were usually under tight time pressure in respect of Adjournment Debates and when the Dáil sat until 10.30 pm we had much more time to get the information than we have had in recent years. My plan was always to get someone working on getting the brief together as a matter of urgency and give some broad direction as to how the draft speech should be set out. While all this would be going on I would be keeping an eye on the clock and calculating the time still available since the draft would have to go through the Secretary General's office and from there to the Minister's Office.

The Department is organised into divisions on a functional basis There are divisions for acute hospitals, blood policy, nursing, personnel, social inclusion, primary care, etc. Each Division will take the work that arises from an issue raised in Parliament -where, for instance, bed closures in acute hospitals is an issue the briefing is prepared in Acute Hospitals Division, as that division will have the information in its files or will be expected to source the relevant information. The Division will have its own network in the wider service and will use that network to find the information in time for a comprehensive brief for whatever Minister will be answering to the Dáil. Usually this is a clear cut decision but at times an issue might cover a number of Divisions and cross divisional working is required with one division taking the lead role. This would have been the case with the controversial issue of waiting times in Accident and Emergency Departments for example. Acute Hospitals Division would take the lead role with assistance from the division dealing with services for the elderly.

The preparation of briefs took a very significant portion of civil servants time but also meant that the Department accumulated in-depth knowledge and a huge amount of information on these issues. This information would go to inform the policy making that is part of the normal estimates cycle that takes place each year.

Traditionally the files and briefs are all held by the division concerned but one of my last jobs was to pilot a system where these briefing files could be held electronically to improve access to the relevant information. That is not a simple task as files have to be constantly updated to allow this to be of use and because of tight staffing files are updated only if major events take place.

There are so many issues that it would take a small army to update all the files on a daily basis and if a file is not fully up to date then it cannot be used without the follow up call to the delivery agency. Updating files is therefore a constant task in the Department. I once did a rough count on the number of issues that would be live in the Department at any one time and came up with a figure of over 2,500. These would not be for individual constituents; these would be issues involving policy-making or service improvements. I believe that anyone today wanting to do the same exercise would find more than that. Thus the raising of issues in Parliament alerts and updates the Department and may shift the focus in policy making.

The new arrangement for a Parliamentary Affairs Division in the Department and the HSE should improve the flow of information and provide a better service for the public representatives. Public representatives only look for this information because their constituents have asked for it and since the parliamentary process is essential to the democratic system the service is actually much more responsive to the public than is apparent.

The Parliamentary Question

The preceding sections describe what can happen during sitting days in the Houses of the Oireachtas. One of the most important ways to hold a Minister to account politically is by way of Parliamentary Question. This allows members to put down questions for written or oral answer. In any one-year the Department would deal with approximately 3,000 such questions. This is a huge workload in the Department and in the Health Service Executive but it is largely viewed as the price of a flourishing democracy. I believe that these questions are of vital importance in allowing the Dáil, which as we know pays the bills for the major part of the health service to interrogate the Minister and through the Minister the actual health delivery system.

Questions may be tabled for written or oral reply. "Written" questions can be tabled for reply with three working days notice being required. The majority of the questions are for written reply and there is a constant flow of these questions when the Dáil is in session. Oral questions are taken once every five weeks or so. The Minister takes these questions in the Dáil between 2.30 pm and 3.45 pm on Tuesdays, Wednesdays and Thursdays when the Dáil is in session. There will be five priority questions at the beginning of the session. The rules allow the member asking the question to ask what are called supplementary questions of the Minister. This means that the brief must be very comprehensive and must contain a full account of all matters relating to the issue. Here the civil Servant is not just worried about misleading the House but has the additional concern that the brief cannot be so big as to be unreadable yet must contain the key issues that may well be raised. There is therefore a balance to be maintained between information overload and getting the relevant facts for ease of reference during the interaction that follows the immediate answering of the question. Ministers take their questions very seriously and quite often refer briefs back where there is not complete clarity in the draft answer. While the Civil Servants prepare the material, the Minister becomes responsible for the content of the reply. The Minister is expected to know everything about the health service down to the smallest detail. It would be impossible to answer in the Dáil without a comprehensive brief. I have always been impressed with Ministers who can field questions on a service that employs more than 100,000 people, costs 8 per cent of our gross national product, has thousands of units, treats over half a million people as inpatients in hospital and another 350,000 on a day care basis and has a presence throughout the country.

Representations

While these arrangements cover major issues, Dáil and Seanad members will be writing constantly to Ministers and Ministers for State to make cases for their constituents (mainly) for various services. These letters are known as "reps" or representations on behalf of constituents. These letters tend mainly to be referred to the Health Service Executive, which provides information to allow the Minister to answer the letters. They are dealt with mainly at Executive Officer and Clerical Officer level and, while important in their own right, they refer mostly to individual cases. While they are of vital importance to those individuals they are rarely matters of policy so do not feature in that frantic rush that goes with immediate parliamentary business. Representations can however provide a barometer on service difficulties particularly where the same issue or service is the subject of several representations. The Minister's Office will notice this also and this will call for closer scrutiny.

Representations and Parliamentary Questions can serve as a very good measure of how services are delivered. For example, during my time in the Hospitals Division there was a major problem with cardiac surgery. This was a very public story at that time. Waiting times were very long and the number of coronary artery bypass grafts being carried out had fallen during the late 1980s. Right through the early 1990s the number of parliamentary questions, adjournment debates and representations on matters relating to cardiac surgery from TDs and Senators increased. It was quite obvious that we had a major problem and this was showing up in the local clinics run by TDs and Senators. The mid-1990s saw a major initiative to resolve these problems being launched and at the time of writing there has been a major improvement in cardiac services with waiting lists reduced very significantly. Looking back on the situation in the late 1980s and early 1990s it is fairly obvious that raising the issue in Parliament had some effect on the decision to improve services in this area.

The Minister's Accountability

The Oireachtas has two key arrangements in place to question the Minister and the Secretary General and to make their views known on ongoing issues in the health service. Since most of the funding to run the service is voted by the Dáil its Public Accounts Committee (PAC) is mandated to follow the money and to ensure best value for money is provided for the taxpayer. I believe that the task of the PAC is very much a stewardship one in that the steward acts on behalf of the owner for the general good of the organisation. I see the PAC as acting on behalf of the owners (the taxpayers) and as such has a very wide ranging brief. Preparing for the appearance of the Secretary General before the PAC is a role that is taken very seriously by senior Civil Servants. This event is preceded by an examination by the Comptroller and Auditor General (C&AG) of the financial accounts of the Department and these accounts are then presented to the PAC.

The PAC has a reputation of taking its remit seriously and questions can be asked about almost every element of the happenings in the health service. The Chairman of the PAC is a very powerful person and will want questions of committee members answered quickly, accurately and comprehensively. Preparing the brief involves almost every section and division of the Department. There is usually adequate time to prepare the brief and most of the work here is not about writing the brief but compiling a brief that the Secretary General can refer to if required for details of issues should a question on some detail or other arise. It is impossible to cover all the detail and have a readable document so the key points need to be highlighted with adequate signposting of where the particular detail can be found. My advice to staff beginning to work on these briefs was to set out the main points in bullet point format and show where the details can be found in a supplementary brief.

From time to time the C&AG undertakes value for money audits on particular service developments or projects and again a comprehensive brief must be compiled. This will usually include senior Civil Servants being in attendance before the committee and giving their account of what happened, what the thinking behind a project was at that time and answering any questions put by the Deputies. Knowing that you yourself will have to answer PACs questions certainly sharpens the mind and all other non urgent meetings or discussions take a back seat on the days before the hearings. Again preparatory work is essential if you are to have a successful appearance before the Dáil committee. The PAC is regarded as having teeth and is always taken seriously.

The second arrangement is the Joint Committee of the Oireachtas on Health and Children. This Committee has a membership drawn from the Dáil and the Seanad and will contain the health spokespeople from the political parties represented on the Committee. This is where policy is discussed and there is often a very general discussion on strategic issues. The Minister appears before this Committee assisted by a small team of Civil Servants. Again if the subject being discussed is within your remit of responsibility, you will be expected not only to brief the Minister but also to attend as part of the Civil Service team.

Lots of groups or indeed individuals are invited to attend by the Joint Committee as it has a broad role in examining all aspects of policy on healthcare. From time to time reports received by the Minister will be sent to the Joint Committee for their attention and this will involve hearings and debates. Any of the relevant people can be called to appear at the hearings and Civil Servants are invariably called at that stage.

I believe that with the abolition of the Health Boards, the Joint Committee on Health and Children will become much more important in future as it has the task of examining spending proposals in the health estimates and it is here that public representatives can query spending on particular programmes before the money is spent. Prior to this the members of Health Boards had the task of agreeing the service plans of Health Boards together with the consequent financial arrangements for each Board. The majority of Health Board members were elected representatives and with the abolition of the Health Boards the elected representatives in the Dáil become the initial "watchdogs" of the political world through the Joint Committee.

My preference is for much more debate on health issues in the Dáil and Senate, which would seek jointly, agreed approaches to healthcare. My criticism is that in political debates and discussions politicians tend always to adopt a position of "for or against" an issue. The accepted view that the role of the opposition is to oppose lessens the value of the debate. This is part of the reality of party politics and perhaps that system simply does not allow productive debates on health issues. The Joint Committee might be a good place to have this type of debate in future.

Politicians from all sides have their networks that inform them, but the Minister needs a Department that can provide a comprehensive factual briefing and recommend the best course of action. I believe that this role of the Department will become much more important in the future and that evaluation of the delivery system will be a far more significant element of the Department's role. In the past the Department was engaged in a lot of operational tasks and evaluation was not seen as the priority. The Department's role now, as set out on its website, is to support the Minister in the formulation and evaluation of policies and that should be welcomed as a significant improvement in accountability in the health service.

The Legislative Process

Legislation is, of course, a major element of the business of the Houses of the Oireachtas and the preparation of legislation is a key function of the Civil Service. Civil Servants are involved at all stages of the legislative process from the time that the Government makes the decision to introduce legislation until it is signed into law by the President. Recent years have seen a very significant body of legislation being drawn up in the area of health and all of the reforms are underpinned by legislation to establish new organisations and to modernise the structures for the provision of healthcare. Major pieces of legislation like the 2004 Health Act require specific teams of Civil Servants to be drawn together for the duration of the task. Again it is a case of the senior Civil Servant having to balance his or her time between the immediate pressures of the day and the longer-term work of legislation. During my time in the Department some progress was made in advancing the Medical Practitioners Bill, amending the Nurses Act and preparing the Health Act (2004).

Any proposal for legislation by a Minister first goes to Government and from there it will normally go to the Office of the Attorney General where the Parliamentary Counsel will begin work on the draft of the Bill. A Bill undergoes five stages of passage through the Dáil and will then normally move through the stages of the Seanad. While undergoing the stages in the Dáil the Civil Servant will be required to be in attendance as amendments may be tabled during the second stage, the third or Committee Stage and the fourth or Report stage as it makes its way through the parliamentary process.

Balancing the efforts of managing day to day issues with the mental energy required to think through the potential longer-term implications of any legislation being developed, required considerable skill from within the Department. Sometimes there would be very tight deadlines for legislation and this would see the team fully stretched over a lengthy day. When, for instance, the Health Act, 2004 was undergoing its various stages in the Dáil the Civil Service team worked all through the night on the amendments and last e-mails to the various key players at 7.00 am would see them have a short respite before being back at work later on during the day.

There has been a lot of debate about how drafting of legislation should take place in a department like Health and Children. Should it be undertaken by a specialist team with legal competency or should a team drawn from the Division familiar with the problem be tasked with the drafting of the Bill? There is no easy answer to this and a mix of these skills might be the best way to tackle the issue. I found, during my period in the Department, that having a dedicated team, freed up from the fire-fighting tasks (provided one could release sufficient capacity) was the most successful way of getting the job done.

Reorganisation of the Department of Health and Children and Making it Relevant to the Early Twenty-first Century

As part of the reforms I was involved centrally in the reorganisation of the Department of Health and Children. This reorganisation was required to allow the Department take on its new announced role as part of the reform programme in June 2003. A number of new divisions were set up. One such new division was the Parliamentary Affairs Division. In arguing for this division to be set up we were anxious to bring modern public service management to bear on the interaction between the Oireachtas and Government. The Oireachtas is constantly in contact with government but it was clear to me that just as public services are not always as responsive to the citizen as they should be, the health service was not as responsive as it should have been to the parliamentarians. A key part of the reforms was putting in place systems that would be more responsive to members of the Oireachtas. This called for clear lines of communication, which could provide the information required in an accurate and timely fashion. It also called for the formation of a Parliamentary Affairs Division in the Health Service Executive. There would be little point in having a new system in place in the department if it did not have a similar arrangement in the Executive, which would feed in the information. Setting up these Divisions called for use of persuasion in convincing all those involved of the importance of managing the relationships with the Parliamentarians. If you were to view their requests for information as an annoyance then the management of the relationship would be a problem but on the other hand if you were to see these requests for information as part of the democratic system then there is a clear cut case to manage the system better.

If the new system works well it should improve the flow of accurate information to public representatives. This should lead to less reliance on Parliamentary Questions as a mechanism for obtaining information.

Cost Containment

It is impossible to divorce healthcare from money. For those that hold the purse strings there is the overriding priority of balancing the books. Since health is part of total Government expenditure the health budget must be balanced like everything else. Good fiscal management of the funds voted for the services is essential in every country where the exchequer foots the bill for the service. Spending on health is subject to the one most important rule of all in that you can't spend what you have not got and if you do you certainly can't continue to do it. Significant overspending beyond that budgeted for in health becomes a threat to the economic stability of the country. (We have learnt this from the experience in the 1980s when overspending led to significant and painful cuts in healthcare in the late 1980s.)

My experiences have led me to believe that all of our national wealth could be spent on healthcare and we could still identify additional services that need to be provided. There seems to be an infinite demand for healthcare but the resources available to any Government are always limited. The Department stands on the ground between the demands for infinite services and the limitation on funding arising from good fiscal management. The World Health Organisation (1997) has described this as a balancing act "between the moral imperative of maintaining solidarity and the social good character of healthcare and the fiscal imperative of cost control". This is happening all over the world and is certainly a feature of all OECD countries.

The huge growth in the cost of healthcare started in the middle of the twentieth century according as new technologies came on the market. Dunning (1996) described the situation where before the Second World War the effectiveness of medicine was limited but was readily available at reasonable cost. Relman (1988) described what followed as a "medical revolution" which saw the emergence of antibiotics, new vaccines, cardiovascular drugs, minimally invasive surgery, lasers, organ transplantation and cancer drugs all with very significant costs. Healthcare costs grew far faster than the normal price increases and this continued over a 30-year period.

Cost containment has been a central feature of healthcare reform throughout developed countries and what we have seen in Ireland is part of an international trend. According as developments in medicine have become standard practice and the costs of these new technologies have had to be paid for, governments have resorted to cost containment to limit costs to the public (Ham, 1997). While no two countries have the same health systems all were dealing with the same set of problems in seeking equity of access while containing costs (WHO, 1997). Gooijer (2007) describes the problem as increased health expenditure being powered by the new technologies during the very good years of European economic growth and reluctance by governments internationally to confront the gap between demands and funding until increased health spending threatened to destabilise whole economies.

In Ireland cost containment in healthcare has become a political issue and this is pretty much in line with the situation in most OECD countries. It has tended to dominate the lives of senior Civil Servants who are right in the middle of the cut and thrust of these battles. The political element of the working lives of the staff in the Department is very much grounded in what happens at service delivery level when spending caps or cost containment methods are put in place and the consequences that arise from these policies. The great flow of parliamentary work is very much driven by these decisions and as such touches the reality of the lives of the members of the public and must be dealt with effectively and efficiently.

Conclusions

We cannot divorce politics from healthcare, nor should we attempt to. Accountability to public representatives and to government is an important part of our democratic process. The public has an entitlement to hold the civil servants and the service delivery professionals to account and to do so through their elected representatives. It is important therefore to respect the roles and responsibilities of all of the actors in healthcare, whether it be a local politician, a health professional, a secretary general, a TD or a Minister. They all have a part to play in improving out health system.

A key skill for all of these actors is their ability to balance – the short term with the long term, the individual good with the collective good, the investment with the impact or benefit, the arguments for with the arguments against. Most importantly each of us needs to pay attention to our accountabilities as well as our responsibilities.

Creating more space for informed debate on health issues is something we all have a role to play in. Such debate needs to take place in the wards and corridors of hospitals and clinics as well as in the Dáil and Senate and the focus must shift from the adoption of hard-line and opposing positions to working together to deliver a better health service.

References

Delivering Better Government (1996). Second Report to the Government of the Co-ordinating Group of Secretaries. Dublin: The Stationery Office.

Dunning, A.J. (1996). "Reconciling Macro- and Micro-Concerns: Objectives and Priorities in Healthcare". In the Organisation for Economic Co-Operation and Development (ed), *Healthcare Reform: The Will to Change*. Paris: OECD, pp. 59-65.

Gooijer, W de (2007). *Trends in EU Health Systems*. Amsterdam: Springer.

Ham, C. (ed.) (1997). *Healthcare Reform: Learning from International Experience*. Buckingham: Open University Press.

McKevitt, D. and Keogan, J.F. (1997). "Making sense of Strategy Statements: A User's Guide." *Administration*, 45, 3, 3-25.

Relman, A.S. (1988). "Assessment and accountability: The Third Revolution in Medical Care". *New England Journal of Medicine*, 319, 1220-1222.

Saltman, R.B. and Figueras, J. (eds). (1997). *European Healthcare Reforms: Analysis of Current Strategies*. Copenhagen: World Health Organisation Regional Office for Europe.

Wood, R. (1995). "Performance Pay as a Co-ordinating Mechanism in the Australian Public Service". *Australian Journal of Public Administration*, 54, 1, 81-96.

Chapter 7

FINDING COMMON GROUND ON WHICH TO BUILD A BETTER HEALTH SERVICE

Matt Merrigan

The role of trade unions in organisational change in the Irish health service has been neglected in most of the writing on health services change and development. For years the high degree of unionisation in the health service was seen as a negative feature and most of the attention on trade unions tended to focus on industrial disputes. On one level, this is not surprising given that the health services have been bedevilled by low levels of trust between management, staff and trade unions and by many high-profile disputes, including the most recent disputes involving nurses and hospital consultants. On another level it is surprising that writers could exclude one of the key dynamics of organisational change, i.e. trade unions and industrial relations, from their accounts of organisational change in this sector. I want to try to redress that imbalance by focusing on the role of trade unions in advancing partnership at national, regional and workplace levels within the health service as an alternative and more co-operative approach to organisational change and improvement.

Notwithstanding some high profile industrial disputes the period since the late 1990s has seen a considerable degree of positive working between health service trade unions, employers and the state, not least in respect to the reform of health service structures and service delivery. Some attribute this relative calm to the booming economy and increased expenditure on health, while others, including myself, recognise the significant role the partnership approach at national level, as well as within the health services, has played in bringing about this stable and highly productive period.

This chapter is mainly concerned with the history, practice, and prospects of workplace partnership in health, and the ability of the main parties – government, management and trade unions – to fundamentally change the industrial relations culture in a way that allows for more innovation and progress. My core argument is that government, health service employers and trade unions need to work together constructively to find common ground on which they can jointly build a better service rather than going around in circles fighting old and new battles.

My role in the Services, Industrial, Professional and Technical Union (SIPTU) has allowed me to observe much of what we do well and what we do less well within the health system. SIPTU represents a very wide range of occupations and professions including psychiatric and general nurses, radiographers, office staff, porters, cleaners, health care assistants, community welfare officers, social care workers, laboratory staff, and others. For this reason, SIPTU sees into the health services from many different perspectives. The union has to balance the interests of different categories of employees rather than simply advancing the interests of one group regardless as to what the implications might be for other groups. SIPTU also has a huge membership outside the health services and we see our role as helping to provide these people as citizens with an excellent national health service. In other words, despite what critics of the trade unions might say, our policies and activities are not simply based on advancing the needs of our members *as employees* but also their needs *as users* of the health services like the rest of the general public.

Clearly, my point of view is heavily informed by my trade union history, but I have also spent many years negotiating with ministers for health, with senior civil servants and with health service managers, including the managers of the new Health Service Executive (HSE). In addition, I have served for many years on the board of a major Dublin teaching hospital and have seen developments from a board room perspective. Finally, I have made a point of visiting many health care facilities, both publicly and privately owned, in other countries to see what can be learned from these different experiences.

The Origins of Workplace Partnership

Increased levels of unionisation and significant cutbacks in the late 1980s played a major role in forcing all parties in the health services – as well as in the wider public services – to recognise the need for a new industrial relations climate. As staff had to work with cuts in frontline services, it was predictable that their anger would manifest itself in a more assertive (or confrontational, depending on one's point of view) negotiating stance with management. Antagonism often leads to further frustrations and retaliatory gestures on all sides, and so it would be fair to say that the delivery of a high quality health service would be severely impeded in this kind of industrial relations environment. At that time, there was no consensus around the idea that it was necessary to have employee and trade union input to plans for change. In essence, management thinking was that it was their responsibility to come up with the plans for change and, in so far as these plans might have implications for pay and conditions of employment, then negotiation might be necessary with the trade unions *after* the key decisions had been made.

There was no sense among most managers that the staff and unions might actually have something positive to contribute in terms of ideas and suggestions, only that our role was to protect what we had won over the years. Many trade unionists also shared this view and even today you will find members who think that we are doing management's job for them when we sit down with them in partnership to plan and implement organisational changes and improvements. Today, however, we have formal partnership agreements that recognise the importance of employee and trade union involvement and we have transposed the European Union's Information and Consultation Directive into the local partnership arrangements thus giving an even stronger underpinning to these arrangements (Health Services National Partnership Forum, 2006a).

By the mid to late 1990s, all parties, including trade unions, acknowledged the need to reform the health services in the best interests of those needing these services. The unions and management knew from past experiences that it was not feasible to handle ongoing changes of a complex nature through adversarial or "across the table" negotiation. We knew that some different model was needed if we were to avoid constant conflict that would reflect badly on all sides and that would continue to sour relations and to impede change. There was a real sense among us that we had to get the right industrial relations climate in place, as the late 1990s had been a torrid time in terms of industrial grievances.

As has frequently been pointed out, the unions and employers acknowledged the benefits of a partnership or "problem solving" approach to resolving differences at national level and in the negotiation of the national programme, *Partnership 2000* (Government of Ireland, 1996), we decided to see if this approach might be transferred down to sectoral and organisational levels. While the unions took the initiative in arguing for partnership in the public services there was no resistance from management in the national talks as they also saw the potential benefits of a new way of doing business at the local level. *Partnership 2000* ushered in formal partnership arrangements right across the public services, most of which still operate today.

Defining Workplace Partnership

At its simplest, workplace partnership is about bringing management, staff and unions together to work out ways to deal with an array of decision-making and problem-solving issues at different levels within the organisation. Instead of assuming that there will always be a "them and us" approach to each issue that arises for discussion, the assumption behind partnership is that if we try hard enough we can discover common ground that may be more fertile for producing acceptable solutions. So the parties are expected to come to the table with more of an open mind than if they were preparing for a traditional set of negotiations.

Needless to say, partnership takes time to develop, involves risks for managers and trade unionists and requires a fairly high level of openness and trust between people. Rather than negotiating, the parties try to talk, listen and explore options to see if they can reach a consensus agreement. Any subject can be put on the agenda provided that there is something positive that the partnership group in question can contribute to that issue (HSNPF, 2000). As a simple way of explaining partnership we say that in partnership the parties work together "around the table" rather than confronting each other "across the table". If you had to sum it up in one term, I think that term would be "problem-solving". Using the language of negotiations, partnership is an "interests-based" process and not a "positions-based" one, interests being the deeper needs and concerns of the parties rather than the surface positions that they adopt in order to satisfy those interests.

The aim of the workplace partnership programme was twofold: to improve responsiveness within the health service and to facilitate the need for staff to see more stimulating work and career paths. It was not intended to use partnership to erode the place of traditional roles and structures on either the management or trade union side, but rather to aid quicker decision-making and problem-solving, as well as fostering an atmosphere of greater trust among all parties within the organisation concerned.

The Partnership Framework Agreement

It was important for unions to have formal partnership structures, otherwise there was the danger that management would decide when and on what issues they wanted to engage with staff and unions through partnership rather than through industrial relations. The first structure that was established was a national partnership group that comprised of the most senior managers and trade union representatives, the Health Services National Partnership Forum or HSNPF.

Some managers initially found the structures a bit frustrating but have got used to them over time. The early structures were straightforward: a partnership committee for each health board, as they then were, and for larger hospitals and other institutions. There were also partnership committees in particular services such as community services, the ambulance services, intellectual disability service providers, etc. These committees basically decided their own agendas within national guidelines and if they chose to they could set up sub-groups, usually called working groups, to address specific issues. This allowed more people to become involved and allowed more knowledge, enthusiasm and expertise to be accessed in the pursuit of organisational changes and improvements.

The basic framework agreement is still in place but has had to be modified to take account of the new HSE structures that were implemented when the regional health boards were abolished.

Partnership Facilitators and Other Supports

Once we had drawn up our model of workplace partnership, we then entered into discussions with the Department of Finance, who agreed to an initial funding package of around €1.8 million to let us recruit workplace facilitators for the health sector. It will probably come as no surprise to readers that even though the enthusiasm was there, it still took us nearly twelve months to set up the HSNPF in 1999. Nominations from both management and trade unions were put forward as participants for the various committees, and an independent chair was nominated to oversee things. Personally, I learned a lot about how the civil service bureaucracy works when trying to set up the HSNPF. Civil servant negotiators are typically used to negotiating on workplace partnership with fellow civil servants or professional public servants, such as teachers; they simply knew less about the form of workplace partnership in health.

Once we had the structure and the funding, we advertised for workplace facilitators. In the beginning, we advertised externally, and made sure not to specify a long list of educational qualifications as prerequisites as this would serve to exclude a significant proportion of the trade union membership. We did not get the funding we wanted to get a full complement of facilitators, so the twenty facilitators we could afford to recruit (for a workforce of nearly 100,000) quickly became swamped with work. These facilitators have received considerable training over the past number of years and are accredited as workplace facilitators through the Further Education and Training Awards Council (FETAC).

Partnership Agendas

The partnership framework agreement suggested certain issues that might be taken on by partnership committees in their early days. It would be fair to say that in the beginning there was an understandable reluctance on the part of managers and trade union representatives to take too many risks by handling difficult or complex issues. Typical early agenda items included communications, human resource projects such as employee assistance programmes, improving training and development provision, providing more information to employees on conditions of service, improving the physical environment, and so on.

Further national programmes such as *Sustaining Progress* (Government of Ireland, 2003) and the current agreement *Towards 2016* (Government of Ireland, 2006) generated change agendas at national level that fall to be implemented through partnership at the local level. Today, with the exception of pay matters and personal grievances, there are few issues that cannot or have not appeared on partnership agendas.

Partnership and Industrial Relations

A tricky issue that arose early on was to decide what the relationship should be between the partnership and industrial relations processes. Many trade union representatives and managers thought that it would be too risky to have newly established partnership groups handling difficult and perhaps contentious industrial relations issues. For that reason it was decided early on not to have these groups handling established industrial relations issues. However, as time passed and managers and union representatives built up confidence in each other and in the partnership process they began to realise that the issues that they most wanted to address were either industrial relations issues or issues that had an industrial relations dimension to them.

So, perhaps inevitably, the parties began handling issues that in the past they would have handled through the formal negotiation procedures. Early examples would have been changes such as the introduction of flexible working arrangements and later issues included extended opening hours of clinics and other services. Having the support of skilled facilitators as well as the support of a national partnership group – the Health Services National Partnership Forum – were clearly important to the partnership groups at this early or "pioneering" stage when they were essentially learning about partnership by doing it and needless to say taking the risks that went along with such experimentation.

In the early days, partnership and industrial relations were seen as two very distinct channels. Today this is less the case. For example, parties to an industrial relations negotiation might agree to refer an issue to a partnership working group because they consider that it has potential for a "win-win" outcome. An example might be a complex issue such as rostering. Equally a group working on an issue through partnership, say moving operations to new premises, might generate some issues such as disturbance money or staffing levels, which they would refer into the industrial relations process for resolution while they continued working on other matters. Today management and union representatives are more confident about moving issues back and forth between the two channels. Where partnership works well it has been found that it has led to better relationships between negotiators and to improved overall industrial relations. There are, unfortunately, in such a large system as health, still many areas where the old adversarial approach with its low trust ethos still holds sway. These are often the areas that are crying out most for change and improvement but where it is most difficult to achieve this.

Performance Verification and Hardening the Partnership Agenda

Sustaining Progress marked the advent of performance verification groups (PVGs) whose role was to verify that changes agreed at national level had actually been implemented on the ground. For the first time ever in the health services as well as in the wider public services, trade unions accepted that pay increases would be linked with change and flexibility. *Sustaining Progress* also laid down a marker for collaborative working and modernisation. It called for "major changes by both sides and an unequivocal commitment by all stakeholders to a culture of co-operation, collaborative working and partnership in the management of the industrial relations climate in the health services". We knew right from the start that we would have to operate within the agreed rules of engagement and be proactive about changing our work practices or risk being cited for non-compliance and thus not get our pay increases.

While the PVG process was initially controversial among workers it is now an accepted part of the pay and change process. It actually puts managers under pressure to ensure that the changes to which they have committed their organisations are actually implemented. It also provides an enhanced role for partnership committees because these bodies have to scrutinise and approve the elaborate reports prepared by management on all of the changes agreed nationally through the national programmes. Again, this led to difficulties in the early days but this is now an established and routine activity for partnership committees. It keeps the need for change and the pace of change at the forefront of management and union thinking across the health services. Where there are difficulties such as non-compliance or differing interpretations we have procedures for involving third parties and for achieving final resolutions.

Spreading Best Practices and Innovations

It is disappointing for me to think that one of the signature problems we have in health in Ireland is that we have never been good at actually replicating good local practice throughout the system. There has always been a sort of "don't tell them what we're doing" attitude, partially because of a competitive atmosphere between the old health boards, but also because of the fear of failure or ridicule. I had first-hand experience of this when I was involved in trying to broaden the range of activities of an A&E department within a major hospital. It was clear that some genuine innovations had taken place and were yielding promising results. However, one of the major professional representative bodies heard about this "deviation" on the ground and were concerned that they may have to coin a new national position, rather than simply and correctly recognising that not every initiative needs to have a national-level imprimatur. Needless to say, when the representatives of the professional body came to talk about the innovation in that A&E department, the whole process slowed down drastically.

It is plain that innovation has never been rewarded in this system, and so one initiative that SIPTU has been central in has been to sponsor the health innovation awards. The Health Services Innovation Awards were established to give national recognition to successful innovations in the health sector. Expressions of interest are invited from all public organisations that have made a positive contribution to health. Last year (2006) was the second year that the Health Services Innovation Awards have had a national forum since its inception.

How Organisational Change has Affected Partnership

Perversely, the direction of organisational change may well have impeded workplace partnership. In the eighteen months or so between the dismantling of the old health boards and the ERHA, and the setting up of the HSE, it appeared that management lost a sense of what was good about the health service and should be kept and what was bad and should be jettisoned. Some of the new CEOs who were coming through the system prior to the setting up of the HSE were prepared to give workplace partnership a chance, and to give staff a say in service planning, a process that had traditionally been confined to senior managers. Being involved in service planning gave staff considerable insights into how their organisations worked and into the resource constraints under which they operated.

For some time, the unions had been putting in a lot of money and time to get buy-in to service plans; but under the HSE, this has reverted back to a single master service plan coming from HSE headquarters. Although the intellectual disability (ID) sector and the Dublin Academic Teaching Hospitals still have service plans, the ability to have individualised plans for regions across the country is certainly hampered by such a centralised structure. In this sense, then, the new structures blocked rather than facilitated greater staff involvement in a critical planning process affecting them in their day to day jobs.

The unions still want workplace partnership, but we have felt that it is becoming a bit of a one-way system and that the HSE is reluctant to fully commit to it with us. However, senior management within the new Primary, Community and Continuing Care area (PCCC) have worked well with us to form a new national partnership body for the PCCC area.

This group will deal with the enormous changes happening within that area, and we will hopefully witness palpable change in terms of the development of community services. The HSNPF have put in around half a million euros to help make that workplace partnership happen and HSE management have agreed to match that sum. A similar package has been negotiated with the National Hospitals' Office and we are optimistic that good workplace partnership will take root there also.

One significant problem has been the amount of people still employed by the HSE who do not want to work under the new organisational structure for whatever reason. Any major change programme is going to have a group that is disaffected, a group that is empowered, and a group that has one eye on retirement. The Department of Finance did not put up the money to enable the HSE to negotiate severance deals with those who did not want to be part of the new system. Some of these reluctant personnel are in reasonably senior positions, and can serve to dampen progress or initiative by their attitude and slow pace of movement. One could say the fault lies solely with the Department of Finance, or that the interim HSE did not argue strongly enough to obtain the resources from the Department of Finance to prune such staff. Although Professor Drumm is on the record as someone who pushes for innovation to be fostered, I doubt if the layers of management below are fully on board – there are many managers who are frightened to take a chance in doing something in a different way for fear that they will get sidelined or sacked – a hang-over from a culture where administrators administered (i.e. did what they were told to do) rather than managed.

Getting Beyond Adversarial Industrial Relations

I was not naïve about the problems the workplace partnership model would encounter, but perhaps all the partners occasionally forgot that we were essentially trying to move from a decades-long history of adversarial industrial relations to a more co-operative environment. At local level, if relationships are sound, one will find good working arrangements between managers, employees and union representatives. The part played by the CEO is critical: if he or she is only half-committed to partnership, then the managers below will pick up on that signal and be half-hearted about running a joint working system. I am in no doubt that one needs leadership on both sides to get any sort of buy-in from staff.

At national level, there has been marked reluctance by vested interests in both unions and management to relinquish the power that goes with their negotiating roles. This is predictable, as some have argued that workplace partnership erodes the authority of traditional management and union structures. A continuous dialogue on all issues in the workplace may lead to some suspicion among the traditional wings of both sides that the old employer/union order is essentially replaced by a new arrangement. I have long thought that some management elements have a vested interest in *not* supporting partnership as they can feel safe in the system they have known and so do not have to engage with staff or explain their vision. The wide variation across services in terms of the scope of staff involvement in service plans is illustrative: the service plan in the former North Western Health Board had the involvement of three hundred staff, whereas the service plan in one of the Dublin Academic Teaching Hospitals involved six staff – the latter was a hand-me-down document which would be very unlikely to attract any staff support or commitment.

A clear management and trade union leadership position, repeatedly communicated, is the only way to establish effective workplace partnership. Senior people on both the management and union side sometimes forget that by the time the message has filtered down through the whole workplace or organisation, the message could be either disjointed or ignored.

It can still come as a surprise to see that some managers view the trade unions as unreconstructed, as being there to drop a load of problems on their desk. I think that instead there is a genuine respect for those managers who manage well, and we would recognise that such people have to be given the space to deliver the high grade service we all want. Innate conservatism frustrates me: we should work to cultivate an environment where managers can try things out and if they do not succeed, then let them dust themselves down and keep going. For too long there has been a preponderance of senior managers who micro-manage rather than letting able staff get on with things. Not changing anything allows those who doubt the raison d'être of public service to voice their constant refrain that the public service is hidebound. The next predictable call is for new money to be directed to the private rather than the public sector. Being open-minded is essential to implement change. It would be fair to say that the vast bulk of people whom I meet within the Department of Health and Children (DoHC) and the HSE are very committed towards the public health sector: they want delivery of a better service. But collectively, they often seem to be ambivalent about their commitment: on the staff side, there can be a sort of hiding behind the representative bodies, rather than thinking and speaking honestly and independently about what can be done within the sector to make things better for the patient or client.

Seeing the value of new ideas or practices, even if they do not fully tally with one's own worldview, is critical if one wants to implement a better health service. For that reason, in the HSNPF we have placed a lot of importance on studying experiences of health services in other countries, particularly the US, and we have initiated studies to establish methodologies for measuring the outcomes of partnership for patients and service users as well as for managers, employees and trade unions. We have termed the evaluation of partnership from a multiplicity of perspectives "interests-based measurement" (HSNPF, 2007a).

Key Findings on Partnership Outcomes

There have been many local and national reviews of partnership in the health services since 1999. It is probably true to say that partnership has been evaluated more rigorously than most innovations in the health services. The most recent of these reviews drew on a number of partnership projects across the health services as a basis for developing effective tools for measuring the outcomes of partnership projects (HSNPF, 2007b). The main conclusions of this exercise were that partnership in the Irish health sector works in that it delivers quantifiable benefits for patients and service users as well as for managers, employees and trade unions.

Patient and service user benefits that were identified in these projects included better physical facilities, the provision of additional therapies, the development of services based on personal outcomes and the provision of additional choices in services. Benefits for managers included reductions in absenteeism, effective implementation of collective agreements, improved communications with staff, and greater frontline staff input to solving problems and developing services. Benefits for staff included better working facilities, improved communications with managers, more input to solving problems and developing services. Benefits for trade unions included the implementation of collective agreements, better administrative and communications facilities for local union representatives and more input into workplace developments generally.

This review also showed clearly that the successful use of partnership projects improved the organisational climate and the industrial relations culture in more than half of the cases concerned. This is important given that organisation climate and industrial relations culture have a significant influence on the effectiveness of organisational change and improvement initiatives. This is not surprising given that partnership provides organisations with a formal and structured channel through which issues and problems can be raised that might otherwise remain unaddressed. It was clear that a number of the projects addressed would not have been undertaken without the presence of these structures. As well as providing a formal channel through which management and unions can engage each other around issues of mutual concern in a non-adversarial way, partnership makes effective use of group processes and techniques for joint working such as joint data gathering, joint analysis and joint problem solving.

This is not to suggest that "everything in the garden is rosy". I have already suggested that much more needs to be done at the level of top HSE management to convince trade unions that they are as serious about partnership as the trade unions are. However, where weaknesses are identified, HSNPF is usually quick to address these weaknesses. So, for example, when it became apparent that many partnership groups were shying away from handling complex or contentious issues because they lacked the confidence and supports for doing so, the HSNPF introduced a new framework agreement and new supports through its *Handling Significant Change through Partnership Protocol* (HSNPF, 2006b).

Challenges for Government and HSE in Developing Partnership

Perhaps the greatest challenge ahead is for governments to resist the temptation to unilaterally decide what should happen on important issues and to then expect the trade unions to engage "through partnership" on a decision that they have been excluded from in the first place. This is not a straightforward matter and unions recognise the role and authority of government in setting policy and budgets. But at the same time, there has to be due regard by policy makers to the likely impact of key decisions on those expected to implement those decisions.

One way of addressing this problem that has been suggested by the trade unions is to have at national level a group comprised of representatives of top management from the Department of Health and Children, the HSE and the trade unions that would meet regularly to chart the introduction of key change agendas and to plan how such changes might be discussed and progressed having regard to the need on the one hand for rapid progress and on the other hand for meaningful involvement of health service employees and trade unions. To date we have not succeeded in getting such a forum off the ground.

Top HSE management also have a critical impact on partnership in terms of their national and local decisions and in terms of the direct involvement of senior managers in partnership committees and working groups. While there are many managers at senior levels within the system who are committed to working in co-operation with the trade unions in the change process and while top management in the HSE are on paper committed to partnership, the signals that they send out to their own managers and to their employees and union representatives are at least mixed if not often contradictory.

Taking the view of "judge me by what I do and not by what I say" leads me to the conclusion that top management are paying lip service to meaningful engagement with trade unions. Their preferred approach seems to be a mix of unilateral management decision-making, combined with direct involvement of employees, and engagement with unions on a "need to" basis. They are currently placing a great deal of emphasis on management leadership. As already indicated, I believe strongly in the value of leadership and in strengthening leadership capability but leadership alone will not generate the type of ownership of change that only high levels of active staff and trade union engagement can generate. If I am right about these mixed signals then it must be a matter of concern as to what impacts these signals are having on those managers who are currently taking risks and working hard at engagement with staff and trade unions.

Trade unions have to accept a measure of responsibility for influencing management attitudes. If we say we are for industrial peace, for service improvements and for change then we cannot be contradicting that through our actions, for example, by resisting changes and by having unnecessary disputes that only serve to copper-fasten negatives stereotypes of trade unions that are only out for their own ends. It is very difficult to convince top management that more active engagement will pay dividends for them when our actions on the ground show that we don't have the discipline needed to stick to agreements reached and to use the established procedures instead of taking to the streets and picket lines.

Challenges for Trade Unions

There is no doubt but that partnership has generated serious challenges for trade unions. On the ideological level, there is the idea that we can and should work together with management to improve the health services. That very idea cuts against the traditional idea that management and unions have separate interests that can only be reconciled through the industrial relations process and through conflicts. We have handled that debate in two ways. Firstly, we have shown that through partnership at national level we could win significant gains in terms of pay and conditions for our members such as the increases secured through the two benchmarking systems. Secondly, we showed that partnership was not just about our helping management with their change agenda but that it was also about their helping us with ours.

Management have probably been more active in pursuing their agendas than we have been but we are putting increasing efforts into having a more strategic approach towards identifying and pursuing the interests of our members through partnership. Traditionally we saw industrial relations as the proper channel for doing that, now we know that we have two channels open to us – partnership and industrial relations. Experience has shown clearly that staff can benefit directly from partnership through improvements in physical accommodation and that unions can also benefit by having agreements implemented more effectively and by having more of a say over developments in the workplace. Staff can benefit by having a better, more open climate in the workplace in which more communications take place and where their views are actively sought by managers and are taken into account in planning and implementing changes (HSNPF, 2006a).

Resourcing partnership has not been easy for trade unions either. Like all voluntary bodies, we find it difficult to attract a sufficient number of eager volunteers to take on what is seen by many as a thankless task. Our full time officials now have to provide backup services to partnership committee representatives as well as shop stewards. At the same time, many representatives say that they like being involved in partnership because it gives them access to issues that are highly relevant to them, to dealing with senior managers and other union colleagues in a climate that is more conducive to good discussion and positive outcomes than traditional negotiation or grievance handling.

Our representatives have had to develop knowledge and skills fairly quickly and without much formal training in new areas such as corporate planning, organisational change, service planning, project management, work organisation etc. It has not been easy for representatives who are not used to being involved in discussions in these areas to play a full role along with managers who have already got the necessary language and ideas, etc., from their daily work as well as from their formal education and training. But we know that if we want to have a meaningful input to decision making that we have to make the effort to ensure that we have confident, articulate and motivated people representing us around the partnership table.

The Effects of the Political System on Partnership

In some respects, people overestimate the effect that the government of the day has on industrial relations within the health sector, as things on the ground are always different from what the people at the centre would have one believe. Against that, ministers have huge influence in the sector as a whole. Currently, I think that I express what many trade unionists would feel in saying that Minister Harney and some of her senior staff have been quite sceptical about the part the unions play in workplace partnership, while the Department of An Taoiseach has been broadly in favour of it. Consequently, workplace partnership is occasionally compromised but not dismissed out of hand. In addition, the outputs are measurable; we have done some study visits to New York hospitals and the results of this and other independent analyses demonstrate a clear productivity and improved industrial relations pay-off for organisations that adopt workplace partnership. As already indicated, the benefits are across the board, including reduced absenteeism and palpably improved morale amongst staff; and in terms of services, extended working hours for laboratories, for example.

Since Minister Harney took office, I cannot remember any real emphasis in any ministerial speech on the positive contributions of the unions. This is not the first time that unions have felt a slightly chilly wind from the Department. I can remember a time, albeit a brief one, when it was made clear to me that I was not welcome to call into Hawkins House to engage in any pre-emptive dialogues SIPTU thought might help.

Minister Micheál Martin was a positive force in terms of organisational change. After the years of underinvestment, more money was poured into health under his stewardship, and he was keen on workplace partnership. The health strategy he launched, *Quality and Fairness for You* (Q&F), seemed to strike all the right notes, but the Department of Finance did not back the plan with the additional resources required, and so it has not really been delivered. I have heard people say that Q&F is succeeding here and there, and those people will invariably point to the implementation of 90 or more of the 140 or so recommendations in the strategy. I reply that the substantive questions have not been tackled and so the system is paying lip service to Q&F. In addition, the signal sent out by the Department of Finance was that they did not trust the Department of Health and Children to utilise any additional resources wisely. That surely engendered a crisis of confidence within Hawkins House. The role of the Department of Health and Children is to do the strategic thinking that will take healthcare into the future, but the degree to which the Department of Finance controls the health budget and the lack of a multi-annual funding basis for health is always going to restrict strategic thinking about how to run the service better.

Conclusion, and an Eye to the Future

It is arguable that the new organisational structures do not seem to have led to a greater impetus to roll out what has been termed "second generation" partnership (Roche, 2002). Although there is some debate as to what second generation partnership entails, it would be fair to say that it arises where partnership is embedded within the organisation and where consultations take place before every major decision is made or implemented: in other words, the *practice* of partnership is mainstreamed within day to day management and trade union behaviour.

Health is likely to be a thorny issue for governments of all hues in the medium term. The population expansion in north Dublin, for example, has simply not been met with sufficient planning and resources for the additional services required. Similar pressures that are now being experienced in the educational system due to the growth in commuter towns will begin to impact heavily on our health services sooner or later.

It is far from being a negative picture, though. The health service today is better than it has been: specialties like cardiology and oncology are much improved, while the capital investment in places like St. James's Hospital is a sign of commitment to better treatment. Despite the current hiatus, which is heightened because of the level of political involvement, I believe that on the whole the industrial relations climate is much better. Negotiations on pay and conditions are better handled than before, and we have built a place for people to work together in negotiations as they have come in contact with each other more, thus making it easier to see the perspective of the other side.

Although the poor relationships between the interim HSE and the unions did damage relationships (and to some extent the approach the nurses have recently taken was influenced by this), I believe these can be repaired given commitment from all stakeholders – we are too far down the road of partnership to return to the old adversarial approach. Ridding the system of mistrust opens the way for working together in a more innovative manner. Such innovation must be encouraged and fostered if we are to continue to see improvements in the delivery of healthcare in this country. We should look to how we can better foster innovative leaders in our health sector. A mentoring programme, where bright young people are advised by a more senior person, could really help to encourage a new generation of leaders to emerge with very robust ideas on how to make things better.

There is strong evidence within health service workplaces of a significant reservoir of goodwill towards the development of partnership. Management, staff and union representatives like the co-operative, problem solving aspect of partnership as opposed to the more adversarial and confrontational ethos of traditional industrial relations approaches.

These are important findings given that the ongoing changes in health services organisation and management structures have to some extent slowed down the progress of partnership within the sector, for example by the concentration of interest on the transformation programme and on changes in organisational structures.

The findings on partnership outcomes to date show that it will be worthwhile for management as well as staff to generate further impetus and effort around the development of partnership in the health services, for example through the new partnership structures being put in place and through the implementation of the new arrangements in "Handling Significant Change through Partnership" and in the many partnership initiatives already underway right across the health services.

References

Government of Ireland. (1997). *Partnership 2000*. Dublin: Stationery Office.

Government of Ireland. (2003). *Sustaining Progress*. Dublin: Stationery Office.

Government of Ireland. (2006). *Towards 2016*. Dublin: Stationery Office.

Health Services National Partnership Forum (HSNPF). (2000). *Working Together for a Better Health Service*. Dublin: HSNPF.

Health Services National Partnership Forum (HSNPF). (2002). *OD2 Consultants Report to HSNPF of Discussions with Union Officials, Directors of HR, Facilitators, Joint Chairs and Forum Members*. Dublin: HSNPF.

Health Services National Partnership Forum (HSNPF). (2006a). *Partnership-Measuring and Evaluating With a View to Learning and Sharing Information: Guidelines and Tools*. Dublin: HSNPF.

Health Services National Partnership Forum (HSNPF). (2006b). *The Health Services Partnership Agreement Incorporating Protocol on Handling Significant Change through Partnership and Statement of Common Interests*. Dublin: HSNPF.

Health Services National Partnership Forum (HSNPF). (2007a). *Evaluating Partnership Composite Report from OD2 Consultants*. Dublin: HSNPF.

Health Services National Partnership Forum (HSNPF). (2007b). *Partnership – Measuring and Evaluating – Evaluating the Effectiveness of Workplace Partnership Projects in the Irish Health Services (EWP Project) – Interest Based Measurement and Evaluation – Guidelines and Templates*. Dublin: HSNPF.

Roche, W. K. (2002). "Whither Partnership in the Public Sector?" *Administration*, 50, 3, 3-26.

Chapter 8

PROFESSIONAL EVOLUTION

Anne Scott

Introduction

Amidst poor staff morale, much industrial unrest and following a recommendation from the Labour Court (Recommendation No. LCR15450), the Commission on Nursing was established by the Minister of Health, Mr Michael Noonan in March 1997. The purpose of the Commission was to fundamentally review the role of nurses in the health service. The remit covered service delivery and managerial roles, professional development, promotion opportunities and difficulties, grading structures and educational and training roles. It was asked specifically that in its recommendations it should seek to "provide a secure basis for the further professional development of nursing in the context of anticipated changes in health services, their organisation and delivery" (Government of Ireland, 1998).

One of the key recommendations from the Commission, on the appropriate preparation of candidates for the nursing profession, was as follows:

> The Commission recommends that the Minister facilitate the transition of pre-registration nursing education into third-level institutes at degree level (Government of Ireland, 1998: 5.19).

The Minister launched the Report of the Commission on Nursing in September 1998, underlining Government support for the recommendation of the Commission. From the point of view of nursing education this led directly to the establishment of the Nursing Education Forum in 1999 (Government of Ireland, 2001). The Forum was tasked with the preparation of a strategy for moving pre-registration nursing education from the three-year diploma programme to a four-year degree programme. After some months delay, the Report of the Nursing Education Forum was launched by the then Minister of Health and Children, Micheál Martin, TD in January 2001. At the launch the Minister announced that the government had agreed in principle to the introduction of a four-year nursing degree programme commencing in September 2002. He also announced the government's acceptance of the Forum's recommendations for the establishment of an Inter-Departmental Steering Committee and a National Implementation Committee. The Inter-Departmental Steering Committee would be composed of members from the Department of Finance, Department of Health and Children, Department of Education and Science and the Higher Education Authority. It would take responsibility for all funding and policy issues associated with the transition to a degree programme. The National Implementation Committee, Chaired by Ms Mary Rose Tobin, Personnel Manager, Institute of Public Administration, and composed of the key stakeholders in nursing education including: An Bord Altranais, the health service providers, and third level institutions, would oversee the implementation of the nursing degree programme nationally.

A further crucial recommendation from the Commission, in terms of developing the discipline of nursing within the university sector was the following:

> The Commission recommends that the Minister provide for nursing
> and midwifery research to be funded through the Health Research
> Board (HRB). The Commission recommends that the Minister make
> funding available to the HRB specifically for nursing and midwifery
> research (Govt. of Ireland, 1998: 6.75).

This recommendation was pushed particularly by the nursing academics on the Commission, who recognised that without an identified funding stream for nursing research, Irish university departments of nursing and midwifery would suffer the same fate as their United Kingdom (UK) counterparts (Rafferty et al., 2002; Rafferty et al., 2003). It has taken nursing and midwifery in UK over 50 years to establish anything like a substantive research agenda. This is in stark contrast to the success of the nursing research agenda in the United States of America, that since 1986 has been funded by the Nursing Research Institute, National Institutes of Health; and from 1945 until the mid 1980s by federal government, through the nursing division within the Office of the Surgeon General (see http://ninr.nih.gov/ninr/about/history.html). It is also in contrast to the rapid development of the nursing and midwifery research in Scandinavian countries like Finland, where nursing research is funded through the Academy of Finland – one of the main academic research funding bodies for Finish universities (Academy of Finland, 2003).

This government acknowledged recommendation of the Commission regarding a research funding stream, was an important gain for academic nursing departments. When taken together with the fact that nurse tutors, eligible for transfer into the third level sector, had a real choice regarding their future (i.e. tutors could choose to move to the universities or they could opt to remain in the health service in newly created centres for continuing education or up-skill to return to clinical practice), university heads of nursing schools could reasonably expect that any tutor who chose to move into a lecturing post in the university would make every attempt to embrace the culture of the university. This included recognising the main-stream university requirement that academic staff engage in teaching, research and academic administration. Part of ensuring that research activity became a possibility for nurse lecturers was the ability to become involved either in funded research projects – with the HRB as the most likely funding body – and/or in obtaining university support for staff development in PhD preparation. Some of the latter was made possible through negotiations, driven by the university heads of nursing, with the Inter-Departmental Steering Group. The university heads of nursing pushed for staff development funding to be agreed as part of the funding package for the staff transferring into the university sector. A staff development fund of £50,000 per university per year for a period of four years was eventually agreed as part of the transfer package for the move of nursing education into the universities.

Though a small amount of funding, when considered on a per institution basis, in most cases this funding provided the necessary impetus for university-based schools of nursing to leverage additional funding – either from the university or externally – to enable the newly arrived nurse tutors to commence PhD study, or to engage in other research activity in the host school. This was managed particularly effectively in the early post-Commission days by both the heads of the School of Nursing and Midwifery in University College, Cork and in Trinity College, Dublin. Both of these schools managed to tap in very quickly to the newly established, Health Research Board funded nursing and midwifery research fellowships. These fellowships could be used to support promising staff to gain research masters and PhD support on a full time basis; thus kick starting the growth of the research capacity in these two schools.

Prior to the transfer of pre-registration nursing education into the third level sector schools, centres or departments of nursing had begun to develop in a number of Irish universities. Apart from the Centre for Nursing Studies, University College, Dublin, which had been established in the 1960s for the preparation of nurse tutors, the development of such centres, departments or schools of nursing was led by the recommendation of the Joint Nurse Education Working Party (University College Galway and the Western Health Board) in 1991 "to establish a Department of Nursing Studies at UCG, to be headed by an academic of some standing in the field of nursing" Feeley (2006: 150). A Centre for Nursing Studies in University College Galway (UCG) was established in 1993 and a Department of Nursing and Midwifery in University College, Cork in 1994. A School of Nursing was established in Dublin City University in 1995. Dublin City University also appointed the first Chair in Nursing in the Republic of Ireland in 1998. The School of Nursing and Midwifery was established in Trinity College Dublin in 1996. Nursing in Ireland can be considered to have made rather slow progress in moving to introduce itself to the university sector, when compared to such moves in the United Kingdom, Europe or the United States. The first university diploma in nursing was established in the University of Leeds in the early 1930s (McNamara, 2005) and the first university department of nursing was established in the University of Edinburgh in 1962; followed rapidly by the University of Manchester and University of Surrey. In the US nursing has existed in the university sector since the turn of the twentieth century (The first university affiliated nursing programme was established in 1902 and in 1907 Mary Adelaide Nutting was appointed first professor of Nursing at Teachers' College, Columbia University (Meleis, 1997) and in Scandinavia since the early 1970s. For example nursing science was first taught in Finland in Kuopio University in 1979. However it should be acknowledged that the Irish Nurses Organisation was interested in supporting university education for nurses in Ireland from the 1930s. McNamara cites a revealing quote from the Irish Nurses' Magazine, 1942 on this issue:

> Another project we have in mind is a Diploma in Nursing and also a
> Diploma for Sister Tutors. We have communicated with the Univer-

sities in this matter ... We have been told that this will not be easy but we have also been told by a very eminent Professor that these difficulties ... are not insurmountable. So we will carry on in spite of any discouragement (Editorial, *Irish Nurses Magazine,* 12, 18, 1, cited in McNamara, 2005).

The multifaceted issues that prevented this vision for nursing from becoming a reality for more than another 50 years is a separate but very interesting sociopolitical study. However this visionary commitment, of the Irish Nurses Organisation (INO), to the professional development of nurses is often missing in Irish health service managers' analysis of the role and impact of the INO on disciplinary and practice development. It is also generally missing from the exposure the INO gets in national media, where mainly industrial relations issues are aired.

The Story

As indicated above the School of Nursing, Dublin City University (DCU) had been established in 1995, following negotiations between the university, the Department of Health and Children (DoHC) and Beaumont Hospital. The primary motivation had been approaches from Beaumont hospital to DCU to accredit the new three-year Diploma in Nursing Programme.

Further contacts with the DoHC and a number of local health services led to formal links being established with James Connolly Memorial Hospital, St Ita's Hospital, Portrane, St Vincent's Hospital, Fairview and The Daughters of Charity Services, Dublin. By 1998 DCU had accredited The Diploma in General Nursing with Beaumont Hospital and with James Connolly Memorial Hospital, The Diploma in Psychiatric Nursing with St Vincent's Hospital, Fairview and St Ita's, Portrane and the Diploma in Mental Handicapped Nursing with St Joseph's Hospital, Clonsilla. The university had a commitment to teach the biological, computing and social science elements of the diploma curricula in DCU and the nursing elements of the programmes were taught in the hospital based schools of nursing.

Thus nursing began to have a presence in the university, hosted by the then Faculty of Science and Paramedical Studies. A School of Nursing was established and a small number of staff were appointed to the Faculty to run the Diploma in Nursing Programmes and teach mainly the year one non-nursing element of the curricula. Other staff in the Faculty, principally from the School of Biotechnology also taught into the nursing programmes. Relationships with both the health service partners and the DoHC were difficult at best during this period. This was not helped by the fact that the newly appointed Chair in Nursing in DCU, and the first Chair in Nursing in Ireland, resigned within three months of taking up post. This led to adverse publicity for the university and further stormy relations with the health service. The DoHC demanded that the university employ external consultants to work with DCU to find a way forward for nursing within the university, if DCU wanted to retain further links with the health service and play its role in the integration of nursing to the third level sector. A consultancy service was engaged to work with the university for a period of six months, following which a structure for the School of Nursing, DCU, was recommended and approved by both the university and the DoHC in 1999.

In September 2000 I took up the post of Professor of Nursing and Head of the School of Nursing in DCU. At that time the School had six full-time permanent members of staff and a project manager on a short-term contract. Emeritus Prof Rosemary Crow, University of Surrey, had also been appointed visiting professor to the university six month earlier and was providing mentorship and staff support on a part-time basis. Six pre-registration diplomas in nursing programmes were running in the school. A Bachelor in Nursing Studies degree (BNS) was also being delivered on a part-time basis to registered nurses wishing to upgrade their education to degree level. There was no postgraduate provision, nor was there any research base in the school.

As a student nurse, in the late 1970s in the newly established School of Nursing in Sligo General Hospital, I had the good fortune to be taught by one of the real visionaries in nurse education in Ireland in the twentieth century – Principal Tutor, Joe Mullen. Joe was to be the prime (and sometimes sole) mover in the development of the first Diploma in Nursing Programme in Ireland. This programme was developed and accredited by University College, Galway – and was to become known as the Galway model. Prior to his move to University College Hospital, Galway, Joe set up the new School of Nursing in Sligo and ensured that the first nursing research monographs produced in either Ireland or the United Kingdom were an important and much used resource in the fledgling School of Nursing library. Therefore I was trained as a nurse in the clear understanding that research and scholarship was part of the meat and drink of nursing practice. It took me many years to realise that my experience as a student nurse was a very rich exception to the normal nurse training experience in both Ireland and the UK.

My journey upon qualifying as a nurse saw me move to Trinity College Dublin and a joint honours degree in Philosophy and Psychology, staffing experience in St Luke's Hospital, Rathgar, Our Lady of Lourdes Hospital in Drogheda and the Royal Hospital in Donnybrook. I spent four years nursing and teaching in a bush hospital in North West Kenya, took an MSc in Nursing Education at the University of Edinburgh and a PhD in Philosophy at the University of Glasgow. This was followed by a lecturing post in the well-established Department of Nursing, Midwifery and Community Health, Glasgow Caledonian University; and a Senior Lectureship in the new Department of Nursing and Midwifery, University of Stirling. This background provided a breadth and depth of experience, and an ideal skills base, from which to develop the School of Nursing DCU; in readiness for the transition of pre-registration nursing education in August 2002. The only real problem was the timeframe.

On my appointment, at the beginning of the academic year 2000-2001, the two most experienced academic staff in the School of Nursing spent six and twelve months respectively on requested leave of absence. This commenced, with my approval, within weeks of my taking up post. The rationale at the time was very simple. If these members of staff did not wish to be part of the school at this crucial time, it was better that they be facilitated with their request for leave. In hindsight this was a very effective decision, though it did not immediately appear to be so. Due to a number of immediate crises remaining staff – lacking any real depth of academic experience – in some sense needed to fall in behind the new leadership, if the school was to continue to function at even the most basic level. Remaining staff in the school, in addition to the senior staff in the university, made clear their support and willingness to work to move the school forward and to re-establish positive relationships with health service partners and the DoHC. The very tight timeframe remaining to develop and accredit the new BSc curricula was, in hindsight an important galvanising focus.

Some crucial issues required immediate attention. Both the BNS and the Diploma in Nursing Programmes were without academic leadership. DCU was approximately one year behind the other university-based schools of nursing in the rest of the country in planning and engaging in the development of the new BSc nursing curriculum. By the end of the year 2000 no real planning for the transition of either students or nurse tutors had begun in DCU. In addition to these necessary and immediate tasks, ten years working in Scotland had absolutely convinced me that if we did not commence growing and developing our base in nursing research and scholarship as we grew the school, research and scholarship would always take a back seat – if it ever became a reality in the life of the nursing school.

Key necessary roles in programme organisation and delivery were allocated to the few permanent academic staff in the school. The very able Project Manager was tasked with linking with Principal Tutors in our partner services and developing a plan to move forward the development of the BSc curriculum, covering pathways in General, Mental Health and Intellectual Disabilities Nursing. I commenced what evolved for a time into weekly discussion and planning meetings with senior management in the university to steer, first the planning and then the mechanisms to enable, the transition of 26 nurse tutors and over 600 nursing students into DCU. As 2001 progressed the project manager, the HR Department, DCU and the Diploma Programmes Co-ordinator became an increasingly important part of the nursing transition team. From December 2000 a professional advisory group was established comprising the Directors of Nursing and Principal Tutors of our partner health service providers, senior representation from the Northern Area Health Board, the Deputy President, the University Secretary and the Registrar of DCU, the Project Manager and myself as Head of the School of Nursing. This group met monthly for the following two years and provided an excellent discussion and trouble shooting forum, as well as a crucial element in keeping our partner service providers on board and informed of progress toward the full integration of nursing into the university.

During this time the first stroke of luck in establishing our research base dawned. Prof Crow, two junior members of academic staff and I made a successful grant application to the Health Research Board (HRB) to carry out a DOHC commissioned study into perceptions and experiences of empowerment in nursing and midwifery in Ireland. This £96,000 research grant was the largest grant ever awarded in Ireland for nursing and midwifery research. It enabled the employment of two full-time research staff (who were also qualified nurses) and so the first funded research activity at the School of Nursing, DCU commenced; and the school began building research capacity for itself and for Irish nursing research. The two full time nurse researchers employed on the research grant were registered for a research masters and a PhD respectively.

The study was very successful and has generated not only a number of conference presentations and publications (Scott et al., 2003; Corbally et al., 2007; MacNeela et al., 2005; Matthews et al., 2006) but also provided the raw material for the first MSc (research) thesis from the school in 2004 (Corbally, 2004) and the first midwifery PhD thesis from the school in 2006 (Matthews, 2006). The old adage of "success breeds success" is completely accurate in terms of the development of the research base in the School of Nursing. The 2001 empowerment grant was followed in 2002 by the award of the first five-year programme of research in nursing and midwifery in Ireland, funded by the HRB. This one million euro grant was awarded to a collaborative research team led by myself as Principal Investigator, School of Nursing, DCU and in collaboration with colleagues in the School of Nursing and Midwifery Studies, UCD.

These early external funding successes raised the profile of nursing in DCU very substantially and markedly increased the confidence of staff in the School of Nursing in engaging in competitive research funding bids. The open team approach used in the development of these two successful proposals also became the dominant model for the development of many other competitive bids. This became very important during the transition of the 26 nurse tutors in to the school in late 2002. By then the staff in the school numbered 17 (academic, administration and research). It would have been easy for the budding research culture and confidence of this small group to be overwhelmed by the influx of 26 staff from cultures where research was almost entirely absent. One of the most exciting and significant early successes within months of the nursing transition was the award of two research grants from the National Advisory Committee on Drugs (NACD) to teams in the school led by two researchers who had played crucial roles in both the empowerment and programme grants, but which also included staff newly arrived from the health service. In the minds of staff these early wins confirmed both the school as one of the most successful and energetic research-active schools of nursing in the country and, probably more importantly, underlined the real possibility of former nurse tutors engaging in and becoming successful participants in mainstream university knowledge generation activities.

To me, knowledge generation, disciplinary development and emersion in research and scholarship are the key reasons to have nursing in the university. Nursing practice and patient care can only benefit from a more educated, more confident nurse who has developed the tripartite package of intellectual, emotional and clinical skills necessary to care, humanely and intelligently, for the vulnerable human beings the student and registered nurse will encounter during her or his clinical career. Such a nurse will be equipped to challenge and shape, rather than simply conform to, the health service structure within which they find themselves. This vision of what is required from an effective, humane nursing input to patient care and into the Irish health service, has received empirical confirmation over the past six years primarily through the work of Linda Aiken and her international team of researchers. Aiken's work looks at the impact on care delivery and patient outcome of nursing skills mix, nurse patient ratios and nurse education levels (Aiken et al., 2002; 2004; Cheng and Aiken, 2006; Clarke and Aiken, 2006; Rafferty et al., 2007). Similar work indicating direct correlations between patient outcomes and nurse education levels was produced in the University of York in 1992 (Carr-Hill et al., 1992) – but was buried as it did not fit with the political agenda of the day.

A vision of what good nursing is and what all nursing can be has driven the development of the School of Nursing DCU. This vision sees the moral dimension of nursing practice (and all healthcare practice) as central. This explicitly demands that the nurse is competent at the so called psychomotor, physical skills aspect of clinical nursing practice; but it also, and at the same time, demands that the nurse recognise and respond sensitively to the patient as a potentially vulnerable human being with psychological/emotional/social needs/dis-ease as well as presenting physical needs.

The vision of nursing and nursing care that has driven the move of nursing into the academic environment of Dublin City University is a pro-active, self-confident and energetic one. It is a vision rooted in a strong belief regarding the value and importance of the nursing contribution to an effective, humane twenty-first century Irish health service. It is a vision that clearly articulates the requirement for members of the nursing profession to stand up and be counted and to be prepared to live with the consequences of our professional decisions.

In this task I think the university can be justifiably proud of what has been achieved. The School of Nursing, DCU is one of the most successful nursing schools nationally using any measures one chooses – bibliometric and otherwise. The School in the space of 6 years also has a profile that many much longer established schools or faculties of nursing would by proud of. Undergraduate student numbers in the school have grown to approximately 1,000. There is a vibrant menu of postgraduate taught programmes and the research portfolio of the school is growing apace. Staff in the school of nursing have published in excess of 200 peer-reviewed papers, research reports, books and book chapters and earned €2.56 million in externally funded competitive research grants from funding bodies as diverse as Enterprise Ireland, Science Foundation Ireland, the Health Research Board, the Irish patient association and National Drug Advisory Council (Stevenson and Gallagher, 2006). Members of staff have international research collaborations in the US, Europe and the UK, as well as established collaborations with colleagues both north and south of the border. Many of these collaborations are multidisciplinary, spanning both biological and social sciences.

A style of management developed and evolved in the School of Nursing that is largely collaborative, demanding, challenging and supportive. Everyone is responsible and accountable to the School, via the Head, for their work, developmental progress and its impact on the reputation of the school, both externally and internally. The school has developed a reputation as a successful, practice-focused, research active, outcome-sensitive school; with good staff morale and with the space for innovation and creativity to grow and flourish. Instilling confidence in staff and holding them responsible and accountable whilst giving them sufficient autonomy to get on with their work was a critical component in building the school. Relationships with partner health service providers are positive with many joint research and practice-development activities in train. This is not merely the author's opinion but was clearly articulated in the Peer Review Report from the first five-year quality review of the School of Nursing completed in 2005, carried out under the auspices of the Quality Promotions Unit, DCU and the Irish Universities Quality Board.

> The organisation of the school reflects the recent history of nurse education in Ireland, principally the move from a hospital to a university-based system of education, the reliance of the School on our partner service providers for clinical teaching and the recent emergence in this country of an academic discipline of nursing. The rela-

tionship of the School with its seven service provider partners is vital
to its success because of its dependence on the partners for clinical
teaching and because the service partners will be employers of the
nurses on graduation. This relationship is defined in memorandums
of understanding which were agreed in December 2002 after much
discussion and negotiation. The PRG (Peer Review Group) was most
impressed by the positive endorsement of the quality of the relationships developed by the School with its service partners, as expressed
to the PRG by leaders of these services (Peer Review Report, School
of Nursing DCU 2005, 10).

A conscious effort to support and build these relationships, although
time-consuming and energy-sapping at times, was essential to the development of the school and its position within the broader environment of
healthcare.

Reflections

In hindsight it is unlikely that much of the above could have been
achieved without a clear vision of what was possible and what was required to make it happen. This vision, in the case of DCU, generated an
extra-ordinary level of commitment and support from initially the small
team of academic staff within the school. Very inexperienced members
of staff were burdened with onerous workloads, which were embraced,
largely unquestioningly and with much good humour. This energy and
commitment was also extended, pre, during and following transition, by
many of the nurse tutors who transferred into DCU under the national
transfer agreement. Mutual support and the willingness to take calculated
risks was evident, at this time, among both senior management in the
university and directors of nursing in its service provider partners.

   The success story of the past six years for the School of Nursing,
DCU is, I would argue, very much about having the right people, in the
right place at the right time. However it is also about a relatively flat decision-making structure within the organisation and the ability to respond
flexibly and with relative speed and ease to a changing environment. Key
staff must have the ability to create the vision and bring others with them
in the realisation of the vision, and they must be given the freedom to do
so. They must know when to lead, when to steer and when to give others
their "head". A leader must also have the ability to turn chance occur-

rences, challenges and crises into opportunities for success; and then they must ensure the success story is told to all the key stakeholders.

As leader of this change I relied heavily on the skills and expertise of my colleagues. My leadership style could therefore best be described by Ancona's (2007: 94-95) concept of the "incomplete leader".

> Only when leaders come to see themselves as incomplete – as having both strengths and weaknesses – will they be able to make up for their missing skills by relying on others… No one person could possibly stay on top of everything. But the myth of the complete leader … makes many executives try to do just that, exhausting themselves and damaging their organisation in the process. The incomplete leader, by contrast, knows when to let go… The incomplete leader also knows that leadership exists throughout the organisational hierarchy – wherever expertise, vision, new ideas and commitment are found…. Incomplete leaders differ from incompetent leaders in that they understand what they are good at and what they're not and have good judgement about how they can work with others to build on their strengths and offset their limitations.

In reflecting on my approach to leading this change, I have found it useful to frame it within Ancona's categorisation of the activities of incomplete leaders, i.e. sense-making, building relationships, creating a vision and cultivating inventiveness.

Sense-making

In sense making, the leader must have the courage and the ability to present a map of the terrain – providing the blueprint for others to follow and highlighting the elements that the leader deems critical. This is important even if the map does not conform to the dominant perspective. This lack of conformance to the dominant perspective was very much the case in the School of Nursing, DCU. The dominant perspective in DCU as an institution, in the DoHC and indeed in nursing departments nationally was focused on nursing education. In the minds of many nursing education moved into the universities in Ireland – not the discipline of nursing. This was largely also the case in UK departments of nursing and midwifery. A focus on the education perspective was particularly evident for example in Scotland, which despite having the first university-based department of nursing in Europe, had, by the beginning of this millennium, largely failed to establish a strong base of research or scholarship for the nursing discipline. The sense-making that I engaged in with my colleagues in the neophyte School of Nursing in DCU articulated a map for the growth of nursing in DCU and in Ireland that insisted that our programmes – undergraduate and post-graduate – be rooted in research, scholarship and clinical practice. There was a requirement to include the rapid development of postgraduate taught programmes in niche areas. This was necessary from a basic economic perspective. It was also necessary in order to show partner services that we were willing to engage, listen and try to meet their service needs in the area of postgraduate educational provision for specialist and advanced nursing practice. This would enable nursing practice development and nurse leadership of new clinical services – especially in the areas of mental healthcare and care of the intellectually disabled. These were areas grossly under served in the Irish system in terms of post-registration educational provision. Equally important and probably more readily achievable was the commencement of research activity among appropriately prepared staff alongside the commencement of post-graduate research training in the School. This could be pump primed from a variety of sources – my own personal research seed fund, negotiated as part of my appointment package, internal grant applications which had just opened to temporary academic staff (this was very significant for the staff in the School of Nursing as one of our few doctorally-prepared staff was on a temporary contract) and external grant applications. As indicated above within six months of my appointment I successfully applied for the largest research grant awarded for nursing research in Ireland at the time. This grant was in collaboration with Prof Rosemary Crow, a PhD-prepared psychologist and a masters-prepared sociologist on the staff in the School. This success in an external research grant application had a dramatic effect on the morale of staff in the school. It generated a belief that we could succeed and that the desire to root our activities in research was more than mere rhetoric. This success enabled the appointment of the first MSc (research) and one of the first PhD students in the School of Nursing and was rapidly followed by a number of other internal and external research funding successes – with increasing numbers of staff as Principal investigators of collaborating applicant teams. Professor Rosemary Crow and I had set the model of open collaborative groups actively drawing in anyone interested and anyone who wished to contribute. This was effective in at least two ways – it drew on the best expertise we had available and it enabled very inexperienced staff to "learn the ropes". This model continues to exist in the School, alongside and integrated into the development of strong, mature research groups with established programmes of research.

A further part of that early sense-making for the School of Nursing was engaging with the person in the project manager role in the School at the time of my appointment, encouraging her to apply for a full time lecturing post in the school to help drive the practice-rooted curriculum development required for the new BSc programme. Once this was achieved, over the period of the first eighteen months following my appointment, the considerable skills of this individual were focused on working with the design team. Such was required in order to ensure that our new nursing building would meet the needs of our clinical undergraduate and post-graduate taught programmes and also support our developing research and practice culture in the School. One key element of this was including space (a shell to begin with) in the new building that would house some type of "live" healthcare facility. This facility could only be developed when funding was gained – from which particular source we could speculate but could not be certain at that time. However it was clear that if we really wished to ensure good practice roots for our programmes, and have a staff commitment to clinical practice and effective clinical linkage, we could not assume that this would all come from our partner services. We needed to drive academic clinical practice from within the school and this included offering staff (and students) the possibility of engaging in some element of live healthcare provision from the school site. The planning and financing of this would take considerable time. However, if the physical shell to enable this vision was built into the new building, the idea would remain visible until it happened – or until conscious decisions were taken to veer from that path. This was alien to normal health service and educational culture in Ireland and the UK. However it is a perspective very common in the United States, where large academic medical centres are part of universities.

A great deal of sense-making went on in those first few years of my term as Head of the School of Nursing in DCU. However as Anconda et al. point out:

> Good leaders understand that sense-making is a continuous process.
> In health organisations, this sort of sense making goes on all the
> time. People have process ... ongoing dialogues about their interpre-
> tation of markets and organisational realities (Anconda et al., 2007:
> 95).

Interestingly, from my perspective after approximately three years of intense activity in this sense-making and other arenas I began to worry that I was no longer seeing DCU or the School of Nursing with fresh eyes. I felt I was losing the required critical, analytical edge that had helped grow what was becoming a very successful school of nursing. I cast around for some months trying to decide what was happening and what I required to clarify a vision for the future. The school was emerging from the transition of pre-registration nursing education into DCU. We needed a new map going forward that would ensure the full integration of staff from the six partner services into DCU and ensure the continued success of the school from the perspective of programmes, practice innovations and research and scholarship. Gradually I came to realise that I needed to identify some of the most successful schools of nursing internationally and go visit them. From an academic, clinical practice and research perspective one such entity was the Faculty of Nursing at University of Pennsylvania. They appeared to have all the elements that I wished to see develop in the School of Nursing DCU. They also had a very significant international profile. It had taken 25 years to establish their current status and reputation. I needed to go and spend some time there. I wanted to speak with Norma Lang, the Dean who had provided the blueprint and the leadership for the development of the Faculty of Nursing at Penn over many years. I wanted to check if I were on the right track at DCU – and I needed to figure out how to create such success in considerably less than 25 years. March 2004 found me at Penn where I spent a number of days meeting with Norma and a number of staff identified by the Penn Director of Academic Clinical Practice. I also visited Faculty of Nursing run health facilities and looked at various research and education programmes. During this trip to the US I also visited or spoke with Deans of Nursing in Ann Arbour and in Maryland. Around the same time I was invited to visit University of South Australia, Adelaide as their colloquium scholar for the year. This gave me the opportunity to spend time not only in the School of Nursing, University of South Australia, but also in Flinders University, and the Catholic University of Australia – at both the Sydney and Melbourne campuses. During my trip to Australia there was a great deal of discussion around the recent decision of the University of Sydney to close their undergraduate nursing programmes. These international contacts were hugely useful to me in confirming a) the need to continue to grow the base of research, scholarship and practice in the School of Nursing, DCU, and b) the need to move to a new vision for the school going forward. This led directly to continuing to crank up support for research and practice activity among staff in the School. It also enabled me to inject energy into the plans to develop a live health facility in the School. The new building was successfully completed and occupied. Staff were delighted with this fantastic new facility and the shell for the "Health Living Centre" was now ripe for development. My gifted Project Officer-cum-lecturer was now taking soundings from staff, partner services and local GPs, as a first step in moving forward with our plans for the development of academic clinical practice. It was time to develop a 10 year plan for the School of Nursing DCU, visioning the School out to 2014. From the long-term vision the annual steps required can be articulated, implemented and evaluated – sense-making on an ongoing basis.

Building Relationships

The need to build effective relationships was a huge issue when I took up post as the Head of the School of Nursing, DCU. As indicated above relationships among the small staff within the School were very fraught. However this paled in significance when compared with the perceived relationships between the university and the partner services. Relationships between senior staff in the university and senior Civil Servants in the Department of Health and Children were also quite fraught. All of this combined with the fact that the School of Nursing was considered something of an anomaly and a problem within DCU itself meant that some serious consideration and effort needed to be spent on identifying allies, building bridges and relating in a constructive, productive manner to all major external and internal stakeholders. The considerable good will, insight, experience and expertise among senior staff in DCU and staff in both the School of Nursing and our partner service providers made this a much easier prospect than might immediately appear. Within two months of my appointment we had managed to establish weekly staff meetings within the School, weekly Steering Group meetings inclusive of the University Secretary, the Deputy President and myself and monthly meetings of the Professional Advisory Group inclusive of all Directors of Nursing of our partners services, BSc curriculum co-ordinator School of Nursing, Diploma Co-Coordinator School of Nursing, all Principal tutors of our partner services, senior personnel of the Northern Area Health Board, the university Registrar, Secretary and

Deputy President, chaired by myself as Head of School. These meetings laid the foundations for constructive relationships, debate, challenge and mutual respect upon which the School of Nursing has developed over the past six years. Various invitations to participate on internal and external Boards were accepted and encouraged, in order to develop both an internal and external perception of the School of Nursing as positive, active, constructive. The fact that this has worked can be clearly identified in the profile of the staff of the School internally in DCU, but also and perhaps more importantly in the external profile of staff on various national boards and in leadership positions in national associations. My own style is to lead by example, be low profile and non-territorial and deliver on promises and I believe that this was an important element in moving the relationship building agenda for the School and for DCU.

Creating a Vision

"Visioning involves creating compelling images of the future. While sense-making charts a map of what is, visioning produces a map of what could be and more important what a leader wants the future to be." (Ancona et al., 2007: 97). To me sense-making and visioning are inextricably linked. In order to chart the map of the future the map of the present must lay the required foundations. Therefore much discussed above under sense-making is relevant to the creation of a vision. However at the heart of my vision for the School of Nursing was and is a strong belief in the importance of good nursing to good patient care and a good patient experience of our health service. To me this meant and continues to mean that our education and research programmes must inform each other and must be relevant to and informed by clinical nursing practice. The School of Nursing, DCU must be outward looking in order to grow in the appropriate way and must be prepared to use clear, acceptable benchmarks if it is to claim local, national and international impact. Peer review of decision-making and performance within the School is to be welcomed and encouraged. This may help us learn from the best of both our own and others performance.

Cultivating Inventiveness

"To realise a new vision, people usually cannot keep doing the same things they have been doing. They need to conceive, design and put into practice new ways of interacting and organising." (Ancona et al., 2007:

98.) There were significant time pressures to be worked with both in the two years prior to the transition of nursing education into the university and in the few years following the transfer. These pressures were mainly to do with curriculum development and accreditation processes for both the undergraduate and the taught post-graduate curricula. However while these deadlines clearly had to be met there were the other issues that needed to be cultivated in parallel: developing a culture of research and scholarship in the School, developing practice links with partner services, participating in faculty and university initiatives and profiling the School as a positive active entity. We had to find ways to enable all these elements to move forward in tandem. Staff needed to be given their head and enabled to get on and try out a good idea. Permission to try and to fail meant that at least new approaches would be tried. Some did not work. Others took off and reaped dividends for the School. Therefore I am entirely supportive of the need to cultivate innovation within a staff group. This notion underlies two of the four principles upon which *Leading Practice: Education Research and Innovation* (DCU School of Nursing Strategy 2004–2014) is based.

Conclusions

Key problems for the health service today are, I suggest, ensuring that the creative capability, the knowledge and the deep commitment of clinical and support staff within the health service is harnessed in a way that will enable the reform agenda to move forward and patients and staff to flourish within the system. There is a grave danger that the grinding bureaucracy, that stymied the real development of a quality health service focused on patient need and good patient outcomes and led to mediocrity in our previous system, will continue to gain foot hold and infect the new structures and system being put in place. The freedom to innovate and to try new approaches is, in my view, fundamental to improving our current system.

The opportunity to lead the developments the Irish health service of the twenty-first century needs to be based on merit rather than disciplinary background, or territorial vested interest. We need to be able to spot the necessary talent, nurture it, support it and use it effectively for patient benefit; and for the overall development of the health service, where possible. All staff needs to be respected and supported. Controlling cliques and vested interests need to be exposed, challenged and tested against the metric of international standards of patient care, patient satisfaction and clinical outcomes.

The arena of high quality patient care in a health service of the 21st century has no room for small-minded territoriality, vested interest and a mindless bureaucracy that requires multiple levels of decision making before something as straight forward as a staff appointment can be confirmed.

A quality product, and an environmental or organisational culture that encourages innovation, intellectual challenge, individual integrity and staff support is worth fighting for. What we do is intellectually and emotionally demanding, as well as important to human well-being and development. It is also likely to be important to the growth and sustainability of a humane, tolerant society. This is as true of academic activity as it is of work in the health service. We each should be active participants in the generation of new knowledge and in helping to put it to individual and societal benefit. It is also the case that we do not work in a vacuum. We should be prepared to do our best to ensure the quality of our service, and to accept that the tax-payer and the government have the right and perhaps the responsibility to ensure "our best" is open to public scrutiny and international peer review.

References

Academy of Finland. (2003). *Nursing and Caring Sciences: Evaluation Report.* Academy of Finland: Helsinki.

Aiken, L. H., Clarke, S.P., Cheng, R.B., Sloan, D.M., and Silber, J.H. (2004). "Educational Levels of Hospital Nurses and Surgical Patient Mortality". *Journal of the American Medical Association,* 290, 12, 1617-1623.

Aiken, L.H., Clarke, S.P., Sloan, D.M., Sochalski, J., and Silber, J.H. (2002). "Hospital Nurse Staffing and Patient Mortality, Nurse Burnout and Job Satisfaction". *Journal of the American Medical Association,* 288, 1987-1993.

Ancona, D., Malone, T.W., Orlikowski, W.J., and Senge, P.M. (2007). "In Praise of the Incomplete Leader". *Harvard Business Review,* February 2007: 92-100.

Carr-Hill, R., Dixon, P., Gibbs, I., McCaughan, D., Griffiths, M., and Wright, K. (1992). "Skills Mix and the Effectiveness of Nursing Care". Occasional Paper Series, Centre for Health Economics, University of York.

Cheng, R., and Aiken, L. (2006). "Hospital Initiatives to Support a Better Educated Workforce". *Journal of Nursing Administration,* 36, 7/8, 357-362.

Clarke, S.P. and Aiken, L.H. (2006). "More Nursing, Fewer Deaths". *Quality and Safety in Healthcare,* 15, 1, 2-3.

Corbally, M. (2004). *Empowerment of Nurses and Midwifes.* Unpublished MSc Thesis. Dublin City University.

Corbally, M., Scott, P.A., Matthews, A., MacGabhann, L., and Murphy, C. (2007). "Irish Nurses' and Midwives' Understanding and Experiences of Empowerment". *Journal of Nursing Management,* 15, 2, 169-180.

Feeley, G.M. (2006). *A History of Apprenticeship Nurse Training in Ireland.* Routledge: London.

Government of Ireland. (1998). *Report of the Commission on Nursing: a Blueprint for the Future.* Dublin: The Stationery Office.

Government of Ireland. (2001). *Report of the Nursing Education Forum.* Dublin: The Stationery Office.

Labour Court. (1997). *Recommendation No. LRC 15450, CD/97/48.*

MacNeela, P., Scott, P.A., Matthews, A., Corbally, M., Walsh-Daneshmandi, A, and Gallagher, P. (2005). "From Structures to Attitudes: a Process Model of Empowerment, Job Satisfaction and Affective Commitment". In: C. Korunka and P. Hoffmann (eds.), *Change and Quality in Human Service Work (Organisational Psychology and Healthcare, Volume 4).* Munich: Hampp.

Matthews, A., Scott, P.A., Gallagher, P., and Corbally, M. (2006). "The Meaning of Empowerment in Midwifery: An Empirical Model". *Midwifery,* 22, 81-91.

Matthews, A. (2006). Unpublished PhD Thesis. Dublin City University.

McNamara, M. (2005.) "'Dr Nightingale, I Presume?' Irish Nursing Enters the Academy". In J.M. Feeley (ed.) *Care to Remember: Nursing and Midwifery in Ireland.* Dublin: Mercier Press.

Meleis, A.I. (1997). *Theoretical Nursing: Developments and Progress* (3rd. Edition), Lippincott and Co.: Philadelphia, PA.

Peer Review Group Report, School of Nursing, Dublin City University. (2005).Available at http://www.dcu.ie/qpu/pdf/2005%Nursing%PRG%final%20 (27%April%202005).pdf.

Rafferty, A.M., Clarke, S.P., Coles, J., Ball, J., James, P., McKee, M., and Aiken, L.H. (2007). "Outcomes of Variation in Nurse Staffing in English Hospitals: a Cross-Sectional Analysis of Survey Data and Discharge Records". *International Journal of Nursing Studies* 44, 2, 175-182.

Rafferty A.M., Traynor, M., Thompson, D., Ilott, I., and White E. (2003). "Research in Nursing, Midwifery and the Allied Health Professions: Quantum Leap

Required for Quality Research". Editorial, *British Medical Journal.* 326, 833-834.

Rafferty, A.M., Newell, R., and Traynor, M. (2002). "Nursing and Midwifery Research in England: Working towards Establishing a Dedicated Fund". *Journal of Research in Nursing* 7, 4, 243-254.

School of Nursing, Dublin City University (2004). *School of Nursing Strategy 2004-2014. Leading practice: Education, Research and Innovation.*

Scott, P.A., Matthews, A., and Corbally, M. (2003). *Nurses and midwives understanding and experiences of empowerment in Ireland.* Department of Health and Children, Dublin.

Stevenson, C. and Gallagher, P. (2006). *Health4Life: the Inaugural Report and Action Plan for Research in the School of Nursing, Dublin City University.* Dublin City University: Dublin.

Chapter 9

SPOTLIGHTING HEALTH

Aileen O'Meara

It was the paper-clips speech that still stands out in my mind. In the dozens, if not hundreds, of speeches, launches, press releases and statements that Micheál Martin issued as Minister for Health and Children, I remember the one that started off with a few lines about the importance of paper clips. At the Government press centre for yet another launch of yet another soon-forgotten Departmental announcement, the Minister opened his speech with a short homily about the importance of little things, like paper clips in an office, written in conversational style, punctuated for an informal delivery. When I saw that, I knew the Minister was reading a speech written not by a Departmental official, but by a PR professional. The Minister was no longer relying on his officials to write his speeches, but had hired an outside PR company to help manage the onslaught of media attention on a Department trying to persuade the public that the huge increase in health spending was reaping dividends, and that a reformed health service was the way forward. In a small way, this speech was part of a growing recognition, if one was needed, of the huge importance of the media in health politics. The public, after all, receives its messages about the health services through the media, and in particular the broadcast media, locally and nationally. Politicians – especially Ministers – rely on the media to relay their messages to their public. It is foolhardy to use the same approach in dealing with all the diverse strands of the media, from local free sheets to influential local radio and national newspapers and television, and it is vital to learn how the media organs work and how they are used.

Irish people listen more to radio, and read more newspapers than most of their European counterparts. In the Republic alone, there are seven daily titles, an evening paper, 10 Sundays, 58 regional titles, 13 local titles and 40 free local titles. There is a rich diversity of broadcast media in Ireland, with a growing number of commercial radio and television stations, and expanding competition for news services through on-the-hour news bulletins and instant online news. The radio industry is vibrant. Nearly 90 per cent of the population tunes into national, regional, local and community radio every day - one of the highest radio audiences in the world. In the regions, stations like Highland Radio in Donegal command almost 70 per cent of the local listenership. Television news has also expanded in Ireland, and RTE 1's dominance is being gradually challenged by TV3 and Sky News services, the latter in particular offering instant news coverage of major events. Items on the news programmes need to be easily digestible to a general audience, short and tightly-written to command attention from both news editors and the viewers, a simple point that is often overlooked by government bodies in their dealings with television. Health news is part of the staple diet of Irish media – to the extent that everyone is familiar with the sight of A&E queues, the rows over the services offered by local and regional hospitals, and the demands of a plethora of interest groups for more resources. In a competitive environment, especially amongst the Dublin commercial radio stations, and amongst the Sunday newspapers, what's happening in health is always of interest to journalists. All the main titles have at least one specialist Health Correspondent, and both news and features regularly include health-related items. The Irish Times Health supplement is indicative of the growing health sector. With a huge state sector complemented by the private sector, and non-governmental agencies, the level of activity amongst both state-run and independent groups is high. A growing media body absorbs health stories as they incorporate high politics, political backstabbing, and the essential human interest angle.

Well-organised and media-savvy interest groups in the health sector use the media to best effect, putting resources into PR professionals, or full-time communications officers, to ensure the media understand their message, or spin, and that their organisation is ready to use opportunities made available when journalists come looking for information. The most effective ones know how to use the broadcast sector in particular, finding ways of getting on the main news television and radio bulletins and programmes on a regular basis, and keeping health correspondents informed of their agendas.

The Micheál Martin Years

Micheál Martin was appointed as Health Minister in January 2000, replacing Brian Cowen. For television journalists, this was good news. A telegenic, media-friendly Minister replaced a politician with an inbuilt suspicion of cameras, microphones and journalists, who despite his articulacy and vision, rarely co-operated with or cared about the soundbite-driven nature of broadcast news. To get a story, radio needs sound and voices; television needs pictures. Micheál Martin was happy to provide both. He made himself readily available, held numerous press conferences, facilitated tight deadlines, and did live interviews at the drop of a hat. The Minister and his team "fed" the stories, and the media responded.

As well as the Department's own media office, staffed by civil servants hired from other parts of the service with little or no media training, the Minister also had his own personal media adviser. Caitriona Meehan's job was to be on round-the-clock call for the health correspondents, news editors, and programme editors looking for a "spin" or the presence of the Minister in the studio or on television that evening. The starting point for every communications adviser is to make sure everyone had a press release; going beyond this straightforward task is essential if the client is to keep on top of the media's demands. Meehan facilitated the tight deadlines that broadcast journalists worked to; she complained if she felt the story did not reflect what the Minister said; she phoned journalists before press events to ensure their attendance, especially the television cameras. In contrast, it was difficult, if not impossible, to get to talk to a policy maker. From the top down, officials were suspicious, or feared, the media, especially the broadcast media.

Accessing the Newsmakers

There are critical differences between the work output of a broadcast journalist and a newspaper journalist. Broadcast journalists with news outlets work within tight deadlines, and so have few opportunities to hang around at events and chat to officials, like print journalists do. Print journalists can use the "off the record" briefing, adding context and analysis within a news or feature article, something rarely available to a news broadcast journalist.

My own experience tallies with the above. I rarely interviewed a policy maker or a health administrator. I rarely saw them quoted by name in the newspapers, or heard them on any radio stations. I can name the number of administrators who spoke to me "off the record" on the fingers of one hand. With one or two exceptions, I was turned down when I sought such interviews. Briefings with officials took a lot of valuable time to organise, and usually resulted in "off-the-record" chats that reaped little in the way of insight or newsworthy information. They made little or no effort to keep journalists informed of events from their point of view, with one notable exception: Dr Muiris Houston of the *Irish Times* was fed a stream of stories from within the Department of Health about the up and coming health strategy, which fuelled expectations of a high-spending era to come. In my time, hospital management and the leaders of the former health boards were especially apprehensive of saying anything, including the addressing of clear distortions by the other side (whoever that may have been). News bulletin after news bulletin would pass before a response (if there was one) came back: the CEO/manager is not available for an interview. The result was a one-sided story with the consultant's view going unchallenged.

In the absence of direct contact with key policy actors who were the newsmakers, I had to go elsewhere for my content. Most of the stories I received came through press events, public relations companies, and from members of interest groups, doctors, nurses, trade union officials, and the public. The relative contribution of the PR professionals is surprising: they were plentiful in number and were clearly on very profitable retainers, and they certainly worked hard to bombard me with press releases and statements. However, I ignored most of their communiqués because they were not newsworthy or merely plugged a product.

Many individual doctors used the media effectively. Unlike nurses, who speak through their trade union officials, individual hospital doctors gave interviews to journalists with their view on what needed to be done to solve the particular crisis at their hospital: nine times out of ten it involved more resources for their particular department/speciality, whose waiting lists were long and growing longer. Rarely were the white-coated ones questioned about management of finite resources, health overspending or whether the lists could be managed more efficiently. In general, this unwillingness to ask tough questions of medics and other health professionals is of a piece with a more diffuse sentiment of deference among the Irish public generally: rarely does one see a top doctor get a rough ride on a show like *Questions and Answers*, or on a radio phone-in. The alacrity with which the professionals produce figures, allied to their defensiveness when questioned as to exactly where and how things are going wrong, probably explain the journalists' relative timidity when confronted with caring professionals.

The imbalance in the use of the media by the stakeholders serves to paint the legislators, civil servants and health managers as the wrongdoers: how could it be otherwise, when they do not engage effectively and determinedly with the media? For example, a doctor in the Mater Hospital in Dublin complained about the outpatient facilities for his public patients housed in crowded portacabins on the edge of the campus, and agreed to do an interview on site. But while the story of his poor facilities and long waiting lists was accurate and provided good visuals for the news bulletins, the hospital was extremely slow in telling journalists that the money had been allocated for a new building in the coming year and his concerns had been taken on board. Some of the major hospitals got better at managing the media: Tallaght (AMNCH) hired its own in-house communications officer, while the Mater, St. Vincent's and St. James's employed PR companies – but such media engagement was not widespread. Disasters can happen in small hospitals as well as large, specialist hospitals as well as general ones: in such cases, there is no sharing of media expertise among the different hospitals; nor was there a central pool of expertise and resources which the CEO of such a hospital could employ.

What Works in the News

Pictures tell stories in television, a fact that seems to be lost much of the time amongst the PR professionals who hire dark hotel rooms in Dublin city centre to hold press conferences which offer just boring shots of men in suits. An illustration of this was when the latest in a series of initiatives to highlight the low uptake in measles vaccinations was launched in spring 2000. Prior to the launch, there had been significant coverage of research by Dr Andrew Wakefield which questioned the safety of the MMR vaccine. (this research was subsequently trounced). A press conference, with the Minister holding the Millennium Baby (the baby who'd been born at the stroke of midnight on 31 December 1999), contained the usual experts giving the usual warnings about the dangers of measles. What was needed to "sell" the story was a picture of a sick baby with measles, and right then, there was an outbreak in Dublin. Dr Peter Keenan, paediatrician in Temple Street Children's Hospital, agreed to be interviewed, and when we came to his emergency unit, there was a sick baby with measles, attached to an oxygen mask, with the worried mother by her side. The pictures of that sick baby, broadcast on the news bulletins that evening, led to a massive surge in vaccinations in the following weeks and months.

A picture that was less well received by officials in the Department of Health featured overcrowding in the accident and emergency (A&E) unit in Beaumont Hospital. Overcrowding is not a new phenomenon, but for reasons that are not fully understood, it periodically raises its head to become a serious media and political problem, and goes on to dominate headlines for days on end. In March 2000, I rang around the various A&E departments and learned that Beaumont was particularly overcrowded on a typically rainy Irish morning; so my crew and I went up to see what was going on. This may come as a surprise to some readers, but I had no preconceived plan of what I was going to report on or what tone I would use in doing so. Instead, there was a topical issue and an opportunistic impulse led me to go with the crew to Beaumont. The new A&E consultant agreed to let us in, asking the public in advance if it was okay to film the 30-odd trolleys stacked up in the centre of the once-spacious unit, and both consultant and hospital CEO agreed to be interviewed against the overcrowded background. When the pictures were broadcast that evening – they were the lead story on the *Nine O'Clock News* – they caused ructions. The pictures were a severe embarrassment to the health authorities, the Minister, and the Government. Of course, the pictures kept the A&E story at the top of the agenda for weeks afterwards. Not surprisingly, the hospitals were then given an immediate directive: don't ever let television cameras into the units, and under no circumstances allow anyone to be interviewed in a unit like that. As a result, nurses and doctors had to leave the campus to be interviewed, and after long negotiations, cameras were only allowed to shoot pictures of trolleys from below. Their refusal to allow cameras show the real conditions did not kill the news cycle, though, as RTE's *Primetime* circumvented the new policy to send in hidden cameras into emergency units around the country. This created an even bigger public outcry as a result.

The recent negotiations on the new consultant contract were stalled for some time due to what was termed the "gagging clause" where HSE as an employer through this contract was attempting to control the consultants' freedom to publicly comment on the health service. This phrase has since been removed from the contract. Yet an unwritten gagging clause has long been in existence for managers and administrators. The lesson is that managers need to understand that if they say "no" to the media, the media won't go away. They will just find another way of getting the shots and the story, usually in a form that the managers won't like anyway and gives them little if no opportunity to input. More media training is part of the answer, but changing the culture of management would be arguably more productive. Managers have to believe that they can challenge any unfair accusations or "slants" in a news report – if they can't, then burying their head in the sand is not the answer.

Ballymascanlon

The day of the special Cabinet meeting at the Ballymascanlon Hotel in Co. Louth was widely reported as the day when the Cabinet would agree to endorse the huge rise in spending that accompanied the Quality and Fairness health strategy announced by the Department of Health and Children. Ballymascanlon was chosen as the regular "outside Dublin" Cabinet meeting to boost the region after the foot and mouth outbreak had cut it off for the previous months. In the weekend newspapers, heavy spinning by Micheál Martin's advisers built up the meeting as a kind of "health summit" – a day when the Cabinet was to rubber stamp the monies needed to fund the huge expansion in beds and services needed for the growing population, especially the increased proportion of elderly. On a quiet news Monday, mostly political journalists, and this Health correspondent, travelled to the venue along with satellite and radio vans to fill the bulletins for the day. What should have been a good news day for Minister Martin and the Department of Health officials who'd spent long months producing the blueprint for the health service into the future turned into a bad news day. By lunchtime, it was clear that the other Cabinet members did not share the Minster's vision. Dermot Ahern, then Minister for Social, Community and Family Affairs, went on the lunchtime news to make the case for social welfare spending, playing down the "spin" that Health was getting a big boost. Embarrassingly, some Department of Health officials who had come to give a presentation to the Cabinet were left waiting outside, were not called in to the hotel to make their case. As the afternoon wore on, and the journalists hung around waiting for news, it became evident that no major announcement was to be made. Expectations of the Taoiseach and his Health Minister giving a joint press conference were quashed.

Shortly after 4.00 pm, Finance Minister Charlie McCreevy appeared from the hotel, and was doorstepped by this journalist as he walked to his car to leave: "What about this health spending plan? Has the Cabinet agreed it?" "What health spending plan?" asked McCreevy in his own direct style, "We didn't discuss any big plan. There were lots of things on the agenda besides health. It wasn't just about health you know." And then he left. There, on tape, was the real situation, *sans* spin. Finance was not giving any extra money to the health services. The Health Strategy was dead in the water. Two hours later, Taoiseach Bertie Ahern left by the back door to avoid the press's questions about the Archbishop of Dublin and his then partner Celia Larkin, and Micheál Martin and Dermot Ahern held a joint press conference that had nothing to say. The weekend build-up to the Ballymascanlon meeting was a spin that had backfired badly for the Health people: it was arguable that what turned the cabinet against it was that the spin had got out of control, alienating other Cabinet Ministers.

The Smoking Ban Campaign

When the Republic of Ireland introduced the smoking ban in March 2004, it was a victory not just for public health, but also for Minister Martin. It was also an example of how the media were successfully handled to change public opinion, and bolster the Minister's resolve to fight opposition in his own party. An alliance of interest groups, backed by the resources of the department of Health, relayed consistent and growing evidence of the health impact of passive smoking, and used focused public surveys to bolster their case. The alliance included the Irish Cancer Society, ASH (Action on Smoking and Health), the MANDATE trade union (for bar workers), the environmental health officers, and the Office of Tobacco Control. They worked individually and collectively in providing a strong and consistent argument for the ban, and always had their "soundbite" clear. They brought in experts from abroad, and produced strong research to back up their case. In particular, they successfully won the argument against the vintners that the evidence of damage from second-hand smoke was conclusive. The campaign was run centrally through a PR company, Montague Communications, who were contracted by the Office of Tobacco Control.

From a media point of view, the campaign provided facts and background, and speakers when required, often at short notice. Their speakers were well briefed, articulate and passionate about their subject: for example, Prof. Luke Clancy of ASH, a doctor with a respectable track record in the previous campaign to introduce smokeless coal in the 1990s. Press conferences were well organised, and typically consisted of a cross section of doctors who provided the evidence; workers who called for the ban; and politicians who backed the plan. The vintners' lobbying of politicians, in particular the Fianna Fáil backbenchers, failed to counter this polished media campaign. Most pertinently, the organised campaign was not just rolled out as the legislation was about to be introduced, but was attaining high media visibility well in advance of the bill. Throughout 2003 it was clear that the battle for public opinion was being won by the proponents of the ban, as public support grew. In several instances, details of the latest public opinion survey of attitudes to smoking were released on early news bulletins on Monday mornings, a good time to shape the day's news agenda, and influence the local radio stations as well. Where possible, this was followed by an interview on "Morning Ireland", and television interviews for the later TV bulletins, thus giving the subject dominance throughout the traditionally "slow" Monday news day. The concerted campaign put the opponents of the ban on the back foot as they sought to react with their own views. Often they made nobody available, leaving the field clear for the pro-ban groups.

The Irish Cancer Society, with a well-staffed press office, was a key group in the campaign. Their reputation in the cancer field was evidently unrivalled, and their work served as a reminder of all those who had suffered and died from smoking-related cancers. Furthermore, their press events were often colourful and inventive, designed for pictures in newspapers and to enliven television reports. One I particularly remember about smoking in the workplace had young children dressed in adult work "uniforms" of suits and ties in an outdoor office in the middle of St Stephen's Green. Of course, in the heart of it was the then Minister Martin, with yet another press opportunity to highlight his support for a ban.

The Hanly Report

The launch and subsequent backlash against the *Report of the National Task Force on Medical Staffing* (Hanly report) (2003) was a good example of poor preparation; the negative response caused the Government to change its mind, and the lack of media groundwork illustrates how and why the central message of Hanly was lost.

Even before the official launch of the Hanly report at the Government press centre, the rumblings against the principles of "centres of excellence" were clear, and nobody should have been surprised at the opposition to plans to close emergency services in small hospitals. However, it was clear at the press conference to launch the report that the supporters of the Hanly reforms were ill-prepared for the opposition. First, the opening question from a political journalist at the press conference asked about Fianna Fáil backbench opposition to the plan, and the Taoiseach and Minister Martin both seemed surprised by the question. By that evening, one of the Government Ministers, Michael Smith (TD for North Tipperary), was opposing the plan, ensuring the story was now a political one, not a health-policy matter. Second, unlike the smoking ban campaign, the proponents of Hanly were ill-prepared for local opposition, particularly in the pilot region in the mid-West. While there was little discussion in the other pilot region in the East Coast area of Dublin – Labour's Liz MacManus warned about long travel distances for Wicklow people, thus hampering the surveying of public opinion at various fora in the region – the anti-Hanly campaign was mainly focused in regional areas outside Dublin, where the Health Services Action Group created an alliance of local groups defending their local services. Third, and again unlike what had been a feature of the smoking ban campaign, the supporters of Hanly did not have a group of readily available articulate speakers with facts and figures at their fingertips to bolster their case. If Hanly was such a good idea, I asked one doctor, where were its supporters amongst hospital consultants and family doctors? Why was it left to Dr. Cillian Twomey, of the Task Force on Medical Manpower, to defend the plan? Where was the groundswell of support in its favour? If doctors supported it, did they get the back-up to take on the opponents? The lack of a cogent pro-Hanly front was particularly important in local radio discussions, where local voices with local knowledge have easy access to local talk shows with high audiences. It allowed the opponents to use the obvious argument that Dublin-based experts were once again dictating plans for the regions.

There was one exception to this poorly organised pro-Hanly report – but it was in Dublin, where the Hanly report was simply less politically explosive. The CEO of St Vincent's Hospital, Nicky Jermyn, agreed to do an interview for a television news feature about how the pilot plan was working on the east coast of Dublin. Mr Jermyn co-operated with filming in the hospital, enabled doctors to talk to RTE and did an interview himself about the advantages of rationalising the hospital services in the region, through creating closer links between St Vincent's, St Michael's and Loughlinstown hospital services. Conversely, the regional hospital in Limerick, or indeed the regional health managers in the mid-West, were publicly silent on the issue of Hanly, in my experience.

It is perplexing to think that the same government and same health service developed a very competent template (the smoking ban campaign) to prepare the ground for a shift in health policy, whilst at around the same time they made few if any media preparations for the launch of the Hanly report. Worryingly, the Hanly failure had clear echoes of the previous plan for regional breast cancer services, written by Prof. Niall O'Higgins, which was also left without political support following local opposition to the loss of breast surgery services: these examples highlight the lack of organisational learning within the health system.

The HSE Era

When there were eleven health boards, each of the boards had their own communications manager and office. Many of the personnel in these offices worked closely with the health board CEOs, and liaised with journalists at a local and national level. They were the "voice" of the health boards, and journalists used their information to inform their stories, particularly the print media. Communications managers issued statements and press releases on behalf of health boards, but rarely offered officials or CEOs for comment to broadcast media. In contrast, the political representatives on the health boards received a high media profile locally from their input at these meetings.

Since the abolition of the health boards, the HSE has taken over the communications role for the country's health services. In the centralising of health services, communications functions have also been centralised. The communications division in the HSE's Parkgate Street and Naas offices run the press services, with close input from the HSE's central management team in Prof. Brendan Drumm's office. As the HSE structures begin to settle down, some senior officials are doing occasional press interviews and briefings, such as John O'Brien, Acting Director of the National Hospitals Office. However, to date, most interviews are still conducted by the CEO, Prof. Brendan Drumm. While many of the for-

mer health board communications managers have remained in the regions, most of the press output is now managed and centralised in Dublin. However, it is not clear what role regional press offices will have in
the future as many roles have not been clearly defined yet. For example,
when the report into hospital services in the north-east, *21st Century
Health Services for the North East*, was launched in summer 2006, it was
done so in the boardroom where the old Eastern Regional Health Authority used to meet, across the road from Prof. Drumm's offices in Parkgate
Street in Dublin, not in the north-east itself. It was at the launch of that
report on the north east that Prof. Drumm gave an insight into his own
views of how the media should work. With local north-east media highlighting the cuts in beds that this report would entail, Prof. Drumm got
frustrated that the media were not concentrating on the benefits of creating regional centres of excellence as outlined in the report, i.e. doctors
working in teams, better services for the patient, more community-based
services. Turning to a group of journalists from the national media, he
said "It's up to you, you know. You have to get that message out. You
are the ones who need to tell this." Actually he was wrong. That is *not*
the job of journalists – to be propagandists. His comment reflected his
frustration that his message was not being reflected in the headlines, that
he was on the defensive again. It also reflected his ignorance of what
journalists do, and how they work. The job of journalists is to provide
news stories to feed their outlet, whether it is the next radio or television
bulletin, or tomorrow's newspaper. And then there is the internet, with
specialised websites, podcasts and weblogs, all of which increase the
insatiable appetite for news. Thanks to mobile and satellite technology,
the era of "instant" news is upon us. A comment made at a press conference at 10.45 am can be on the 11.00 am news bulletins around the country, and on internet websites within minutes. News journalists – and their
public – want stories in short, bite-sized pieces. To compete, news must
be sharp, dramatic and entertaining, as well as informative. Health managers have to work hard to adapt to these criteria and to make sure that
they are capable disseminators of what they see as the right news agenda.

My Reflections on the Story – Television

Television news can be good and bad: it skims the surface. It allows for
little analysis, instant opinion, and no depth. Deadlines dictate the content, in many cases. One of my colleagues calls it "laser journalism" –

journalists with little background in health, or an understanding of the history or complexity of a story – scan (or "laser") a press release, turning it around fast for the next bulletin, get the instant soundbite and onto the next story. Few difficult questions are asked ("Minister, what is your reaction to the [fill in the gap]?" is the standard question asked by journalists with little knowledge of the subject they are covering that day).

On good days, television news gives an accurate and vivid account of events, or reports. In one-and-a-half minutes, a 300-page report can be synopsised into easily understood points, without losing the essence of the report. On bad days, dramatic predictions of dire results from policy decisions go uncontested and unchallenged because either a journalist has not attempted to find balance in a story, or because the attempts have failed to get a response from the relevant health authority.

Personal stories of experiences of the health services – usually critical of a hospital or health authority – can go unchallenged because the manager who knows the full story was in a meeting all day and the press officer failed to get the relevant information – another example of failing to prioritise media queries.

A sketch of broadcast political and policy journalism shows how intense the pressure is to feed the requirements of television – striking pictures, tight deadlines, pitch-perfect sound, boiled down information, the right amount of context. Television and radio journalists operate under intense deadline pressure, and RTE journalists in particular who work for both radio and television outlets simultaneously, are required to produce stories for hourly radio bulletins, and three if not four television news programmes a day. It gives them little or no time for detailed briefings by officials, or long explanations about the nuances of policy. Anyway, all too often, their public isn't interested, neither is their news or programme editor. The news message must be clear and simple to relate, one that can fit a 10-second introduction. Broadcast journalists are NOT interested in the minutiae of policy, in the grey area of "maybes." Digestible news makes the headlines; if the stories offer conflict and an edge – all the better, that's what makes it news and not a memorandum.

Local Radio

Local radio has become an increasingly influential medium in Irish life, particularly outside Dublin. Their emphasis on local issues, local voices and local audience is matched by strong talk-based morning programmes which mix music with local and national issues. Health is a big subject on local radio, and interest groups have learnt that access can be direct and powerful.

Local radio can give more time to a subject, and programmes typically broadcast audience reaction, as well as allowing the participant space to give details and respond to opposition. The programme hosts like a good discussion and are willing to hear both sides of the argument. However, in many cases, producers struggle to find a health manager who is willing to go on live radio against someone who opposes their policy. The result is that the audience is left with only one side of the story. A short written statement giving the health organisation's points is totally inadequate in the era of live radio.

Interest Groups and the Media

The health community is made up of vibrant community and interest groups with constant demands for more resources and changes of policy. Groups like the Irish Cancer Society and other charities reliant on public support, employ their own communications managers to ensure they have a profile.

Groups like the Irish Haemophilia Society have also learnt the valuable lesson that keeping an issue in the public eye can keep the pressure on a Minister or Government to deliver. All groups like these either have dedicated press officers, or senior executives who retain a good relationship with key health journalists and programme editors, available for interviews or briefings with journalists when required.

It is not that difficult to access the media, even the national media, when the subject is newsworthy. The Irish Patients Association is one example of a small but powerful lobby group who use the media to good effect to get their voice heard and have an input into policy. Without any resources or experience, a group called Parents for Justice created a national profile for themselves within a matter of weeks, when the controversy over organ retention was uncovered in late 1999. The group, formed by parents whose children had organs retained without their knowledge or consent by Irish hospitals, quickly saw how media interest in the initial stages helped them get the attention of the Minister. By keeping in close contact with journalists, whom they regularly briefed with their side of the story, they ensured the matter stayed in the public interest. Prior to and after each meeting with the Minister, and his officials, they gave interviews and made a number of speakers available to the journalists, and kept the matter in the public eye for some time. However, in the longer term, their expectations were not met, as the subsequent Minister decided against a public inquiry into the matter.

Rising to the Challenge

Much of what I found frustrating about my job as RTE's Health Correspondent was the failure of policy makers to take time to understand how the media works, and what its needs and demands are. Instead of finding ways to use the media, management criticised and complained that it was biased or one-sided. In my experience the view that a report was one-sided was mainly because the journalists' efforts to get the other side of the story were rebuffed, or ignored. Ireland is a small country, and it is possible to pick up the phone and make contact with journalists easily. Influential journalists need to be informed when they are commenting and reporting on events, and they rely heavily on their sources for that information. In an era of huge change in the health services, managers and other significant healthcare actors need to become more available for discussion with the public, who pay for the health service through their taxes, and less defensive of the criticisms being made of them. It is impossible to ignore the media. It shapes policy, helps inform public opinion, and is an essential part of any democracy. Managers have to learn how to use the media, and learn how the media works. Otherwise the PR types have the field to themselves, and Ministers end up giving speeches about paperclips.

Chapter 10

CITIZEN PARTICIPATION IN
IRISH HEALTHCARE

Fergus O'Ferrall

Ireland has a deep tradition of active engagement by its citizens in
every aspect of our national life and culture... We need to identify
and understand how public policy helps and hinders active engagement... At the beginning of the 21st century, Ireland needs to reimagine a new culture of active citizenship to build a vibrant civic society... Active citizens shape strong societies – An Taoiseach, Bertie
Ahern, TD, *The Irish Times*, 10 April 2006.

Introduction

"Active citizenship" is now firmly on the public policy agenda in Ireland. The Taoiseach established a Task Force on Active Citizenship in
April 2006 'to recommend measures which could be taken as part of
public policy to facilitate a greater degree of engagement by citizens in
all aspects of life and the growth and development of voluntary organisations as part of a strong civic culture'.[1] The National Economic and Social Council (NESC) in two key reports has emphasised the importance
of the community and voluntary sector if the economic and social challenges confronting Irish society are to be met. In May 2005 NESC in
The Developmental Welfare State analysed Ireland's welfare state and
advocated harnessing "the characteristic contributions of non-profit organisations" particularly in respect of what it terms "activist measures":

> This requires giving greater recognition to community and voluntary
> groups who pioneer ways of addressing the marginalised positions of
> individuals, families and communities – creating the right framework
> for their continuing emergence while engaging them in networks and
> processes which raise their standards, increase their effectiveness
> and ensure transparency and accountability in return for medium to
> long-term security in funding.[2]

The most recent key strategic analysis NESC has provided NESC Strategy 2006: People, Productivity and Purpose has for the first time in a NESC document designed to lay the basis for social partnership agreement, included a key section on "Enabling Voluntary and Community Activity" as this is considered "an important requirement for overall economic and social development". NESC sets out the rationale for deepening "partnership between statutory bodies and voluntary and community organisations" as part of the necessary wider change in government, public governance and civic organisations.[3]

In addition to this Government and social partnership policy arena, independent policy studies and European policies are turning increasingly to "active citizenship" for a range of reasons. In Ireland an independent Democracy Commission produced in 2005 a very significant report entitled *Engaging Citizens: The Case for Democratic Renewal in Ireland* which highlights the value of "active democratic citizenship" and the need for "accessible opportunities and mechanisms for participation".[4]

In the European Union work is well advanced on a European Charter of Active Citizenship; in 2002 a European Charter of Patients' Rights was issued which contained a section on "Rights of Active Citizenship" which included "the right to participate in policy making in the area of health".[5]

It is in this context of increasing attention to the concept of "active citizenship" in relation to public services that it is important to consider the implications for Irish health policy and practice of this new awareness of citizenship. Many analysts have drawn attention to "the civic deficit in Ireland" over recent decades. Tom Barrington, the former Director of the Institute of Public Administration, in a prophetic lecture in 1992 stated:

> The "civic deficit" is not a single thing. It is the accumulation of the
> deficits, the liabilities over the assets, in our civic culture. That civic

culture contains in itself a number of intertwining sub cultures – the civic, the intellectual, the democratic, the institutional and the moral. We can say that, taken together with perhaps some others, these constitute our attenuated civic culture.

What do we mean by "culture"? It is a shared collection of values, principles, conventions and priorities that determine decision-making, especially collective decision-making.[6]

If such a deficit is indeed a characteristic of Irish life then it exists also in the Irish health system and it is valuable to assess how recent health reforms in Ireland have addressed it. This chapter will, therefore, make a brief evaluation of the reform process in the Irish health system in regard to citizen participation. It will go on to seek to understand in a more rigorous fashion what is meant by "active citizenship" in political theory. It will explore the potential benefits of greater public participation in healthcare and the future challenges posed to health policy-makers and practitioners if "active citizenship" is to be placed at the centre of our health services.

A personal note by the author may help appreciation of my angle of vision. I have been deeply involved with many others in the community and voluntary healthcare sector in Ireland in seeking greater understanding of this sector's contribution to the health and well-being of our people; in addition such organisations have long sought for an agreed framework for the optimum relationship between community and voluntary organisations and statutory bodies.[7] In particular I participated in the work of the "Health Spoke" of The Wheel (the social partner organisation which seeks to network and service the whole community and voluntary sector in Ireland) which between 2002 and 2005 has developed a database of the extensive community and voluntary healthcare sector and sought to represent this sector's common policy issues. We also sought to research the scope of the sector.[8] The "Health Spoke", through a series of "roundtable" meetings with large numbers of community and voluntary healthcare organisations, identified a range of common issues including the need for active partnership between the Department of Health and Children, through a well-staffed Voluntary Activity Unit, and the voluntary healthcare sector. Detailed submissions were made to the Department of Health and Children in this regard and also on the new Health Bill in 2004 establishing the Health Services Executive (HSE) as to how it could be strengthened from the point of view of the community and voluntary healthcare sector's links with the new health structure. It quickly became obvious to the Health Spoke that from the Minister of Health and Children down through the Department of Health and Children and the interim HSE Board and staff that there was little or no interest in public participation or in the community and voluntary healthcare sector's structured involvement in the reform process. It is arguable that this should be so because of the weak "intellectual sub-culture", to use Barrington's phrase, within Irish health policy circles and in particular the impoverished view of citizenship that has obtained in our political culture. It is natural that my reflections will be informed by this involvement on behalf of what I have elsewhere described as "the sleeping giant in Irish healthcare".[9]

The Irish Health Reform Process and the Citizen

Since 2001 the Irish health system has been the subject of a remarkable number of Government health policy statements.[10] In addition there have been a number of new critical studies of the Irish health services.[11] There continues to be a deep and general malaise in respect of the structures and performances of our healthcare services.

The Health Strategy published by the Irish Government in 2001 introduced the new principle of "people-centredness" in addition to equity, quality and accountability as the governing principles of Irish healthcare provision. The Health Strategy influenced the production of two highly valuable papers: Community Participation Guidelines published in December 2002 by the Health Boards Executive in response to Action 52 of the Health Strategy that "provision will be made for the participation of the community in the decisions about the delivery of health and personal social services" and Public and Patient Participation in Healthcare A Discussion Paper for the Irish Health Services published in December 2002 by the Office for Health Management. The new horizons and new vision behind the Health Strategy employed remarkable rhetoric about a new "people-centred" approach; this is the vision set out for the Irish health system:

> A health system that supports and empowers you, your family and community to achieve your full health potential.
>
> A health system that is there when you need it, that is fair, and that you can trust

A health system that encourages you to have your say, listens to you, and ensures your views are taken into account."

The Health Strategy describes a "people-centred health system" as one which:

- Identifies and responds to the needs of individuals

- Is planned and delivered in a co-ordinated way

- Helps individuals to participate in decision-making to improve their health.

It states: "The "people-centred" healthcare system of the future will have dynamic, integrated structures which can adapt to the diverse and changing health needs of society generally and of individuals within it. These structures will empower people to be active participants in decisions relating to their own health." From this rhetoric it appears that a public participation perspective triumphed in the widespread consultation and detailed preparation undertaken in preparation for Ireland's new Health Strategy in 2001. The reality of practical implementation since 2001 totally belies the rhetoric. The major structural reforms announced in The Health Service Reform Programme by the Irish Government in June 2003 and now underway consolidates a growing democratic deficit in Irish healthcare provision. The indirectly elected regional health boards were abolished and a new single Health Services Executive was established to manage the national health system as a centralised single entity. In fact this major reform of the Irish health system is following a classic late twentieth century "modernising government" agenda with these key characteristics:

- Central co-ordination/control

- Use of "value for money" rhetoric

- Use of business models and "consumer" language

- Seeking to have public sector services compete with a private sector freshly supported by the State.

It is perhaps not surprising that the rhetoric of the Health Strategy was so quickly subordinated to the prevailing neo-liberal "reinventing government" ideology. In Ireland as noted by Barrington and others, a civic cul-

ture of "active citizenship" is weak as far as public participation is concerned in public policy formation or the design and delivery of public
services and the very centralised Irish political system has a deeply in-
grained clientalist culture: in this regard users or potential users of public
services rely very heavily on political representatives and their "advice
centres" to secure their access. Eligibility to "medical cards" for free
health services is one clear example where political representation can
help secure the "medical card" as there exists some discretion as to who
may qualify. In return politicians expect their "clients" to vote for them.

Centralisation and clientalism both erode the concept and practice of
active citizenship especially for the large socially and economically excluded population groups in Ireland. They serve to personalise "grievances" or needs and encourage people to ignore systemic analysis and
rational discourse about public policy. Public service reform in Ireland,
including health reform, has been strongly influenced by "new public
management" ideology particularly the attempt to apply market principles and terminology to the provision of public goods and services. So
the language is about "customers" or "consumers" rather than citizens. In
the key documents and reports issued after 2001 on Irish health reform –
for example, the Health Service Reform Programme of June 2003 or the
Health Act, 2004 based on this – it is clear that there is no strong commitment to develop effective citizen engagement and participation in
either policy formation or in the design and delivery of healthcare services. The effects of a centralised political culture are reinforced. The
Irish health reform process illustrates a controlling state and the further
erosion of citizenship.

There are many frustrated community and local groups, such as local
hospital action groups struggling in this "command and control" health
system to have a say or to protest about lack of consultation. By and
large it is true to note that they exercise negative "blocking" power such
as in the case of the proposed Hanly reform of hospital structures, but
there are almost no consultative and continuing channels for citizen engagement in the design and delivery of Irish health services. Recently the
Health Services Executive (HSE) has mooted the establishment of ad hoc
Expert Advisory Groups described as follows:

> These independent groups will enable health professionals and clini-
> cal experts, patients, clients and service user groups play an active
> role in healthcare policy development, implementation and monitor-

ing within the HSE. Each group will focus on a specific area such as diseases (e.g. cancer), conditions (e.g. mental health), practice (e.g. surgery) and users (e.g. community care). [12]

While such Expert Advisory Groups may have a valuable role as part of public participation, they fall far short of rectifying the democratic deficit in Irish healthcare. The Health Act, 2004 provides for "Public Representation and User Participation" in Part 8 of the Act, including a National Health Consultative Forum, Regional Health Forums (for local authority members) and it empowers the HSE to take "such steps as it considers appropriate to consult with local communities or other groups about health and personal social services." [13] While the Act makes possible fuller public participation it is solely at the discretion or invitation of the Minister for Health and Children or is controlled by the HSE itself.

The approach to Irish health reform in respect of public participation underlines the almost total lack of appreciation of the essential benefits to be obtained by such participation in healthcare. The table below summarises what has been well established in practice in other health systems to result from effective public participation. [14]

Table 10.1: Value of Greater Public Participation in Irish Healthcare

Benefits to the health services
➢ Restoration of public confidence
➢ Improved outcomes for individual patients
➢ More appropriate use of health services
➢ Potential for greater cost effectiveness
➢ Contribution to problem resolution
➢ Sharing with the public responsibilities for healthcare

Benefits to people
➢ Better outcomes of treatment and care
➢ An enhanced sense of self-esteem and capacity to control their own lives
➢ A more satisfying experience of using health services
➢ More accessible, sensitive and responsive health services
➢ Improved health
➢ A greater sense of ownership of the HSE

Benefits to public health
➢   Reduction in health inequalities
➢   Improved health
➢   Greater understanding of the links between health and the circumstances in which people live their lives
➢   More healthy environmental, social and economic policies

Benefits to communities and to society as a whole
➢   Improved social cohesion
➢   A healthier democracy – reducing the democratic deficit
➢   A health service better able to meet the needs of citizens
➢   More attention to crosscutting policy issues and closer cooperation between agencies with a role to play in health promotion

If these benefits are to be gained then we must address more rigorously what is understood by "active citizenship" and what implications and challenges must be addressed. To this task the rest of this chapter is devoted.

Citizenship Theory – A Practical Need

The revival of citizenship theory stems from the evident problems of western democratic societies in relation to the nature of the welfare state and the determination of the respective rights and responsibilities of citizens in relation to the state. The crisis laden Irish health services may be seen as just a local example of very pervasive issues and concerns in relation to public services in western and European societies.[15] The increasing attention to citizenship theory highlights what appears to be substantial theoretical confusion in health policy discourse as to how "people" are described. This is exemplified by the terminology to describe those served by healthcare systems: "consumers", "users", "clients", "patients", "the public" or "citizens" are variously and often loosely employed. All of these terms are freighted with theoretical or ideological implications, however correctly or poorly understood by healthcare policy makers, managers or practitioners.

It is important, therefore, to make explicit the ideological or theoretical underpinnings of these key linguistic terms in healthcare, otherwise our health systems are in danger of importing ideologies which may be inappropriate to the provision of human care in a democratic society.[16]

An obvious example is the use of the term "consumers" which is imported from economics and is quite appropriate to a market but may be of questionable value in respect of the provision of healthcare particularly in a non-market context.

Healthcare managers, policy-makers and practitioners need to acknowledge more explicitly that political and social theory is of immense practical importance in shaping our health systems. J.M. Keynes in his famous The General Theory of Employment Interest and Money, published in 1936 wisely observed:

> Practical men, who believe themselves to be quite exempt from any intellectual influences, are usually the slaves of some defunct economist. Madmen in authority, who hear voices in the air, are distilling their frenzy from some academic scribbler of a few years back.

More positively it has been succinctly stated that: "there is nothing so practical as a good theory".[17] It may be argued that much that is dysfunctional in our health systems stems ultimately from theoretical confusion or political illiteracy, for we never govern or manage in the absence of "intellectual influences".

Marshall Marinker has drawn attention to the need to develop an analytical and non-adversarial discussion in regard to health policy in order to have a "constructive conversation" and to avoid the "systemic ambiguity in the way we talk about health".[18]

We need to be more rigorous in the way we use loaded words such as "citizen" in respect of health policy and practice. A theory of citizenship must be fully outlined and then examined as to what it has to offer in terms of health outcomes for the whole population.

The revival of citizenship is related to the increasing concern about the vigour of western democratic societies which depends upon the behaviours, qualities and attitudes of its citizens. There is the related concern, such as that identified by NESC, that welfare states require "partnership" with citizen-based or voluntary organisations to develop or sustain public services.[19] As Thomas Janoski has noted:

> A theory of citizenship, properly conceived, should provide the tools
> to explain the development and balancing of public rights and obli-
> gations in advanced industrialized societies. The promise of citizen-
> ship theory is that it will also illuminate a large range of behaviours

and processes concerning rights and obligations in industrialized societies.[20]

The richest discussions in citizenship theory have occurred in the move
beyond reflections upon the formal rights attaching to citizens as accorded by state law to the social and political capabilities of individuals
for collective action in the common good. As stated in The Well-being of
Nations report to the OECD:

> The realisation of human capabilities is therefore vital for a broader
> notion and measure of human and social development. Human well-
> being is more than the sum of individual levels of well-being since it
> relates to individual and societal preferences regarding equality of
> opportunities, civil liberties, distribution of resources and opportuni-
> ties for further learning.[21]

Citizenship as a process or practice has assumed increasing importance
in social and political science over citizenship simply as a status within a
state.[22]

Civic republican theory concerning the "active citizen" and how citizenship contributes to the common good provides, I will now suggest,
the optimal approach to the development of healthcare services. This will
be seen to be so in at least two key respects: first, in terms of public participation and involvement in the governance, management and delivery
of services and secondly, in addressing the key social and economic determinants of health so as to raise the health status of the population.

The Civic Republican Theory of Active Citizenship

Civic republicanism has a "strong" conception of citizenship in place of
the "weak" conception associated with liberalism; this "strong" conception
may also be reflected by the liberal theorists who favour participatory democracy. However, in respect of our understanding of the norms of voluntary action by "active citizens" in society civic republicanism is richer: it
moves on from liberalism in the sense that it is post-liberal rather than
anti-liberal and is distinguished by at least seven characteristics:

- The "republican citizen" is based on a view of human nature which
  recognises the social constitution of human beings and accounts for
  motivations other than self-interest.[23] Clarke wryly observes: "the
  liberal human, one might say, is distinguished by being non-political

most of the time and inadequately human for all of the time". Clarke's "deep" or civic republican citizenship "shifts the centre of politics away from the state and so recovers the possibility of politics as an individual participation in a shared and communal activity".[24] In civic republicanism life goals are attained in the public sphere and are not merely centred upon the private domain; autonomy and activity are linked as human beings are seen as "political" beings indicating the intrinsic value of participation.

- The "republican citizen" is based upon a clear commitment to "the common good" and a strong sense of each citizen's obligations and duties to others and to the community and to the public interest; in contrast liberalism is neutral as to conceptions of the human good or struggles to articulate such a concept.[25] The best case in liberal theory for the "virtuous" citizen is that presented by Galston who properly distinguishes the liberal and civic republican concepts of the citizen:

  The liberal citizen is not the same as the civic-republican citizen. In a liberal polity, there is no duty to participate actively in politics, no requirement to place the public above the private and to systematically subordinate personal interest to the common good, no commitment to accept collective determination of personal choices. But neither is liberal citizenship simply the pursuit of self-interest, individually or in factional collusion with others of like mind. Liberal citizenship has its own distinctive restraints - virtues that circumscribe and check, without wholly nullifying the promptings of self-aggrandizement.[26]

- The "republican citizen" is based upon republican civic liberty (or "freedom as non-domination" as Pettit describes it) in which the "arbitrariness" of the state is sought to be eliminated;[27] civic republicanism seeks a polity in which not only is citizen participation essential but the "business" of the state and society is seen as the "business" of citizens. As Pericles famously put it: "we do not say that a man who takes no interest in politics is a man who minds his own business, we say that he has no business here at all";[28] citizenship and self-hood are intricately linked.

- The "republican citizen" is based upon a concept of civil and political life as "a free way of life" yet which has as its core an ethic of care guided by concern for others; a citizen in this context is one who develops the "civic virtues" to sustain a political culture - a culture in which a prime value is to use one's independence and autonomy in the public domain and orient actions towards the common good.[29] While liberalism tends to erode the public domain by emphasising individualism and privacy civic republicanism see human actions as carrying always an ethical and moral dimension which depends on social interaction. Republican theory, however, is not naïve about issues of power; it recognises that those in positions of power are always corruptible and that citizens are required to protect their liberty through eternal vigilance.

• The "republican citizen" is based upon a broader understanding of what is "political" than is available generally in liberalism: in civic republicanism the boundaries between public and private, state and civil society are blurred and in flux and these spheres are embraced by a public philosophy which understands how they overlap; in effect "civil society" is also "political society". As Clarke notes in this perspective:

> The new politics, the development of deep citizenship and the citizen self, occurs not in spite of but because of the social: it occurs as a consequence of shifting the political into the social [30]

In this context voluntary action is an opportunity to practice the civic virtues – politics occurs when individuals act in a shared and communal activity. To be engaged in voluntary action is to be engaged as a citizen: to live an engaged life is to live politically; to be a "republican citizen" is to participate both in the operation of one's own life and in some wider social spheres; to be conscious of acting in and into a world shared by others; to be conscious that the identity of self and the identity of others is co-related and co-creative; while also opening up the possibility of both engagement in and enchantment with the world.[31]

In this way civic republicanism has the potential to alter the modern conception of politics as a limited activity for "shallow" citizens in a "weak" democracy. As Barber has noted:

The major devices by which liberal theory contrives to guarantee liberty while securing democracy - representation, privacy, individualism, and rights, but above all representation - turn out neither to secure democracy nor guarantee liberty. Representation destroys participation and citizenship even as it serves accountability and private rights.[32]

Barber argues that liberalism lacks a theory of citizenship and his prescriptions for active citizenship are in effect civic republican prescriptions: "strong democracy" is a civic republic.

- The "republican citizen" is based upon an enlarged view of human capacity for living a civil and humane life. The ideal of humanitas, which informs civic republicanism, includes doing that which people are uniquely by their nature fitted to do and voluntary action ("political action") is a distinctively human response and results in eudaimonia ("well being"); this ideal is one which can accommodate and utilise human struggle and diversity within a conception of laws not simply imposed by the state but developed by public participation and consent in a well-ordered state.[33] Pettit emphasises that a republic needs a "politics of difference" and that "contestability" is more a feature of republics than mere "consent" but this occurs where there is widespread, group-centred society-made norms in civil life about how differences are resolved in the public interest and for the common good.[34] There is, in this perspective, an awareness of the fragility of republican government and society. As Rousseau observed in a chapter entitled "the death of the body politic":

  The constitution of man is the work of nature; that of the state is the work of artifice. It is not within the capacity of men to prolong their own lives, but it is within the capacity of men to prolong the life of the state as far as possible by giving it the best constitution it can have.[35]

- The "republican citizen" is based upon the scope which a republican state and society leaves for what Pettit has termed "the intangible hand" which is akin to what Pericles called the "unwritten code" which "cannot be broken without acknowledged disgrace"; the use of approval or disapproval and the benefits of being well regarded by others to motivate citizen action. Liberal societies have hitherto relied upon either the "invisible hand" (based on market concepts) or the "iron hand" (based on state management) that is either a free market or an imposed order. Pettit notes that these approaches have "particularly affected the attitude taken to the various autonomous and quasi-autonomous bodies that belong to civil society but that states are generally expected to support or subsidize"; these include hospitals, schools, universities, research institutions, broadcasting stations, public utilities, and welfare organisations. Those voluntary organisations require "a regulatory environment within which the intangible hand flourishes", one which supports the supply of civic virtue rather than undermining it as the "invisible hand" or the "iron hand" tends to do.[36]

Implications and Future Challenges

The application of the concepts embedded in the seven characteristics of the "active citizen" outlined above to health policy and practice will require a fundamental paradigm shift in all "the intertwining sub-cultures – the civic, the intellectual, the democratic, the institutional and the moral" which make up the current "civic deficit" in our civic culture as described above by Tom Barrington. This shift will require great persistence at a number of levels, including the European Union (such as the European Charter of Active Citizenship movement), the national level (such as NESC, social partnership support, the Task Force on Active Citizenship), the Health Services Executive (to compel action on the existing possibilities in the Health Act, 2004 for citizen engagement leading to democratic reform of the HSE in the medium to longer term), the local or agency level (seeking more and more scope for citizen involvement in the governance and design of health services as well as the delivery of health services).

As the Taoiseach's quote at the head of the chapter indicates, we need "to reimagine a new culture of active citizenship to build a vibrant civic society" and this requires an identification and an understanding of "how public policy helps or hinders active engagement". If fully thought through the Taoiseach's rhetoric points to a transformative paradigm shift from a liberal managerialist state to a civic participatory republic.

Citizenship as a concept provides a way of constructing competing understandings about the relations between the people, the state and welfare. The fundamental question relates to what ought to be the relationship between citizenship (both rights and duties), the role of the state and the demand and need for healthcare.

The social constitution of human beings which is a characteristic insight of civic republican "active citizenship" is increasingly confirmed by epidemiologists, such as Michael Marmot and Richard Wilkinson, as being fundamental to human health and well-being both individually and at societal levels. In particular social standing and income inequality affects health outcomes and the health status of particular social groups in a decisive way.[37] Social epidemiology has now made more explicit that how we organise our lives, or have them structured by society, affects our health and that of the people around us. It is inequalities in human capabilities that we need to focus upon if better health outcomes are to be achieved- central to these capabilities are autonomy and social participation. This is especially relevant to how people are able to exercise such capabilities in respect of healthcare. Epidemiological research is rediscovering what civic republican political theory recognised as vital to human flourishing as Wilkinson has illustrates in *The Impact of Inequality: How to Make Sick Societies Better*, published in 2005. The evidence now available as to the social determinants of health outcomes makes it imperative to consider how citizens relate to each other (whether equally or not) and also how citizens are effectively engaged in shaping their own lives and how they share responsibility for healthcare services. This requires a fundamental change of perception in the design of the governance, management and delivery of healthcare from a centralised "command and control" model towards a devolved public participatory model, albeit one which is highly integrated as to standards and available supports to responsible local providers.

Engaging citizen-based community and voluntary organisations and fostering social networks with the norms and values that facilitate co-operation becomes a paramount requirement in what will be, in effect, a new population health model to secure better health outcomes and to raise the health status of the whole population. Fine Gael's policy on health, *Restoring Trust: A Health Plan for the Nation*, published in November 2000, contained an innovative set of proposals on "citizen involvement in the health services" and details of a new covenant of patient rights and responsibilities; this policy called for "citizen-based boards" for all healthcare providers in a reformed Irish healthcare system and for a Voluntary Activity Division within the Department of Health and Children to provide active partnership arrangements with the community and voluntary healthcare sector. This latter proposal echoes the stalled White Paper entitled *Supporting Voluntary Activity*, published in 2000, which stated that such Units would be established.[38] The only resources that people have for voicing their needs and for exercising influence over the health services they require is through their social relationships, social networks, community and voluntary organisations or through their political representatives. The latter, as we have seen, operate in a centralised clientalist political system which does not co-exist happily with a participatory democracy such as "active citizenship" would create. It is especially important in healthcare, as in other key domains of life, to recognise that the rights of marginalised or excluded social groups may only be vindicated through their own forums of collective action to achieve optimum health and well-being. "Re-imagining" or reconceptualising citizenship must address the deeper basis of economic and social dominance, in particular growing income inequality, in Irish society where the ideas of equal citizenship and "the common good" have become greatly diminished.

If such "active citizenship" is to be seriously taken as a fundamental building block of Irish society and a new civic republic then the State must be reconceived as an "enabling state". Liberal democracy has allowed a "controlling state", under "new public management" or "reinventing government" rubrics to emerge – a state which conceives of people as "consumers" of state services.[39] It is important to understand that the State is not a neutral force in respect of citizenship development. The policies and actions of the State greatly influence the possibilities of "active citizenship": the state shapes its citizens. Healthcare is a fundamental part of what Janoski calls "the social mechanisms to create citizenship".[40] The scope provided for voluntary action by citizens to create and provide public goods and services is the critical factor in this regard.

In *On Liberty* John Stuart Mill famously draws attention to the great dangers of government replacing citizen action

> ... a State which dwarfs its men, in order that they may be more docile instruments in its hands, even for beneficial purposes – will find that with small men no great things can really be accomplished.[41]

Citizen-based voluntary organisations have been described as "oases of civic initiatives" which invigorate and complement representative democracy.[42] In healthcare such organisations are essential in any society which values the principles of freedom, plurality, inclusion, equality, participation and social solidarity. They are also crucial if we are to achieve optimum healthcare outcomes. Citizen buy-in to the "smoking ban" is an obvious example where citizen co-operation is vital to better health outcomes.

Active citizenship in the first instance will require "the recovery of civism in public administration".[43] This will mean challenging the "managerial" mindset which currently pervades public service reforms and processes. As Frederickson observes, the effective public administration of the future "should be intimately tied to citizenship, the citizenry generally and to the effectiveness of public managers who work directly with the citizenry". He spells this out clearly:

> For public administration both in practice and in education, this will mean a return to an emphasis on the *public* aspects of the field and to the basic issues of democratic theory. If public administration is to be effective, persons who practice it must be increasingly familiar with issues of both representational and direct democracy, with citizen participation, with principles of justice, and principles of individual freedom.[44]

The requirements of democracy's political institutions such as associational autonomy, inclusive citizenship, freedom of information and expression together with free and fair elections are all heavily reliant upon voluntary organisation and action together with citizen competence. Dahl, for example, notes that independent associations are "a source of civic education and enlightenment. They provide citizens not only with information but also with opportunities for discussion, deliberation and the acquisition of political skills". Dahl states that:

> One of the imperative needs of democratic countries is to improve citizens" capacities to engage intelligently in political life...these older institutions will need to be enhanced by new means of civic education, political participation, information and deliberation that draw creatively on the array of techniques and technologies available in the twenty-first century.[45]

Voluntary organisations which have public purposes are one key means of civic education for citizenship and participatory politics. It is, of course, recognised that they need to be supplemented by other forms of civic education and citizen development.[46]

Tocqueville had the crucial insight that *administrative* centralisation "which would restrict the self-regulation of free associations" would frustrate "the competence and responsibilities of citizens who participate in these associations".[47] Tocqueville's concept of the role of the state in facilitating active citizenship is echoed in Oldfield's work on civic republicanism in respect of the need for appropriate constitutional settings for the practice of citizenship:

> There have to be arenas where potentially everyone can take part, where everyone can do something. In the modern state, this means the decentralization of political tasks and functions... What is to be sought is the creation and widening of opportunities for responsible self-government by citizens... Self-government can refer to any public tasks and activities that a community wishes to engage in.

A range of conditions need to be met for the practice of citizenship; these are summarised by Oldfield:

> These conditions are that individuals need resources: they need empowering – in terms of knowledge, skills, information, time and well-being – to become effective agents in the world. They need opportunities – in terms of the decentralization of both political and economic power – in which they can be effective agents, that is citizens. Finally, they need to be provided with the required motivation to take the practice of citizenship seriously, in terms of performing the duties which they owe to the political community of which they are members.[48]

Conclusion

The Irish experience in healthcare reform illustrates the impoverished consequences of inadequate citizenship theory and of unexamined assumptions when using rhetoric such as "people-centredness". In fact Irish society is characterised by a very extensive citizen-based voluntary or "non-profit" healthcare sector.[49] The failure of the current health reform process to engage with this extensive and diverse citizens sector to deliver better health outcomes must surely rank as one of our major "blind spots" only latterly addressed, as we have seen, by NESC in regard to the potential value of the community and voluntary sector.[50]

The Health Strategy 2001 adverted to the concept of "social capital" but did not sufficiently develop the policy implications of this concept for citizenship development in healthcare. Social capital may be defined as "networks together with shared norms, values and understandings that facilitate co-operation within or among groups".[51] Active citizens and citizen-based organisations which seek to provide or meet health needs represent precious social capital and indeed are essential to secure desired health outcomes and to raise the health status of various groups in the population. There is indeed a close association between the civic republican concept of the "active citizen" and the concept of social capital. As has been noted one of the key aspects of civic republicanism is the belief in an ideal of "the common good" which is achieved through the exercise of "civic virtue" by the citizenry as well as by "institutional design" whereby the best institutions are developed to facilitate citizens in seeking the "common good".[52] "Civic virtue" as the disposition to further public good over private gain as outlined in republican theory is one crucial way to set out the "shared norms, values and understandings" of citizens that facilitate co-operation within or among groups as they seek the common good and secure their "self-interest properly understood" to use Tocqueville's phrase which echoes Aristotle.

A key element in both civic republicanism and in the literature of social capital relates to trust and how to develop trustful relations in society. We need social and political institutions that through public participation facilitate citizens in judging where to place their trust: we need to trust our health systems perhaps even more than other systems given that health and well-being is at stake. The recent history of Irish healthcare is replete with examples of the breakdown of trust whether in regard to doctor-patient relationships, such as evidenced by the *Lourdes Hospital Inquiry Report* (Jan 2006), or by State failure to vindicate rights of citizens as evidenced by the failure of the Department of Health and Children in relation to nursing care payments since the 1970s documented in the *Travers Report* in 2005. Accountability mechanisms and increased regulation appear not to generate trust; in fact as Onora O'Neill has argued they may serve to diminish or erode trust and good governance. Healthcare is complex and reforms based upon simplistic modernising agendas fail to recognise the public policy implications of a "complex adaptive system" such as healthcare.[53] As a warning to the mindset which produces centralised bodies like the new Health Services Executive in Ireland Onora O'Neill has wisely observed:

> We try to micro-manage complex institutions from the centre and
> wonder why we get over-complex and inadequate rather than good
> and effective governance.[54]

It is through civic engagement and participation in healthcare services
that social trust is most likely to be developed and sustained. The evidence for this may be traced in the social capital literature but common
sense and experience would make it intuitive in any event: frequent interactions and experience of co-operation lead us to be able to trust those we
encounter more than those we do not meet or know. Civic virtue has a
positive relation towards social trust.

If we put the logic of social capital at the centre of healthcare systems the "empowered citizen" has a central role. The key to success in
health outcomes is the active capacity of people and their organisations
for self-transformation: the capacity within organisations, communities,
and within whole societies to learn and to turn that learning into adaptive
change. It is important to link this with what has been learned about governance and public policy. The seminal work of Rhodes indicates that
policy outcomes should not be sought in the actions of central government. Governance best occurs as a function of self-governing networks
of disparate interests and agencies negotiating and collaborating for
agreed outcomes.[55] Such an approach leads to more innovation, flexibility and adaptability to local circumstances. This means empowering citizens and their organisations to undertake a comprehensive range of services and actions affecting lifestyle and all the social determinants of
health. This poses a key challenge for existing centralised structures:
they have to let go of some power and authority and see this redistributed
into other networks. The state must become "an enabling state" rather
than a "controlling state". It is not possible to advocate the positive development of social capital in order to achieve better health and at the
same time hold onto the inherited state structures and the instinct of central top-down authority and power.[56] Outcomes and solutions in public
policy rely at least in part on the citizens themselves and their capacity to
take shared responsibility for positive outcomes.

Active participation by citizens is itself one of the healthiest things
that people do. Robert Putnam states that "of all the domains in which I
have traced the consequences of social capital, in none is the importance
of social connectedness so well established as in the case of health and

well-being". Active citizenship and social connectedness is a powerful determinant of health and well-being.[57]

Civic republican "active citizenship" has very profound and practical consequences for public policy and services. The civil renewal agenda in the United Kingdom, led by David Blunkett, MP, as Home Secretary with its vision of strong, active and empowered communities provides one early practical example of how "active citizenship" as a normative theory might be translated into public policy and practical implementation.[58]

As a normative theory of active citizenship in healthcare civic republicanism requires healthcare policy makers and practitioners to make a major cultural shift in perspective towards what has been called "the adaptive state" – a state which develops public services through citizen engagement and participation to create more "public value".[59] A key distinction between the current approaches to health systems and their development as exemplified by the Irish case and a "public value" approach to public services is the way in which individual members of the public – the citizens – are regarded. As Chapman observes:

> Within economic theory the public are regarded as consumers, expressing their individual preferences in their actions and purchases. This focus has been incorporated into the new public management (NPM) as an emphasis on public choice - .... The view of the public from the public value perspective is much richer....[60]

Civic republican "active citizenship" invites a "much richer" consideration of the human person than one who simply "consumes" health services. It sees the person as a citizen who engages in healthcare in a multi-dimensional fashion: as a citizen who requires that taxes are spent appropriately, as a citizen with an interest in issues of equity and fairness, as a "co-producer" of the outcomes of health services, as a participant in governing healthcare organisations and as an active voice in health policy formulation at various levels. "Active citizenship" is no doubt the next "big idea" for public services such as healthcare if health outcomes are to be the measure of success:

> At no point in the modern history of public services have there been more resources, or a better range of tools, to use in the creation of public value. But if public services are going to achieve their full potential over the next generation, they must be reshaped through an open, evolutionary process. This process will not arise from the per-

petual efforts to restructure existing arrangements without changing the dominant assumptions governing models of organisations.[61]

I suggest that the key "dominant assumption" that needs to be changed in healthcare is the one we make about the human person as citizen.

Endnotes

[1] Government Press Release, "Taoiseach appoints Task Force on Active Citizenship", 18 April 2006 and "Group chosen to promote civic work", *The Irish Times,* 19 April 2006.

[2] National Economic and Social Council, *The Developmental Welfare State* Report No 113, May 2005, p. xxi.

[3] National Economic and Social Council, *NESC Strategy 2006: People, Productivity and Purpose,* Report No 114, December 2005, pp. 220-232 which is essential reading in respect of the argument of this chapter.

[4] *Engaging Citizens: The Case for Democratic Renewal in Ireland,* ed. Clodagh Harris (TASC at New Island, Dublin 2005); this is the report of The Democracy Commission, chaired by David Begg, which was established in 2003 as an initiative of two think tanks, TASC and Democratic Dialogue.

[5] See draft "European Charter of Active Citizenship", March 2006 and "European Charter of Patients' Rights, 2002 at *www.activecitizenship.net*; see D. O'Mathúna et. al., *Healthcare Rights and Responsibilities: A Review of the European Charter of Patients' Rights,* a report prepared by Dublin City University for the Irish Patients Organisation, April 2005.

[6] See Tom Barrington, "The Civic Deficit in Ireland" in *People Power: Proceedings of the Third Annual Daniel O'Connell Workshop* M.R. O'Connell (Institute of Public Administration on behalf of DOCAL – Daniel O'Connell Association Ltd, Dublin 1993) pp. 1-18; there is a critical analysis of Irish political and civic culture in J.J. Lee, *Ireland: 1912-1985 Politics and Society* (Cambridge University Press, Cambridge, 1989) chapter 8 "Perspectives", pp. 511-687.

[7] See Fergus O'Ferrall, *Citizenship and Public Service Voluntary and Statutory Relationships in Irish Healthcare* (Adelaide Hospital Society/Dundalgan Press, Dundalk, 2000); ibid "Civic Republican Citizenship and Voluntary Action", *The Republic A Journal of Contemporary and Historical Debate* No 2 Spring/ Summer 2001 pp126-137; ibid, "People Centredness: The Contribution of Community and Voluntary Organisations to Healthcare", *Studies An Irish Quarterly* Vol .92, No. 267 Autumn 2003, pp. 266-277.

[8] See, for example, *Directory of Community and Voluntary Healthcare Organisations Compiled by The Wheel 2003-2004* (The Wheel, Dublin 2004) and *Scoping the Community and Voluntary Healthcare Sector in Ireland: A Literature Review* published by The Wheel, 2005; The Wheel website is *www.wheel.ie.*

[9] See Fergus O'Ferrall, "People Centredness: The Contribution of Community and Voluntary Organisations to Healthcare", *Studies an Irish Quarterly,* op.cit. p. 271.

[10] The key document is the *Health Strategy 2001* entitled *Quality and Fairness: A Health System for you,* Department of Health and Children, Stationery Office, Dublin 2001; this was accompanied by a strategic policy for primary care entitled *Primary Care: A New Direction,* Department of Health and Children, Stationery Office, Dublin 2001. Subsequently, three key reports were published and these underpin the Health Service Reform Programme, announced by the Irish Government in June 2003: (i) *Audit of Structures and Functions in the Health System,* Prospectus Report on behalf of the Department of Health and Children, Stationery Office, Dublin 2003 (ii) *Commission on Financial Management and Control Systems in the Health Service,* "The Brennan Report", Stationery Office, Dublin 2003 (iii) *Report of the National Task Force on Medical Staffing,* "The Hanly Report", June 2003.

[11] See T. O'Sullivan, M. Butler, *Current Issues in Irish Health Management: A Comparative Review* (Institute of Public Administration, Dublin 2003); Maev-Ann Wren, *Unhealthy State: Anatomy of a Sick Society,*(New Island, Dublin 2003); A. Dale Tussing & Maev-Ann Wren, *The Health Report: An Agenda for Irish Healthcare Reform* (Irish Congress of Trade Unions, Dublin, 2005); *Just Caring, Equity and Access in Healthcare: A Prescription for Change* (An Adelaide Hospital Society Policy Paper, 2005).

[12] Health Services Executive website, www.hse.ie.

[13] Health Act, 2004, Sections 41-44.

[14] Adapted from Ruth Chambers, Chris Drinkwater, Elizabeth Boatt, *Involving Patients and the Public: How To Do It Better* (Radcliffe Medical Press, Abington, 2003) p. 2.

[15] See W. Kymlicka and W. Norman, "Return of the Citizen: A Survey of Recent Work on Citizenship Theory", *Ethics,* Vol. 104, January, 1994 pp. 352-381; J.M. Barbalet. *Citizenship* (Open University Press, London, 1988).

[16]For the effect of wider values and beliefs on the development of healthcare services see, for example, M. McKee, "Values, beliefs and implications" in *Health Targets in Europe: Polity, Progress and Promise*, ed. M. Marinker, (BMJ Books, London 2002) pp. 181-205.

[17] J. Gill, P. Johnson, *Research Methods for Managers,* 2nd Edition (Paul Chapman, London 1997) p. 23.

[18] See M. Marinker, "The Madrid Framework" *Eurohealth* Vol. 11, No. 1, 2005 pp. 2-5 and his *Constructive Conversations About Health Policy and Values* (Radcliffe Medical Press, Abington, 2006) which examines in depth the underlying values and principles of health policy and posits more enlightened public and political discourse in relation to health.

[19] See, for example, two valuable OECD reports: *The Well-being of Nations: The Role of Human and Social Capital* (OECD, Paris, 2001) and OECD *Citizens as Partners: Information, Consultation and Public Participation in Policy-Making* (OECD, Paris, 2001).

[20] T. Janoski, *Citizenship and Civil Society: A Framework of Rights and Obligations in Liberal, Traditional and Social Democratic Regimes* (Cambridge University Press, Cambridge, 1998) p. 3.

[21] *The Well-being of Nations: The Role of Human and Social Capital* (OECD, Paris, 2001) p. 11.

[22] The great debate generated by Robert Putnam's *Bowling Alone The Collapse and Revival of American Community* (Simon & Schuster, New York, 2000) and the development of an extensive literature on "social capital" reflects this widespread focus upon the voluntary action of citizens and its role in western societies.

[23] See important article by Jane Mansbridge, "Self-Interest in Political Life" *Political Theory*, Vol. 18, No. 1, 1990, pp. 132-153 which identifies the "mini revolt in political science against the self-interested model of the way a democratic policy works" raising the question "what political forms encourage individuals to replace self-interest with a concern for the collective good".

[24] Paul Barry Clarke, *Deep Citizenship* (Pluto Press, London, 1996) pp. 4, 123.

[25] On this see Michael J. Sandel, "The Procedual Republic and the Unencumbered Self", *Political Theory*, Vol. 12, No. 1, 1984, pp. 81-96.

[26] William A Galston, *Liberal Purposes: Goods, Virtues and Duties in the Liberal State* (Cambridge University Press, Cambridge, 1991) p. 225.

[27] See the very important theoretical statement of republicanism by Philip Pettit, *Republicanism: A Theory of Freedom and Government*, Clarendon Press, Oxford, 1997.

[28] Pericles "Funeral Oration"; various translations exist – see whole speech in Thucydides *The History of the Peloponnesian War* (Wordsworth Classics of World Literature, Ware, Hertfordshire, 1997) pp. 94-100; some translations read

that the uninvolved person is a "useless character" (Jowett's trans) quoted in G.H. Sabine, *A History of Political Theory* (George G. Harrap & Co Ltd, London, 1963) p. 14.

[29] See important discussion by Shelley Burtt, "The Politics of Virtue Today: A Critique and a Proposal" *American Political Science Review* Vol. 87, No. 2 1993, pp. 360-368 which distinguishes between "publicly oriented civic virtue" and "privately oriented civic virtue" and argues that the latter is "well within the reach of contemporary citizens" while the former is unrealistic.

[30] Paul Barry Clarke, *Deep Citizenship* (Pluto Press, London, 1996) p. 110.

[31] Clarke, op.cit., p. 6.

[32] Benjamin R. Barber, *Strong Democracy: Participatory Democracy for a New Age* (University of California Press, Berkeley and Los Angeles, 1984) p. xiv.

[33] There is an important recent literature on "the good life", see *The Good Life* Demos Collection 14, 1998 ed. I. Christie, L. Nash (Demos, London, 1998; J. Kekes *Moral Wisdom and Good Lives* (Cornell University Press, Ithaca, New York, 1995); J. Annas, *The Morality of Happiness* (Oxford University Press, Oxford, 1993).

[34] See Pettit *Republicanism* op.cit., especially Chapter 8, "Civilising the Republic".

[35] J.J. Rousseau, *The Social Contract* (Penguin Books, Harmondsworth) 1968, Book III ,op.cit., p. 135.

[36] See Pettit *Republicanism,* op.cit., pp. 256-257; and Thucydides, *The History of the Peloponnesian War* ,op.cit., p. 95.

[37] See, in particular, the key works Richard Wilkinson, *The Impact of Inequality: How to Make Sick Societies Healthier* (The New Press, New York, 2005) and Michael Marmot, *The Status Syndrome: How Social Standing Affects Our Health and Longevity* (Times Books, Henry Holt & Co, New York, 2004).

[38] For examples of policy recommendations with a population health approach see *Just Caring Equity and Access in Healthcare: A Prescription for Change* (An Adelaide Hospital Society Policy Paper, Dublin, 2005).

[39] See, for example, the Irish approach to public service reforms in 1990s, *Delivering Better Government: Strategic Management Initiative Second Report to Government of the Co-ordinating Group of Secretaries – A Programme of Change for the Irish Civil Service* (Government Publications, Dublin, 1996); The Public Service Management Act, 1997; see on this generally, C. Pollitt *Manageralism and the Public Service: The Anglo-American Experience,* Second Edition (Blackwell Publishers, Oxford, 1993).

[40] Janoski, op.cit., pp. 107-8.

[41] John Stuart Mill, *On Liberty* (Penguin Classics Edition, London, 1985) pp. 180-187 is crucial to this argument; see also my chapter, "Theories of Voluntary Action in Society; Active Citizenship and Pluralist Democracy" in *Citizenship and Public Service,* op.cit., pp. 77-121 which includes a brief analysis of Mill's contribution.

[42] J.C. Isaac, "Oases in the desert: Hannah Arendt on democratic politics" *American Political Science Review* Vol. 88, No. 1 (March 1994) pp. 156-168.

[43] See H. George Frederickson, "The Recovery of Civism in Public Administration" *Public Administration Review*, Vol. 42, No. 2 November/December 1982, pp. 501-8; for a current assessment in Europe see *Public Institutions Interacting with Citizens' Organisations: A Survey on public policies on civic activism in Europe* edited by G. Mori, Active Citizenship Network, Rome, March 2004 and *www.activecitizenship.net* for this and for *European Charter of Patients' Rights* published in 2002 which has a key section on "rights of active citizenship".

[44] Frederickson, op.cit., pp. 501-3.

[45] R.A. Dahl, *On Democracy* (Yale University Press, New Haven & London, 1998) pp. 83-99; 187-88.

[46] See Benjamin R Barber, *Strong Democracy: Participatory Politics for a New Age* (University of California Press, Berkeley and Los Angeles, California, 1984) pp. 233-244.

[47] See H.E.S. Woldring, "State and Civil Society in the Political Philosophy of Alexis de Tocqueville", *Voluntas: International Journal of Voluntary and Non-profit Organisations*, Vol. 9, No. 4, 1998, p. 364.

[48] Adrian Oldfield, *Citizenship and Community Civic Republicanism and the Modern World* (Routledge, London and New York, 1990) pp. 28, 145.

[49] See the recently published *Directory of Community and Voluntary Healthcare Organisations*, The Wheel, Dublin, 2004 and the extensive database of such organisations in The Wheel database of the voluntary sector.

[50] I have outlined the contribution of these organisations to healthcare in Fergus O'Ferrall "People-Centredness: The Contribution of Community and Voluntary Organisations to Healthcare", *Studies An Irish Quarterly*, Vol. 92, No. 367, Autumn 2003, pp. 266-277.

[51] See *The Well-Being of Nations,* OECD Report, Paris, 2001 p. 42; see the history of the concept of social capital; see J. Farr, "Social Capital: A Conceptual History", *Political Theory,* Vol. 32, No. 1, February 2004, pp. 6-33; in the Irish

context see *The Policy Implications of Social Capital*, National Economic and Social Forum Report, No 28, Dublin, 2003.

⁵² See R. Dagger, *Civic Virtues: Rights, Citizenship and Republican Liberalism*, (Oxford University Press, New York and Oxford, 1997).

⁵³ See the very important series of articles in the *British Medical Journal* (BMJ): P.E. Pisek and T. Greenhalgh, "The challenge of complexity in healthcare, *BMJ* 323, 15 September 2001, p. 625; T. Wilson and T. Holt, "Complexity and Clinical Care" *BMJ* 323, 22 September 2001, p. 685; P.E. Pisek and T. Wilson "Complexity, leadership and management in healthcare organisations" *BMJ* 323, 29 September 2001, p. 746; and S.W. Frazer and T. Greenhalgh, "Coping with complexity: Educating for capability" *BMJ* 323, 6 October 2001, p. 799; see E. Donnellan, "Department in Shock", *The Irish Times Weekend Review* 12 March 2005 for analysis of successive failures of Department of Health and Children and its inability to deal with complexities of healthcare services.

⁵⁴ Onora O'Neill, *A Question of Trust,* The BBC Reith Lectures 2002 (Cambridge University Press, Cambridge, 2002) p. viii.

⁵⁵ See Robert Rhodes, *Understanding Governance – Policy Networks, Governance, Reflexivity and Accountability* (Open University Press, Milton Keynes, 1997); this needs to be linked to the recognition that "public value" is created not delivered; see M.H. Moore, *Creating Public Value: Strategic Management in Government* (Harvard University Press, Cambridge, Mass., 1995).

⁵⁶ See *The Adaptive State: Strategies for Personalising the Public Realm*, edited by T. Bentley and J. Wilsdon (Demos, London 2003) for an important set of essays concerning the sharper moral and political vision required in reforming public services; see also discussion in G. Mori, "The Citizen's Side of Governance" *The Journal of Corporate Citizenship*, Issue 7, Autumn 2002, pp. 18-30.

⁵⁷ R. Putnam, *Bowling Alone: The Collapse and Revival of American Community* (Simon & Shuster, New York, 2000) p. 326; increasingly epidemiologists are stressing the social factors such as exclusion, relative income inequality and relative status within societies as key factors determining health outcomes; see R. Wilkinson, "Putting the Picture Together: Prosperity, Redistribution, Health and Welfare" in *Social Determinants of Health,* eds. M. Marmot and R. Wilkinson (Oxford, 1999).

⁵⁸ See Rt. Hon. David Blunkett MP, *Active Citizens, Strong Communities Progressing Civil Renewal* (Home Office Communication Directorate, London, 2003) for overview of various policy initiatives in the United Kingdom.

⁵⁹ "Public value" has been defined as "what the public values – what they are willing to make sacrifices or money and freedom to achieve"; see Jake Chap-

man, "Public Value – the missing ingredient in reform?" in *The Adaptive State* op.cit., p. 124.

[60] ibid., p. 125.

[61] T. Bentley and J. Wilsdon, "Introduction to the adaptive state" in *The Adaptive State*, op.cit, p. 34.

Chapter 11

EFFECTING CHANGE IN HEALTHCARE

Kenneth McKenzie and Eilish McAuliffe

In trying to extract the threads of wisdom from the various contributors to weave together a pattern of the enabling and inhibiting factors that are an integral part of the healthcare environment, we draw on the institutionalist framework we introduced in Chapter One – a framework that has been popular in all domains of policy analysis (Rothstein, 1996). We referred to the idea of implicit or explicit political institutions, and in these chapters we have seen how something as explicit as our electoral system affects the kind of strategic thinking we have in healthcare (Ahern), as well as how an implicit rule such as how actors react to deviations from national structures in local situations (Merrigan) can shape the industrial relations landscape. In adopting an institutionalist perspective we use March and Olsen's (2005: 4) definition of institutionalism as "a set of theoretical ideas and hypotheses concerning the relationships between institutional characteristics and political agency, performance and change." Institutionalism emphasises the endogenous nature and social construction of political institutions and claims that institutions are more than mere "equilibrium contracts among self-seeking, calculating individual actors" or "arenas for contending social forces". Instead March & Olsen view institutions as "collections of structures, rules and standard operating procedures" (2005: 4). This institutional framework allows us to analyse the interplay between the actors and the environment and identify the personal, interpersonal and situational factors that are critical to succeeding in the quest to improve healthcare.

The most immediately visible commonality amongst our contributors is that they held to a long-term goal or vision, despite being very aware of and exposed to short-term strictures. Having built up knowledge, contacts and experience of what worked and did not work, they all were clear about where they wanted to take their ideas and knew what they would be likely to encounter by way of opposition or setbacks. This ability to read the institutional (health service) framework seems to be a critical first step to implementing change. Kelly's chapter shows how his cumulative learning through the development of various policy and strategy documents enabled him to develop this skill, likewise with Barrington's story. Owens's chapter sets out a thorough analysis of the institutional climate, highlighting limited political and public interest with an ensuing media silence; stigma; professional self-interest and inter-professional rivalry as some of the factors that inhibited the development of a mood for change. His message is that despite this national reluctance to move mental health services into the twenty-first century, several local services have managed to modernise. A critical aspect of reading the institutional framework is the ability to identify levers for change and to recognise that these can occur at any level of the system. Owens's chapter demonstrates that there may be room for incremental change, even when the institutional climate appears negative in every respect.

Identifying leverage points and using them to effect change, knowing when to act and when to sit tight, are skills that some would argue only develop with long experience. However, we would argue that a greater emphasis on retrospective analysis of policy changes and the processes of achieving such changes could create a climate of learning that propels managers towards change. The rules and practices of the institution need not be hidden in such a way that it takes years to stumble upon an understanding of how they might be used as an empowering rather than a constraining force. One suggestion offered by Matt Merrigan is to develop a mentoring system as a way of trying to ensure that new people are allowed to push their fresh analyses to the fore.

The need to lay the foundations for significant change is a recurring theme: it is not enough to hope that a good idea will find favour within the healthcare sector. Michael Kelly, Anne Scott and John Owens all point to the work they did in advance of any significant changes they espoused. Moreover, there is a palpable sense of the wisdom of incremental change: in the majority of initiatives mentioned in this book, change had to be "geared". Even a change such as the smoking ban, which seemed to be implemented in a very short timeframe, we now understand from Howell and Allwright's chapter was long in the making in terms of the collection of evidence and support from both national and international actors. A too-rapid pace of change may frighten different actors within healthcare to retreat to their entrenched positions. The all-too-obvious drawback to slower change is that sometimes it can be remarkably slow, as in the case of reform of mental health services (Owens) or indeed the shift towards active citizenship, something that O'Ferrall and many other voluntary sector actors have been working towards for some time. One senses that it is on the horizon, particularly with the establishment of the Task Force on Active Citizenship, but it will take a long time to rise. As with the mental health services and indeed *within* the mental health services, one is heartened to see several local examples of the active engagement of citizens in healthcare planning. The message here is that whilst accepting that substantial change takes much preparation and needs long time-horizons in any institution, it is critical to build from the bottom-up as well as preparing for institutional change from the top-down. The identification of appropriate leverage points is an essential component.

Working with and through other people, being able to persuade people towards a vision and a new way of doing things is something that most leaders aspire to. Matt Merrigan alludes to the beneficial working relationship he has built up with various people in management, the professions and the Civil Service, something that helped him in his subsequent efforts to establish workplace partnership. Having worked on similar protocols in AMiNCH (Tallaght Hospital), Merrigan was aware of what tended to work and what didn't in negotiations. John Owens knew of the advantages to be gained from a strong multidisciplinary perspective, and acted as a champion of what could be done when a holistic view of the patient's needs was reflected in an agreed treatment programme that went beyond a purely psychiatry-led approach. Anne Scott recognised that she needed to bring the university stakeholders, the Department of Health and the School's health service partners on board to build a vibrant milieu where teaching, research and service delivery provide the synergistic relationship that is essential for nursing development. Institutional theory sheds little light on this process – is it the personality or the idea that people are drawn to?; does the institution shape the individual or the individual shape the institution? As March and Olsen surmise "new institutionalism" tries to avoid unfeasible assumptions

that require too much of political actors, in terms of normative commitments (virtue), cognitive abilities (bounded rationality) and social control
(capabilities)" (2005: 20). Many of the contributors to this book were
reluctant to engage in discussion about their personal leadership abilities,
attributing more weight to the confluence of circumstances that enabled
them to act. Thus we return to the position we set out in the opening
chapter of this book – it is the *interplay* between the actors and the environment that is critical and; as clearly demonstrated by this collection of
authors, this interplay involves environments shaping actors and collections of actors shaping environments or institutions.

Another dominant theme from the contributors is breaking the pro-
cedural mould to move beyond involvement of the usual suspects. At
both government and service planning level, policy and strategy had previously been devised by a relatively insular team, removed from stakeholder input: at government level, both Frank Ahern and Michael Kelly's
chapters partly serve to illustrate how we expect central government to
be all-knowing and all-powerful, and indeed some would contest
whether central government wants to loosen the control it has had over
health. Owens mentions that psychiatrists were very much in charge of
mental health on the ground to the exclusion of other professionals and a
patient-advocate perspective. Fergus O'Ferrall observes that the established practice has been to isolate citizens from healthcare planning and
service evaluation. Kelly's enlightened approach to the development of
Quality and Fairness, O'Ferrall's work with the Health Spoke of The
Wheel and Owens's inclusive approach to reforming mental health all
demonstrate what can be achieved when one questions and takes risks
with the institutional rules and procedures.

The use of legislation to achieve policy goals perhaps is not as visible a strand as some people may have first thought. For example, significant changes in the role of the nurse as discussed by Anne Scott were
partly precipitated by legislative change, but it could be said that the legislation was both preceded and accompanied by shifts in training and in
attitude. The relative legislative inertia since the mid-1980s on mental
health is a feature of John Owens's chapter; it is arguable that the voice-
less constituency of people with mental health problems partly explains
the lack of effective and timely policy shift in this area. An exemplar of
how legislation changes the health landscape is the smoking ban: Howell
and Allwright show that solid legal foundations, a strong research base,

and concerted effort by interested parties can come together to sizeably alter a maladaptive health behaviour.

Looking beyond the national horizon and learning from other countries' experiences is a feature that has slowly crept into our health system over the past decade. Merrigan writes about the utility of looking abroad for best practice and cites the research carried out in the New York hospital system and the action research on partnership conducted at Cornell University. The weight of evidence and of a prior legislative record is referred to by Howell and Allwright in their tracing of the origins of the smoking ban. Ruth Barrington details how, through referencing international practice, she fought for a broader conception of how research could be gainfully deployed in the health sector as a whole, even when the dominant view was against that of the Health Research Board. She writes of the imperative to develop a solid research platform in Ireland. Economic arguments for exporting our own researchers to be trained abroad with the expectation that they will return, along with the doubt that a small country like Ireland could hope to mount its own valid medico-scientific research programme, have underlain a collective and perpetuated unwillingness to invest in frontier-grade health research (Ireland's parlous economy until the late 1990s must also be invoked, of course). Hard work by scientist-practitioners and senior administrators enabled the case to be made for expanded funding of research; early initiatives by charities and philanthropists prepared the ground for the subsequent significant cash injections. There is no doubt that research-led health practice has shifted to become the norm in acute and chronic care and is on track to doing so in public health and health planning (cf. Butz and Boyle Torrey). Additional research posts in health have also come on stream and the face of health research as a whole is unrecognisable to what it was even ten years ago. With the government committed to massive funding of wet lab, 'bench to bedside' and other applied scientific research as part of its knowledge economy strategy over the medium-term future, it is clear that Barrington has helped to position the HRB to the fore in this new thriving research climate.

Howell and Allwright detail a case where outside expertise, in the form of both a committed public health lobby and professional public relations input, helped to win the argument for the introduction of smoke-free pubs. Goodin (1996) references elements of design, competitive selection and "the accidents of external shocks" as contributors to the dynamics of institutional change. What we see here is more intentional than accidental and more pricking than shocking. How the proposed legislation would have fared if these two groups had not been brought in is worth considering, particularly in light of the inability to successfully implement the Hanly strategy. If ever an initiative demanded international reference points and a clearly articulated evidence-base, it is Hanly. Explaining to people the benefits of regionalisation and higher patient throughput in large centres must happen if people are to accept that small and less specialised facilities are to be closed. The counterfactual case of how things will not be better if they are left as they are has not been forcefully made by the professions or by politicians. Emotive contributions from an angry public will continue to feature in local media as long as Hanly is on the table in one form or another; seriously confronting the evidence base for the validity of these fears is a task for all our senior people in health if we are to implement what best practice compels us to do.

Related to this is the critical value of a positive media strategy, as highlighted by Aileen O'Meara. Judging by the viewing figures for medical dramas and documentaries, it is evident that we find medical stories gripping; the challenge for health leaders is to find a way to engage enthusiastically with the media and thus the public; all too often health is reported negatively as there is only negative news for the journalists to report. Relaying the positive news about 'bench to bedside' research; improvements in cardiovascular and cancer specialties; and significant rises in front-line staff numbers and capital project investments is a vital and underused method to reassure the public that the picture is not bleak. The contractual obligations surrounding managers and health professionals and their relations with the media must of course be made to work for everyone's benefit in as much as this is possible; but as O'Meara's story illustrates, a strategy of hoping negative events in a hospital will not become news is too passive and defeatist.

The role of democracy in health policy is expressly articulated by Fergus O'Ferrall but serves as a background in Frank Ahern's chapter. The flood of Dáil questions on health and the often-frantic pace of work to respond to them via Minister's briefings are cited by Ahern as an overriding reason why it is hard for civil servants to focus on policy. The sense that something bad on the news could derail the working day for the senior civil servant is plain in this chapter; however, no-one in the book (or probably in the health sector as a whole) seems able to recommend what needs to be done to balance the competing needs of responsiveness and leadership in health policy-making. It is hard to envisage a time when health will not be a key election issue; single-issue candidates on health are increasingly prevalent, and the political class seemed genuinely at a loss as to how to persuade people of the argument for centres of excellence in place of local hospitals (cf. the case of the Hanly Report). O'Ferrall notes that our political system is marked by a clientelist relationship between the constituent and the representative. The PR-STV structure exposes all TDs to the significant risk of not being re-elected unless the constituency is spared any major upheaval.

As we see it, there are two competing routes of accountability at play here – the short route is the direct relationship between the citizen and the service. O'Ferrall makes strong accusations on the extent to which this has been ignored in healthcare. The long route is through the elected political representative back to the citizens who elected him or her. Ahern's argument is that this long route is equally if not more important in the daily work of the civil servant. Accusations of excessive "political interference" in healthcare and "local clientelism" come from those who place less importance on this long route. What is becoming clear is that the solution lies in the balance, the long and short routes both need to be part of the frame, both our politicians and citizens are legitimate actors in shaping healthcare and both should be enabled to play their parts.

Concluding Comments

The stories in this book bring a diversity of experience and perspective to the critical question of how we effect change in healthcare. There is universal agreement that healthcare is a complex environment or institution. Some would argue that because of the path-dependant nature of this institution it is impossible to achieve any significant degree of change. Others would claim that the greater forces of design and environment limit the human potential to effect change. However, the experiences outlined in this book point to the need to "go beyond rational design and environmental dictates as the dominant logics of institutional change" (Brunsson and Olsen, 1998). We see how a variety of actors develop a growing awareness of the institutional framework, identify leverage points, and reference points, garner support, break the moulds, challenge the rules and procedures and take risks whilst maintaining a steady course towards a vision held fast. These individuals are not "knights in shining armour", and none of them could be described as "new blood".

Neither are they all-powerful or dominant. Many would not even lay claim to being charismatic. They are however, competent, committed people that worked with the environment and through other actors. Thus, we return to our claim that it is the interplay between the environment, the actors and the actions that is critical to effecting change. It is about reading the environment, preparing the ground and nurturing a vision. As March and Olsen (1989) so aptly put it: "reformers are often institutional gardeners more than institutional engineers".

References

Butz, W. P. and Boyle Torrey, B. (2006). "Some frontiers in social science". *Science*, 312, 1898-1900.

Brunsson, N and Olsen, J.P. (1998). "Organization Theory: Thirty years of dismantling and then?" in N. Brunsson and J.P. Olsen (eds), *Organizing Organizations*. Bergen: Fagbokforlaget, pp. 13-43.

Goodin, R.E. (1996). "Institutions and their design"'. In R.E. Goodin (ed.) *The Theory of Institutional Design*, Cambridge: Cambridge University Press, pp. 1-53.

March, J.G. and Olsen, J.P. (1989) *Rediscovering Institutions*, New York: Free Press.

March, J.G. and Olsen J.P. (2005) *Evaluating the "New Institutionalism"*, Working Paper No. 11, Arena, Centre for European Studies, University of Oslo. www.arena.uio.no.

Rothstein, B. (1996) "Political Institutions: An Overview". In R.E. Goodin and H.D. Klingemann (eds), *A New Handbook of Political Science*. Oxford: Oxford University Press, pp. 133-166.